JBoss RichFaces 3.3

Enhance your JSF web applications using powerful
AJAX components

Demetrio Filocamo

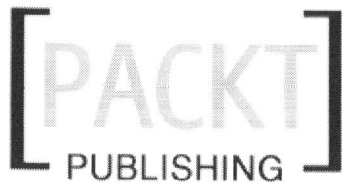

[PACKT]
PUBLISHING

BIRMINGHAM - MUMBAI

JBoss RichFaces 3.3

First published: November 2009

Production Reference: 1231009

Published by Packt Publishing Ltd.
32 Lincoln Road
Olton
Birmingham, B27 6PA, UK.

ISBN 978-1-847196-88-0

www.packtpub.com

Cover Image by Filippo (filosarti@tiscali.it)

Credits

Author
Demetrio Filocamo

Reviewer
Allan Lykke Christensen

Acquisition Editor
Sarah Cullington

Development Editor
Swapna V. Verlekar

Technical Editor
Charumathi Sankaran

Copy Editor
Sanchari Mukherjee

Indexers
Rekha Nair

Monica Ajmera

Editorial Team Leader
Gagandeep Singh

Project Team Leader
Lata Basantani

Project Coordinator
Srimoyee Ghoshal

Proofreader
Lynda Sliwoski

Graphics
Nilesh R. Mohite

Production Coordinators
Adline Swetha Jesuthas

Dolly Dasilva

Cover Work
Adline Swetha Jesuthas

About the Author

Demetrio Filocamo is a computer science engineer with more than 10 years of experience with both Desktop and web applications development. He works as a consultant in London and collaborates with some companies and universities in Italy. Demetrio has been developing Enterprise Java Applications using open source solutions for the last five years.

About the Reviewer

Allan Lykke Christensen is the vice-president of Danish ICT Management, an international consulting firm with its focus on ICT in developing economies. He is responsible for daily management of teams in Uganda, Bangladesh, and Denmark. In his daily work, he is also responsible for project planning, initiating, and overall implementation. He has been developing and implementing IT projects for more than 10 years. His expertise covers a wide range—he has developed workflow systems, information systems, e-learning tools, knowledge management systems, and websites. He has worked as a team leader on several major European Commission-financed ICT projects in various developing economies. He has co-authored *The Definitive Guide to Apache MyFaces and Facelets* (Apress, 2008) and made countless presentations and training sessions on programming-related topics around the world.

To my grandfather Demetrio, my family and Maria Chiara.

Table of Contents

Preface

JBoss RichFaces is a rich component library for JavaServer Faces and an AJAX framework that allows easy integration of Ajax capabilities into complex business applications. Do you wish to eliminate the time involved in writing JavaScript code and managing JavaScript-compatibility between browsers to build an Ajax web application quickly?

This book goes beyond the documentation to teach you how to do that. It will show you how to get the most out of JBoss RichFaces by explaining the key components and how you can use them to enhance your applications. Most importantly, you will learn how to integrate Ajax into your applications without using JavaScript, but only standard JSF components. You will learn how to create and customize your own components and add them to your new or existing applications.

First, the book introduces you to JBoss RichFaces and its components. It uses many examples of Ajax components which, among others, include: Calendar, Data Table, ToolTip, ToolBar, Menu, RichEditor, and Drag 'n' Drop. All these components will help you create the web site you always imagined. Key aspects of the RichFaces framework such as the Ajax framework, skinnability, and **Component Development Kit (CDK)** will help you customize the look of your web application. As you progress through the book, you will see a sample application that shows you how to build an advanced contact manager. You're also going to be amazed to know about the advanced topics you will learn such as developing new components, new skins, optimizing a web application, inserting components dynamically using Java instead of XHTML, and using JavaScript to manage components. This book is more than a reference with component example code: it's a manual that will guide you, step by step, through the development of a real Ajax JSF web application.

What this book covers

Chapter 1: *What is RichFaces* covers the aims of the RichFaces framework, its components, and what you can do by using it in a web application.

Chapter 2: *Getting Ready* explains how to configure your environment by creating a simple project using the seam-gen tool, adding support to Seam and Facelets, and the manual configuration for the RichFaces libraries. We will understand the IDE that we can use while developing with the framework.

In Chapter 3: *First Steps*, you will learn to build Ajax applications by developing a simple example, the basics of RichFaces step by step, from creating the project to editing the code, using very important components and their Ajax properties.

Chapter 4: *The Application* covers how to create the basics of our project by having a look at the side technologies we might know, in order to build good applications. It will cover templating with Facelets, JBoss Seam authentication, and customization of the entities.

Chapter 5: *Making the Application Structure* explains us how to create the login and registration system of the website. We'll look at all the features that a real application might have.

In Chapter 6: *Making the Contacts List and Detail*, we will develop the core feature of our application—contact management. We'll learn about Ajax interaction and containers, and about new Ajax components that RichFaces offers.

Chapter 7: *Finishing the Application* explains how to finish building the application using the RichFaces components, and about customizing them.

In Chapter 8: *Skin Customization*, we'll see all the powerful customization capabilities that the RichFaces framework offers.

Chapter 9: *Creating a New plug 'n' skin* covers how to create, customize, and package and deploy a new pluggable skin.

Chapter 10: *Advanced Techniques* explains you how to use and implement pushing, partial updates, and session expiration handling in order to develop advanced applications.

In Chapter 11: *Component Development Kit,* we'll see how to start a project in order to develop a simple JSF Ajax component in a simple and effective way using the features the CDK offers.

Appendix: *RichFaces Components Overview* covers a list of all the components of RichFaces with their functionalities.

Who this book is for

This book targets Java Developers who want to enhance their JSF applications by adding AJAX, but without having to use JavaScript. If you want to learn how to use the wide set of AJAX components that you find in the RichFaces framework, this book is for you.

You are expected to have basic knowledge of JSF, but no previous experience with AJAX is necessary.

Conventions

In this book, you will find a number of styles of text that distinguish between different kinds of information. Here are some examples of these styles, and an explanation of their meaning.

Code words in text are shown as follows: "Notice that the `myNewSkin.skin.properties` file contains the properties of the skin."

A block of code is set as follows:

```
<jsp:scriptlet>
  <![CDATA[
    Float ratingValue =
                      (Float) component.getAttributes().
get("value");

    variables.setVariable("ratingValue", ratingValue);
]]>
</jsp:scriptlet>
```

When we wish to draw your attention to a particular part of a code block, the relevant lines or items are set in bold:

```
<f:resource
    f:key="org.richfaces.renderkit.html.CustomizeableGradient">
  <f:attribute name="valign" value="middle" />
  <f:attribute name="gradientHeight"
              value="22px" />
  <f:attribute name="baseColor"
              skin="myNewProperty" />
  <f:attribute name="gradientColor"
              skin="headerGradientColor" />
</f:resource>
```

Any command-line input or output is written as follows:

```
mvn install
```

New terms and **important words** are shown in bold. Words that you see on the screen, in menus or dialog boxes for example, appear in the text like this: "clicking the **Next** button moves you to the next screen".

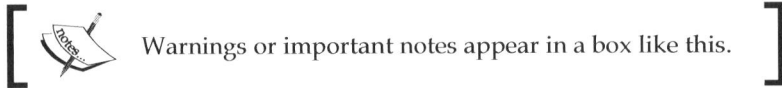

> Warnings or important notes appear in a box like this.

> Tips and tricks appear like this.

Reader feedback

Feedback from our readers is always welcome. Let us know what you think about this book—what you liked or may have disliked. Reader feedback is important for us to develop titles that you really get the most out of.

To send us general feedback, simply send an email to feedback@packtpub.com, and mention the book title via the subject of your message.

If there is a book that you need and would like to see us publish, please send us a note in the **SUGGEST A TITLE** form on www.packtpub.com or email suggest@packtpub.com.

If there is a topic that you have expertise in and you are interested in either writing or contributing to a book on, see our author guide on www.packtpub.com/authors.

Customer support

Now that you are the proud owner of a Packt book, we have a number of things to help you to get the most from your purchase.

> **Downloading the example code for the book**
>
> Visit `http://www.packtpub.com/files/code/6880_Code.zip` to directly download the example code
>
> The downloadable files contain instructions on how to use them.

Errata

Although we have taken every care to ensure the accuracy of our content, mistakes do happen. If you find a mistake in one of our books—maybe a mistake in the text or the code—we would be grateful if you would report this to us. By doing so, you can save other readers from frustration, and help us to improve subsequent versions of this book. If you find any errata, please report them by visiting `http://www.packtpub.com/support`, selecting your book, clicking on the **let us know** link, and entering the details of your errata. Once your errata are verified, your submission will be accepted and the errata added to any list of existing errata. Any existing errata can be viewed by selecting your title from `http://www.packtpub.com/support`.

Piracy

Piracy of copyright material on the Internet is an ongoing problem across all media. At Packt, we take the protection of our copyright and licenses very seriously. If you come across any illegal copies of our works, in any form, on the Internet, please provide us with the location address or web site name immediately so that we can pursue a remedy.

Please contact us at `copyright@packtpub.com` with a link to the suspected pirated material.

We appreciate your help in protecting our authors, and our ability to bring you valuable content.

Questions

You can contact us at `questions@packtpub.com` if you are having a problem with any aspect of the book, and we will do our best to address it.

1
What is RichFaces?

In this chapter, we are going to learn about the RichFaces project and how it can help us develop better Ajax web applications faster.

First, we'll go through a bit of the story of its birth and growth. Thereafter, we'll learn how it works (in general), which components are inside its framework, and what we can do with them. Finally, we'll explain some advanced techniques and start looking at the CDK (Component Development Kit) with a simple example.

An overview of RichFaces

RichFaces is a very useful open source framework that allows you to add Ajax capability to your JSF application (using the standard JSF components) without the need to write JavaScript code and manage JavaScript compatibility between browsers. It is integrated with the JSF lifecycle and other standard JSF features such as validation, conversion, and resource management.

Moreover, RichFaces offers the very powerful **skinnability**. This customizes the look and feel of your JSF applications. You can define different color schemes to create your custom skins or use the predefined ones. Also, you can manage the predefined CSS styles (or add your own ones) to change the appearance of UI library components in a simple and consistent way (you can even use XCSS to dynamically customize the CSS styles). The skinnability feature of RichFaces can apply skins to standard HTML elements such as `input`, `select`, `textarea`, `fieldset`, and so on.

RichFaces provides two sets of component libraries:

Core Ajax: The Core library contains components that are useful to "ajaxize" JSF pages and standard JSF components. It is very simple to define Ajax areas and to invoke Ajax requests in order to update those areas (we'll see how this is done very soon). Also, it provides a component to generate binary resources on the fly (for example, code-generated images, `pdf` files, `csv` files, and so on).

UI: The RichFaces UI library is a set of advanced JSF Ajax components used to add rich user interface features to your applications. The components support Ajax out of the box and perfectly integrate with the Core library. Also, they fully support skins and can be completely adapted according to the users' needs.

Another feature included in the RichFaces framework is the **Component Development Kit (CDK)**—the set of tools used for UI library creation that can be used to make new components with built-in Ajax and skinnability support.

Other extras are the Facelets support, the possibility to create components from Java code (with documented API), the JavaScript API of components to interact with them from the client side (if you want to use JavaScript), and last but not least, the very strong community support.

As you can see, RichFaces has a lot of very powerful features that can help you with rich application development. In the following paragraphs, we'll do a short overview of the framework to start understanding all the possibilities you have.

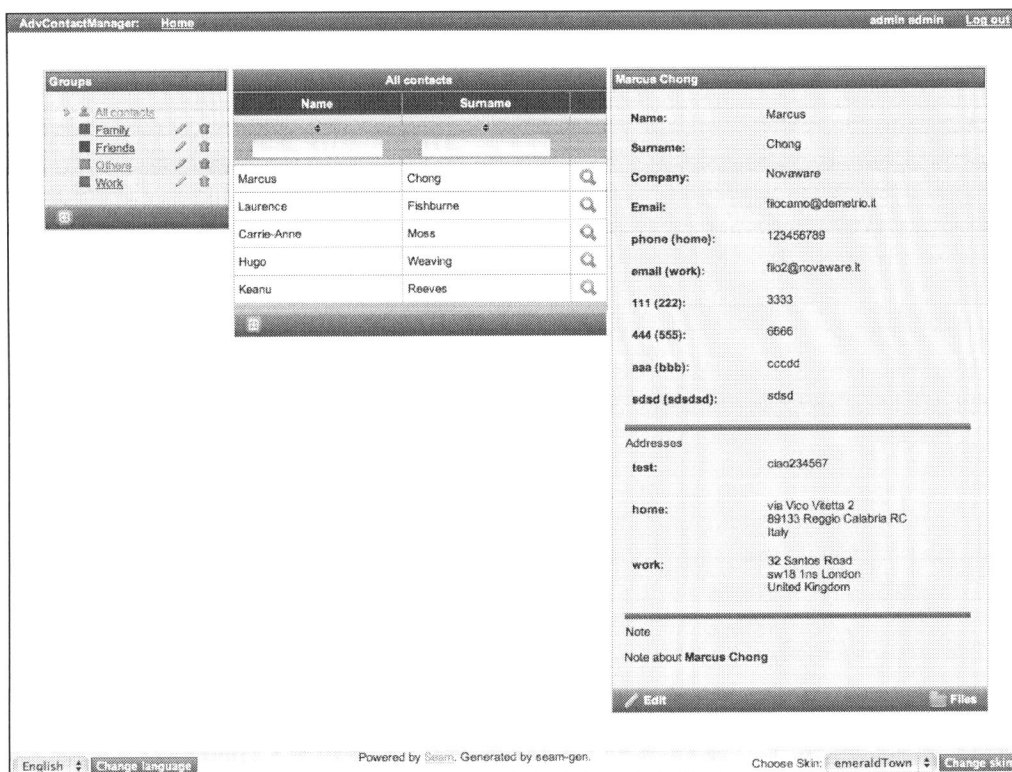

A bit of history

RichFaces comes from the Ajax4Jsf framework. It was created by Alexander Smirnov who joined Exadel in 2005 in order to continue the development. The idea was to put together the "cool" Ajax techniques with the new JavaServer Faces framework.

The first commercial version was released in March 2006 with the name of Exadel VCP. In the same year, it was split into two projects—Ajax4Jsf (open source) and RichFaces (commercial).

Ajax4Jsf provided the Core Ajax framework and the Ajax components to "ajaxize" JSF components in a page (page-wide Ajax support). RichFaces was a commercial JSF Ajax components library.

In March 2007, Exadel and JBoss (a RedHat division) announced a partnership to open the source code of RichFaces, and the two projects were merged into a single open source project called just "RichFaces". It was a good move to solve the version compatibility issues that the two separate projects had.

Nowadays, the project is moving really fast with the help of the community of users involved with the RichFaces team who also decide what the future developments of the framework will be (such as which feature to develop further, which new component to make first, and so on).

For more information, visit the main web site at http://www.jboss.org/jbossrichfaces/), and the user forum at http://jboss.com/index.html?module=bb&op=viewforum&f=261.

The Ajax framework

The RichFaces Ajax framework is a JSF component library that adds page-wide Ajax support to your pages, unlike the traditional and limited component-wide Ajax support. It means that you can use Ajax components to invoke Ajax requests that are automatically synchronized with the JSF component tree, and update single areas without reloading the entire web page. The following image, taken from the JBoss documentation, shows the request processing flow:

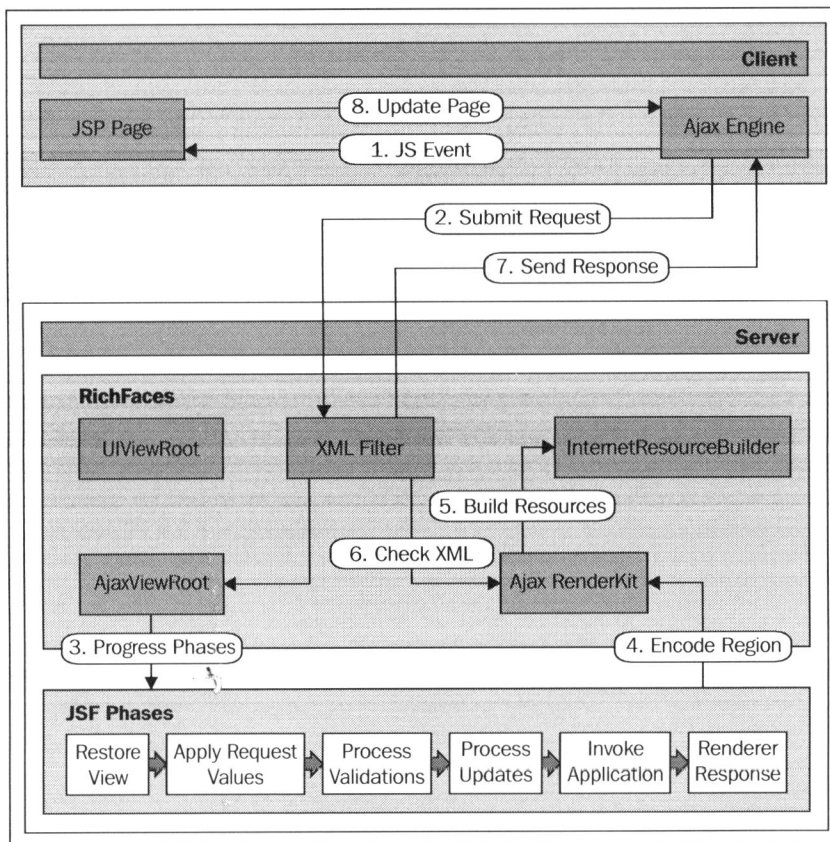

It is not different from a standard JSF page, and you don't even need to write JavaScript code by using the RichFaces Ajax components. Inside the page you can define different areas you want to update, after the Ajax request.

The framework architecture is composed of five parts:

1. **Ajax Filter**: This is essential to add Ajax capabilities to your JSF application using RichFaces. It manages all the requests (both Ajax and standard JSF), corrects and validates the markup code sent, manages the script and style loading, the resources cache, and so on. You have to register the filter in the web.xml file.

2. **Ajax Action Components**: They are standard JSF components that you can use in order to send Ajax requests (we'll see them very soon).

3. **Ajax Containers**: The framework supports the AjaxContainer interface that describes an area ("region") of the page, which should be decoded during an Ajax request. The biggest region is the whole view of a JSF page, but you can define how many regions you want inside the page.

4. **Skinnability**: This is a very useful part of the framework and adds skinning capability to your application (later, we'll see it in detail).

5. **RichFaces JavaScript Engine**: It runs on the client browser and manages Ajax requests and responses. It is automatically managed by the framework, so you don't have to use it directly.

You can decide when to use a standard JSF request (with a full reload of the web page) or when to use an Ajax request. In the latter case, only the involved Ajax region is processed, and the Delta Ajax markup is sent back to the client after the filter has parsed and verified it.

The verification is done because the XMLHTTPRequest JavaScript function sends the request in XML format; the markup inside the XML request is not validated or corrected. The XML filter can automatically remove HTML code problems, but it's a good practice to write standards-compliant XHTML and HTML code.

Components of the RichFaces framework share a lot of Ajax attributes, which are very useful to manage the Ajax options that you have.

The following component attributes are very important and you can find them in all the Ajax-enabled components of the RichFaces framework:

- reRender: In order to decide which area must be updated after an Ajax request.

- ajaxRendered: If it is true, the area is updated after every Ajax request (even if it is not in the reRender attribute).

- limitToList: In order to force the JavaScript Engine to update the areas only in the reRender attribute.

We'll see these attributes in a lot of components of the framework. Therefore, it is useful to know how they work.

Ajax Action Components

As we have said, these components are used to send Ajax requests to the server. Some examples of these components are:

- `a4j:commandButton`: It is the Ajax version of the standard JSF `h:commandButton`. This produces Ajax requests instead of standard ones and has attributes to manage the Ajax options.

- `a4j:commandLink`: The Ajax version of `h:commandLink`. It works like `a4j:commandButton`, but renders a link (HTML `<a>` tag) instead of the `input` element.

- `a4j:poll`: Using this component, you can periodically poll the server for data and update the page using an Ajax request.

- `a5j:push`: It simulates push data from the server.

- `a4j:support`: The most important Ajax component of the library; attaching it as a child adds Ajax capabilities to standard JSF components.

Ajax Containers

The RichFaces Ajax framework contains specific components that describe Ajax areas and implement the `AjaxContainer` interface. The main Ajax container is the view root by default; therefore, you don't need to define an Ajax container for the whole page. However, it's very useful to know how to use the `a4j:region` component to set new Ajax regions and optimize Ajax requests.

Ajax placeholders

A very important concept to keep in mind while developing is that the Ajax framework can't add or delete elements, but can only replace existing elements in the page. So, if you want to append some code you need to use a placeholder.

RichFaces has a component that can be used as a placeholder: `a4j:outputPanel`.

Inside the `a4j:outputPanel` component, you can put other components that use the "rendered" attribute to decide if they are visible or not. When you want to re-render all the included components, just re-render the output panel, and all will work without a problem.

Ajax validators

Another feature of the Ajax framework is the Ajax validators. They work with the JSF validation system. However, as it is event based you can use it to trigger the validation while you are typing, or when you move to another field, and so on. You can mix standard and custom validation and also use the Hibernate Validator framework (so you can just annotate the entire properties to add new validators).

RichFaces components overview

The RichFaces framework contains many JSF components to add Ajax to our applications in a very simple way, without needing to know anything about JavaScript (but if you know it, you have more features to use the framework inside your personalized JS code).

There are a lot of components for different kinds of tasks (such as interaction, input, output, drag-and-drop, validation, and so on). We are going to explain how they work every time we use them in the forthcoming chapters.

Throughout the book, we are going to develop an application using RichFaces. While doing so, we'll see how those components work in practice using real examples that cover all of their functionalities.

RichFaces skinnability overview

In standard CSS, you can't define a particular value (for example, a color or a font size) to "reuse" it in more than one selector—you have to copy and paste it where you need it.

So, if you have to change it, you have to search for the value and manually replace it every time it occurs. As you can figure out, this is an error-prone process that can bring lot of problems and layout inconsistencies.

Moreover, if you need an interface that supports multiple sets of color and must be adjusted on the fly , you have to work with a lot of CSS files having the same declarations but different colors, and you would also have to maintain them for other updates.

The RichFaces skinnability feature is here to help us; it's not a CSS replacement, but integrates it by adding more capabilities.

Summary

In this chapter, we've learnt what the aims of the RichFaces framework are, what are its components (the Ajax framework, the RichFaces components, and skinnability), and what you can do by using it in a web application.

In the next chapter, we will learn how to use those components while developing a real Ajax application. We are also going to learn the most useful programming pattern and optimization techniques, in order to use this framework at its best for our Ajax web applications.

2
Getting Ready

In this chapter, we are going to set up and understand our project in order to get ready to develop an application using the RichFaces framework.

We'll explain how to create a project (both automatically and manually) and the **Integrated Development Environments (IDEs)** that you can use to boost your productivity during the development.

We are going to talk a little about other technologies such as JBoss Seam and Facelets. You don't have to know them to understand this book, but we suggest you to learn them as they really can boost your productivity.

Creating a RichFaces JSF project the simple way

Obviously, we can create the project from scratch using our preferred IDE, but it is a boring and long task, as you have to set a lot of configuration files and check all the library dependencies. The most convenient method of creating a new project is to use an IDE that supports it (for example, Eclipse with the JBoss tools plugin) or use a tool such as seam-gen.

In real life, you would use RichFaces together with other technologies such as JBoss Seam, Facelets, JPA, and so on. The task of creating a complete and ready-to-run project (for different IDEs) is done very well by this tool, which is included in the JBoss Seam distribution.

Of course, we can just configure everything manually (and we'll see how later in the chapter), but for 90% of "real" projects, this is a good starting point, which means you will save a lot of time.

Seam-gen

We strongly recommend the use of seam-gen for your first project creation. By using it, you will be able to create "in seconds" a new project, which is ready to deploy and to be opened using the Eclipse, IntelliJ Idea, and NetBeans IDEs!

Seam-gen generates an ANT build script, common configuration files, and a basic structure with Facelets templating support.

Moreover, it can automatically generate the JPA entities from a database using the Hibernate `hbm2java` tool and a simple CRUD (Create, Read, Update, Delete) application (using a Ruby on Rails approach), although we don't want that at this time.

Seam-gen uses RichFaces as the default component library (both seam-gen and Richfaces are JBoss projects) and automatically configures it into the project. We are going to use it to have a fast start and concentrate on the RichFaces features.

The project we are going to develop has support for EJB, JPA, JSF (of course!), Facelets, JBoss Seam, and RichFaces. All of the libraries are put into the `lib` directory of the generated project, and you can update them by just overwriting them (see the *Update RichFaces libraries in a seam-gen generated project* section).

Download and install seam-gen

Seam-gen is a command-line tool and is very simple to use. First, let's download and install it in the following way:

- Go to `http://seamframework.org/Download` and download the latest version of JBoss Seam (now Version 2.2)
- Decompress the zip (or `tar.gz`) package into your local drive

That's it; as you can see, it is not a real install, because seam-gen is included in the JBoss Seam distribution package.

Generating a project using seam-gen

Creating a project with seam-gen is quite simple. Just open the terminal window, navigate inside the JBoss Seam folder where you have decompressed the package, and launch the following command if you're using Microsoft Windows:

```
seam setup
```

If you are using a Unix-like system such as GNU/Linux or Mac OS X, enter the following command:

```
./seam setup
```

Seam-gen will ask some questions, which you will have to answer. Be sure to say *no* when it asks if you want to use ICEFaces instead of RichFaces (no is the default answer), and *yes* to the question "Are you working with tables that already exist in the database?", if you want to generate the entities from an existing database.

In the next chapter, we will develop an example starting from a seam-gen project, and we will see the meaning of every question.

When the setup is complete, you can call seam-gen again to create the project with the following command, if you are using Microsoft Windows:

```
seam create-project
```

If you are using a Unix-like system, such as GNU/Linux or Mac OS X, use the following command:

```
./seam create-project
```

This command creates an empty project with all the things we need in order to start coding.

To generate the JPA entities, you can enter the following command if you are using Microsoft Windows:

```
seam generate-model
```

If you are using a Unix-like system, use the following command:

```
/seam generate-model
```

You can use other commands in order to generate a CRUD application, new actions, forms, and so on. For a complete list of commands, type the following command if you are using Microsoft Windows:

```
seam help
```

If you are using a Unix-like system, use the following command:

```
./seam help
```

For more information about seam-gen, you can also consult the official documentation for JBoss Seam at `http://docs.jboss.org/seam/2.2.0.GA/reference/en-US/html/gettingstarted.html`

The seam-gen generated projects can be opened using your preferred IDE (or if you use Eclipse, you can import them into your workspace), and are ready to be edited in order to implement new features.

Update RichFaces libraries in a seam-gen generated project

Whenever a new version of the RichFaces framework is released, updating your project is very simple, as shown in the following steps:

1. Download the latest ZIP package of RichFaces (the `bin` version) from `http://www.jboss.org/richfaces/download/stable.html`.

2. Unzip the package onto your hard drive.

3. Enter into the `lib` directory of the RichFaces folder you've just unzipped.

4. Rename the library files, by removing the version number (For example, `richfaces-api-3.3.1.GA` becomes `richfaces-api.jar`).

5. Copy all of the three files into the `lib` directory of your project, overwriting the old ones.

6. Call the `deploy` ANT target in order to deploy the new libraries into the Application Server.

Overview of the project structure

Once we finish generating seam-gen, we have a complete project to start working on. Here is a screenshot of the project structure as we can see it when it is opened in Eclipse:

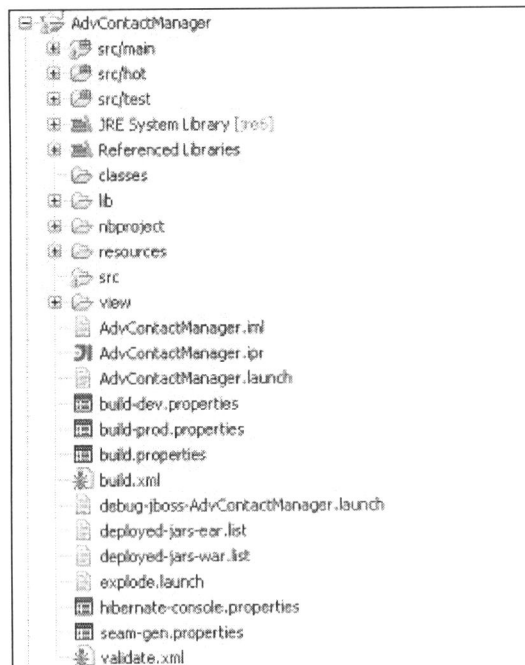

You will notice that there are three source folders (**src/main**, **src/hot,** and **src/test**) and other folders described as follows:

Folder	Description
src/main	Contains the model classes (the JPA entities we have seen).
src/hot	It is the source folder for session beans, Seam components, and everything that your project needs in order to control the model and the view.
src/test	It contains the test classes.
/classes	It contains the compiled classes (it is used by Eclipse, you don't have to worry about it).
/lib	It contains all the libraries of the project. If you want to add a new library, just add it here and then add the library name into **deployed-jars-ear.list** and **deployed-jars-war.list** (depending on whether you want to add the library into the EAR package or the WAR package).
/nbproject	It contains the project information for the Sun NetBeans IDE.
/src	This is the folder containing the source files (that you see on the top as source folders).
/view	It is the root for published web files and contains web-related stuff such as XHTML files, images, other folders, swf, and all the things that you need to make visible from your web application path.

Besides these folders, we can see other files in the previous screenshot, such as the **AdvContactManager.ipr** file (that is, the project file for the IntelliJ Idea IDE) and the **build.properties** file (to configure the JBoss home directory and the domain where the application will be deployed). After these, you can see the **build.xml** file (an ANT script that manages the deploying phase and other actions), some launch configurations, the library deployment list that we have seen, the properties file for the Hibernate console, the seam-gen file, and the ANT file for the validation task.

Incremental hot deployment

Actually, there isn't complete out of the box, hot deployment support. You can enable the `debug` mode on Seam and Facelets by adding the following line to the `components.xml` file found in the `resources/WEB-INF/` folder:

```
<core:init debug="true">
```

During the `debug` mode, you can change any Facelets XHTML and `pages.xml` file, and immediately see the changes.

Unfortunately, you can't do the same with **Enterprise Java Bean (EJB)** components, but there is a medium support for POJO Seam components. In fact, you can change the content of methods in a class and immediately see the modifications without the need to restart the application. However, the only limitation is that if you change the signature of the component (for example add, remove, or change method names), you have to restart the application in order to see the modification. This is not a big development limitation, but they are working to fix it anyway.

Seam and Facelets support

JBoss Seam is becoming very popular, because it can really do what it promises: it simplifies the use of EJB/JPA frameworks with JSF.

It stays on top of Java EE 5, extending it and solving integration problems, and simplifying the development of enterprise applications. One of the most important things in JSF development is that Seam provides an approach to integrate EJB and JSF in a clean and consistent solution, adding many new features and reducing configuration steps.

Besides the integration of EJB and JSF, Seam also has very interesting, new features and we suggest you to consider this technology while developing a JSF application.

As a plus, a lot of ideas coming from Seam will be integrated into the new Java EE specification (the core features of Seam will be in a new standard framework called **Web Beans JSR-299**). Therefore, using and understanding this technology is an investment for the future too.

Facelets is a very useful open source framework that enables the use of XHTML for JSF web pages, improving performance, readability, and productivity. While using Facelets, you don't have to enclose the free text into the `f:verbatim` tag. Also, it offers a complete (and advanced) templating system, debugging support, better error pages (with the exact position of the error), and very useful components. JSF 2.0 specification got many ideas from Facelets.

RichFaces works out of the box with Seam and Facelets. In the case of Seam 2, you just have to define the Facelets view handler `context-param` (as we have seen in the Facelets support), and then use the Seam filter without configuring anything else.

The real world application that we are going to develop in the coming chapters will use JBoss Seam and Facelets technologies (but you don't have to know them to understand the code, and they can also be used with other frameworks). You can get the `web.xml` file for JBoss Seam, Facelets, and JBoss RichFaces support from the source code of the application.

Adding RichFaces manually to your existing JSF project

Adding RichFaces libraries to an existing project is safe, and you won't see any different behavior in your existing non-RichFaces code.

In this section, we are going to discover how to integrate the RichFaces libraries manually in your projects.

Downloading RichFaces

The latest release of RichFaces can be downloaded as a ZIP (or `tar.gz`) package from `http://www.jboss.org/jbossrichfaces/downloads/` (pick the `bin` version). Extract the file onto your hard drive and you're done.

You will find the **lib** folder inside the distribution package, which contains the library JAR files and three other documentation folders:

- **apidocs**: It contains the javadoc generated document about the Java classes, which come with the library

- **tlddocs**: It contains documentation about the tags (and their attributes), which come with the library (generated by the Tag Library Documentation Generator)

- **docs**: It contains the user guide, FAQ document, migration document, and CDK guide

From the same address, you can also download the three plug 'n' skin examples in order to add new skins to your application (however, in the standard package you can choose from a standard set of skins), we'll see how to do that in the Chapter 9, *Creating a New plug'n'skin*.

Basic configuration

This section explains how to configure a basic JSF project in order to add RichFaces support manually.

Where to put the libraries

The first thing to do is (obviously) to add the RichFaces libraries into your `lib` folder.

The framework libraries are:

JAR library	Description
`richfaces-api-X.Y.Z.GA.jar`	Contains all of the interfaces and base classes of the framework
`richfaces-impl-X.Y.Z.GA.jar`	Contains the implementation classes of the framework
`richfaces-ui-X.Y.Z.GA.jar`	Contains the implementation classes of the components of the framework

The other optional libraries are the skins (we used `laguna` in our example) and are:

- `laguna-X.Y.Z.GA.jar`
- `glassX-X.Y.Z.GA.jar`
- `darkX-X.Y.Z.GA.jar`

If you develop your own skin, you will need the skin's JAR file to be in your classpath. Here is an example image of the web application we are going to develop using the **laguna** skin:

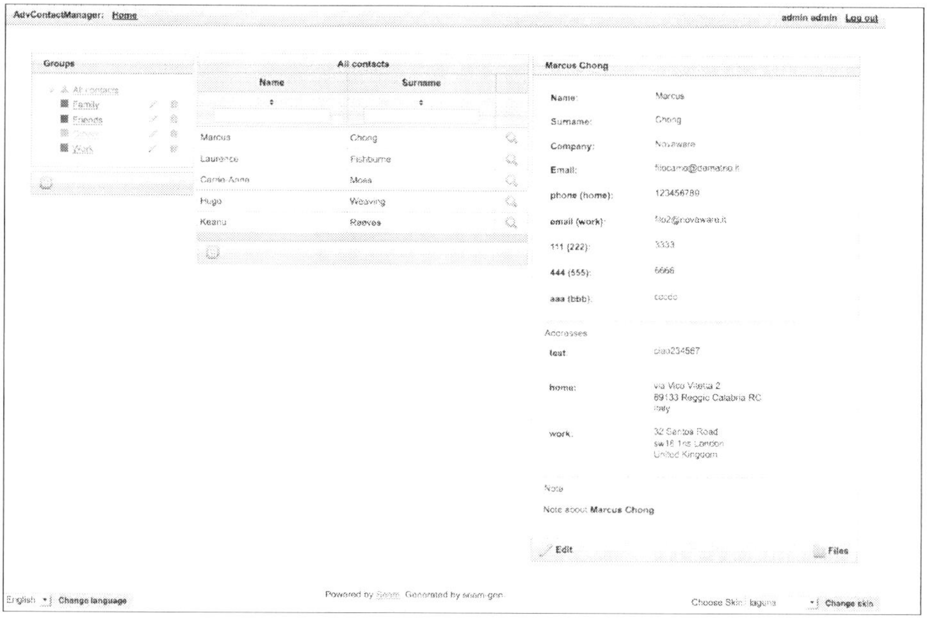

The next screenshot, instead, shows the same application using the **darkX** skin:

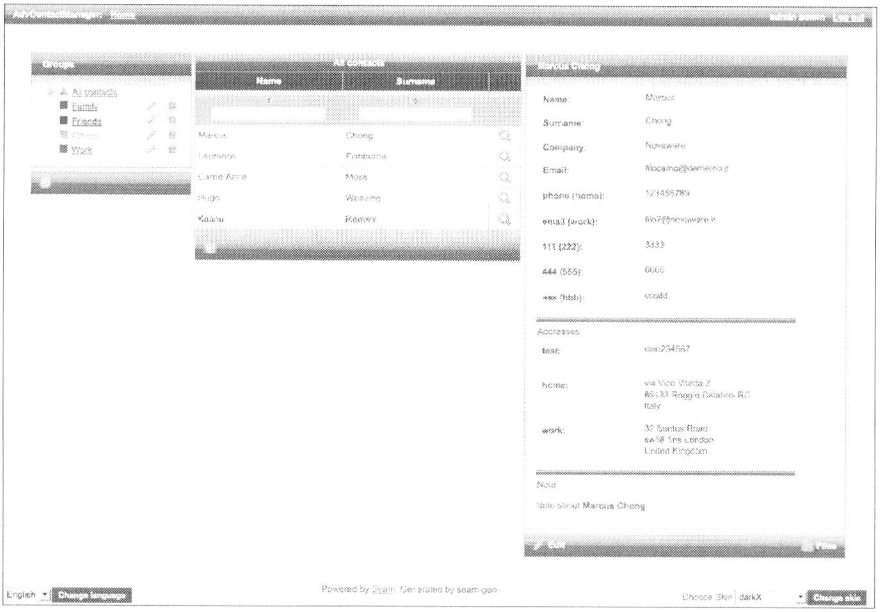

And the **glassX** skin as shown in the following screenshot:

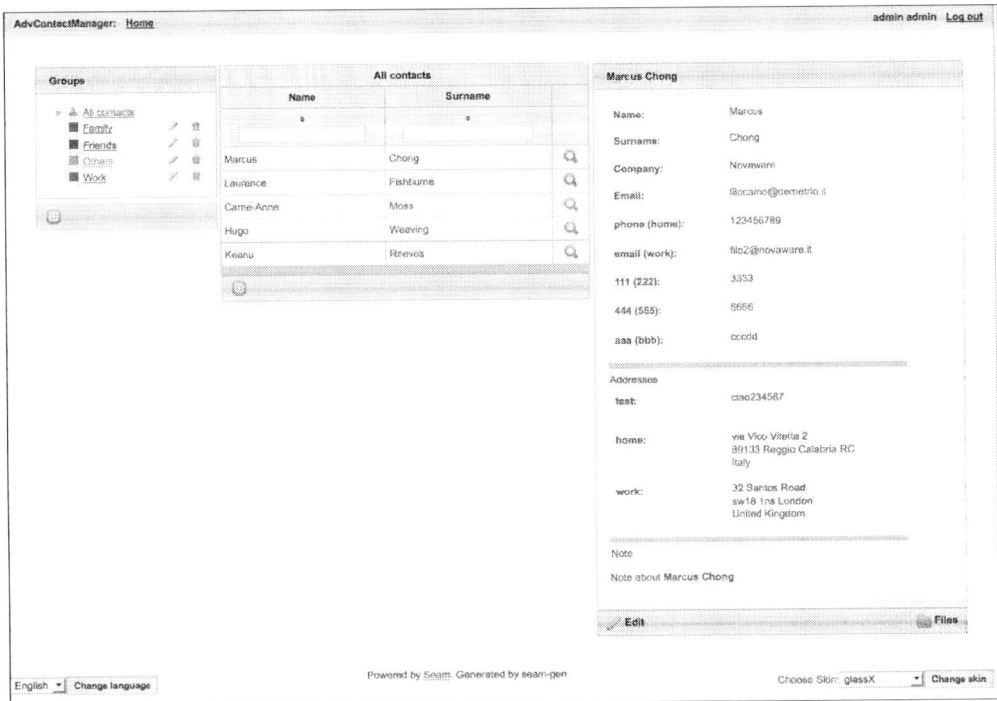

The libraries might stay in the classpath, so if your project deploys a **Web Application Archive (WAR)**, all of the libraries might stay in the WEB-INF/lib directory.

If you are deploying an **Enterprise Archive (EAR)**, your EAR/lib directory might contain the richfaces-api-X.Y.Z.GA.jar library and the other ones might stay in WEB-INF/lib of the WAR contained in the EAR.

To summarize, we have the following table:

Deploy on	Insert RichFaces libraries into	RichFaces libraries to be inserted
WAR package	`<war-root>/WEB-INF/lib/`	• `richfaces-api-X.Y.Z.GA.jar` • `richfaces-impl-X.Y.Z.GA.jar` • `richfaces-ui-X.Y.Z.GA.jar` (all RichFaces libraries)

EAR package	`<ear-root>/lib/`
	
	`<ear-root>/<war-root>/WEB-INF/lib/`
		`richfaces-api-X.Y.Z.GA.jar`
		• `richfaces-impl-X.Y.Z.GA.jar`
		• `richfaces-ui-X.Y.Z.GA.jar`

Registering RichFaces

The second step is to register RichFaces by adding some configuration code to your `web.xml` file.

We are going to add RichFaces classes and configuration into our JSF application using a standard filter.

First of all, we set some context parameters (just add it inside the `web-app` element):

```
<!— Skin used by RichFaces -->
<context-param>
  <param-name>org.richfaces.SKIN</param-name>
  <param-value>laguna</param-value>
</context-param>

<!-- Use RichFaces also for standard HTML controls -->
<context-param>
  <param-name>org.richfaces.CONTROL_SKINNING</param-name>
  <param-value>enable</param-value>
</context-param>
```

org.richfaces.SKIN and org.richfaces.CONTROL_SKINNING are skin-related parameters. The first parameter sets the skin that RichFaces has to use, and the second tells the framework to also apply the skin to the standard controls. We'll see the other options in the later chapters.

After that, we have to register and map the RichFaces filter using the following configuration code:

```
<filter>
  <display-name>RichFaces Filter</display-name>
  <filter-name>richfaces</filter-name>
  <filter-class>org.ajax4jsf.Filter</filter-class>
</filter>

<filter-mapping>
  <filter-name>richfaces</filter-name>
  <servlet-name>Faces Servlet</servlet-name>
  <dispatcher>REQUEST</dispatcher>
  <dispatcher>FORWARD</dispatcher>
  <dispatcher>INCLUDE</dispatcher>
</filter-mapping>
```

If you are using a different name for the Faces servlet, you should change it accordingly.

The RichFaces filter can now work properly and you can start coding using its components!

Facelets support

As we have said, RichFaces supports Facelets without problems.

In order to add it to your project, you don't have to define the FaceletViewHandler in the faces-config.xml file as with the standard Facelets configuration. You just have to configure the org.ajax4jsf.VIEW_HANDLERS context parameter and the RichFaces filter will manage it correctly.

This is the code that you have to insert into your web.xml file:

```
<context-param>
  <param-name>org.ajax4jsf.VIEW_HANDLERS</param-name>
  <param-value>com.sun.facelets.FaceletViewHandler</param-value>
</context-param>
```

As you can see, we have just set the org.ajax4jsf.VIEW_HANDLERS context parameter in order to tell RichFaces to use the Facelet view handler.

IDEs

You can code JSF by hand, but obviously it is better and more productive to have an IDE that automates repetitive tasks. Popular IDEs support the basic JSF functionalities, so RichFaces components are recognized without a problem. However, as RichFaces is a JBoss product, there is extra support for it in their IDE (they have an open source version and a commercial one, we'll talk about them in the next section), and you can add RichFaces automatically to JSF projects. Furthermore, they have visual component development support that can be useful in some cases.

Eclipse/JBoss Tools

JBoss Tools is a collection of Eclipse Plugins made by JBoss to support most of their own technologies such as RichFaces, Seam, Hibernate/JPA, JBoss Application Server, and jBPM. It adds a lot of features to Eclipse **Web Tools Platform** (**WTP**), making life easier for those who want to use those frameworks. Of course, you also have all of the Eclipse platform features and the possibility to add different plugins into the same development environment.

It is completely open source and freely downloadable. The supported platforms are Windows, Linux, and Mac OS X.

You can discover more at `http://jboss.org/tools/`.

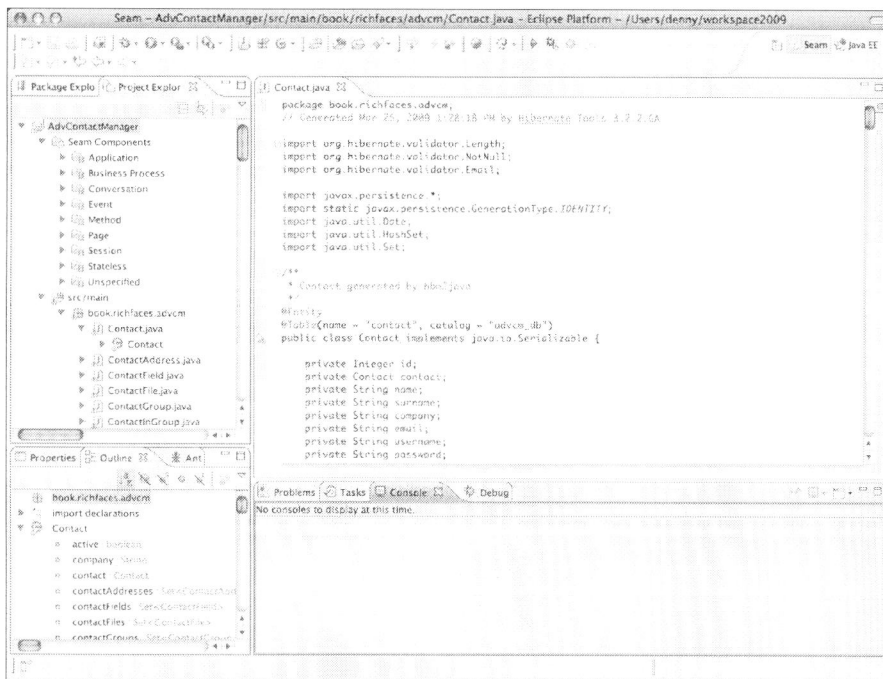

Where to download and how to install it

JBoss Tools is a set of Eclipse plugins, so, to install it we have to first install the Eclipse IDE. You can do everything starting from the JBoss Tools web site, by following these simple steps:

1. Go to `http://jboss.org/tools/`.

2. Select the **Downloads** menu, then **Stable Releases**, then click on the latest one (it is now 3.0 GA).

3. You will be redirected to a page with a list of all plugins (you can also install just a subset of all the distribution plugins). Select the first one, that is **All Plugins,** and download the right version for the platform you are using (the links are on the right side of the table under the **Download** column).

4. While downloading JBoss Tools, click on the link at the top of the table (now the link is **Requires Eclipse Ganymede 3.4.2**), in order to download Eclipse.

5. You are redirected to the Eclipse project web site.

6. There is a table with all the Eclipse versions that you can download.

7. Download the first one (**Eclipse IDE for Java EE Developers**), clicking on the link on the right according to your platform by following the download instructions.

Once you finish both the downloads, let's install them:

1. In order to install Eclipse, just unzip the Eclipse package and copy the `eclipse` folder into your final drive location and you are done.

2. Now unzip the JBoss Tools package, you have a folder called `eclipse` containing two folders (namely `features` and `plugins`).

3. Copy the content of the `features` folder of JBoss Tools into the `features` folder of the Eclipse installation folder.

4. Now do the same with the `plugins` folder (copy it from JBoss Tools to Eclipse installation).

5. You are done, start Eclipse by entering into the folder and double-clicking on the executable file.

JBoss Developer Studio

Like JBoss Tools, JBoss Developer Studio provides Eclipse plugin support to JBoss technologies. It uses the same plugins as JBoss Tools, but they are certified with five years RedHat support (JBoss is a RedHat company). It also has an installer that simplifies the installation phase (the installation is a step-by-step wizard).

JBoss Developer Studio is a subscription-based commercial product (but it is very cheap). The supported platforms are Windows, Linux, and Mac OS X.

If you choose to use it for development, you can access the home page `http://www.jboss.com/products/devstudio`.

Importing a seam-gen generated project into Eclipse

After generating a project using seam-gen, if you are using Eclipse (with JBoss Tools or JBoss Developer Studio), you can import it into your workspace.

This is a simple task shown as follows:

1. Select **Import** from the **File** menu.
2. Open the **General** tree node and select the **Existing project into Workspace** option.
3. Select the parent folder (root directory) where the generated project located is, by clicking on the **Browse** button.
4. The project would be selected for the import.
5. Also select the **Copy projects into workspace** checkbox if the project is not in your workspace directory.
6. Click on the **Finish** button.
7. Your project is now ready in your workspace.

IntelliJ Idea

IntelliJ Idea is a very good commercial IDE that supports many features (from J2SE to J2EE and more) and offers good tools to work with. It supports many languages and frameworks (JSF, Seam, Hibernate/JPA, Spring, Struts, Struts 2, and so on.) and they are well integrated into the platform itself.

The developing experience is very good and if you are using JBoss Seam and seam-gen, you'll get out-of-the-box support for this IDE.

If not using seam-gen you have to add and configure the project by hand to add the RichFaces support (however, as we've seen it's a very simple task).

It is a license-based commercial product (there are different prices based on the license type) and it runs on Windows, Linux, and Mac OS X.

You can find more information about this at `http://www.jetbrains.com/idea/`.

Where to download and how to install it

Installing IntelliJ Idea is very simple, just go to `http://www.jetbrains.com/idea/download/` and download the version for your operating system:

- On Windows: Run the downloaded `.exe` file and follow the installation wizard

- On Mac OS X: Mount (by double-clicking) the downloaded `.dmg` file and copy it to your application folder

- On Linux: Decompress the `tar.gz` file and run `idea.sh` inside the unpacked folder

Summary

In this chapter, we learned how to configure our environment by creating a simple project using the seam-gen tool, adding support to Seam and Facelets. Also, we had a look at the manual configuration for the RichFaces libraries and started understanding the IDE, which we can use while developing with this framework.

In the next chapter, we'll create a simple example to see how all of these things work in practice.

3
First Steps

In this chapter, we will start understanding how to write a rich application using RichFaces.

In order to do this, we've chosen to start with a simple example that implements an Ajax contact list. The user will be able to list, add, and delete contacts without the need of reloading the browser page.

We'll see how some important Ajax components work and how to ajaxize a JSF application by using the RichFaces framework concepts.

The features developed in this example will be seen in depth in the coming chapters.

A simple contact manager

The example application is a simple contact manager—it has a list of contacts and a form to add new contacts. Also, you can delete a specific contact from the list.

The example shows how the Ajax framework works and how you can use the RichFaces Ajax components. It also uses some graphic RichFaces components such as `rich:panel`, `rich:spacer`, and `rich:separator`. It uses the `rich:calendar` component for date input, and the RichFaces version of `dataTable` (`rich:dataTable` and `rich:column`) with automatic filtering and ordering capabilities.

We also use the Ajax validation component (`rich:beanValidator`) to ajaxize and enhance the standard JSF validation.

The skin we have chosen can be changed by editing the skin name in the `web.xml` file (we'll see how to do that in the following chapters).

Creating the new project

As we've seen in Chapter 2, *Getting Ready*, in order to use seam-gen, just open a terminal window and navigate to the JBoss Seam distribution directory.

From that point, you can execute seam-gen commands. Before giving seam-gen the command that creates a new project, we have to configure it using the following commands.

If you are using Microsoft Windows, use the following command:

```
seam setup
```

If you are using a Unix-like system such as GNU/Linux or Mac OS X, use the following command:

```
./seam setup
```

After the welcome text, seam-gen will ask us some questions regarding the project configuration we would like to have; for every question, there is a default answer (in square brackets) that you can choose by pressing the *Enter* key.

The questions are not difficult to understand; let's go through them and create our project for the example:

Question	Description	Answer
Enter your Java project workspace (the directory that contains your Seam projects)	This is the directory in which we want to save our new project (it depends on our environment and preferences)	(The new project directory path)
Enter your JBoss AS home directory	It is the directory where the JBoss Application Server is installed	(The JBoss directory path)
Enter the project name	The name of the application	SimpleContactManager
Do you want to use ICEfaces instead of RichFaces [n]	Seam-gen also supports ICEFaces (another component framework), but we want to use RichFaces, so just press *Enter*	No
Select a RichFaces skin [classic] (blueSky, [classic], deepMarine, DEFAULT, emeraldTown, japanCherry, ruby, wine)	We can select one of the provided skins for our project; we can change it later, for now classic skin is okay	(Let's press *Enter*)
Is this project deployed as an EAR (with EJB components) or a WAR (with no EJB support) [ear]	We can generate a WAR package or an EAR package for our application. We would like a complete EAR application with EJB support	(Let's press *Enter*)
Enter the Java package name for your session beans	The package name containing our session beans (generated by Seam-gen)	book.richfaces.scm
Enter the Java package name for your entity beans	The package name containing our entity beans (generated by Seam-gen)	book.richfaces.scm

Question	Description	Answer
Enter the Java package name for your test cases	The package name containing our test cases' beans	`book.richfaces.scm.test`
What kind of database are you using?	For this simple example, we don't use the database at all	(Let's press *Enter* for default (hsql))
Enter the Hibernate dialect for your database	Not used for our project	(Let's press *Enter*)
Enter the filesystem path to the JDBC driver jar	Not used for our project	(Let's press *Enter*)
Enter JDBC driver class for your database	Not used for our project	(Let's press *Enter*)
Enter the JDBC URL for your database	Not used for our project	(Let's press *Enter*)
Enter database username	Not used for our project	(Let's press *Enter*)
Enter database password	Not used for our project	(Let's press *Enter*)
Enter the database schema name (it is OK to leave this blank)	Not used for our project	(Let's press *Enter*)
Enter the database catalog name (it is OK to leave this blank)	Not used for our project	(Let's press *Enter*)
Are you working with tables that already exist in the database?	Not used for our project	(Let's press *Enter*)
Do you want to drop and recreate the database tables and data in import.sql each time you deploy?	Not used for our project	(Let's press *Enter*)

Okay, we've completed the configuration of the project. We will see how to configure a project for a MySQL DBMS connection in Chapter 4, *The Application* (when we will start making the real application); for now it's okay to use the default answers.

We are ready to create the project using the following commands. If you are using Microsoft Windows, use the following command:

```
seam create-project
```

If you are using a Unix-like system such as GNU/Linux or Mac OS X, use the following command:

```
./seam create-project
```

If you are using the Eclipse IDE, you have to import the project into the workspace (we described how to do that in Chapter 2). With other IDEs (such as IntelliJ IDEA or NetBeans), you can open the project from the location specified while executing seam-gen.

Templating and Facelets

Our new project not only has the Facelets support included, but also a first template file, which we can edit in order to add our features. You can find it at the path /view/layout/template.xhtml.

It is the structure we use in other pages to avoid repeatedly writing the same components across pages.

This is how it looks:

```
<!DOCTYPE html PUBLIC "-//W3C//DTD XHTML 1.0 Transitional//EN"
http://www.w3.org/TR/xhtml1/DTD/xhtml1-transitional.dtd">
<f:view contentType="text/html"
        xmlns="http://www.w3.org/1999/xhtml"
        xmlns:ui="http://java.sun.com/jsf/facelets"
        xmlns:h="http://java.sun.com/jsf/html"
        xmlns:f="http://java.sun.com/jsf/core"
        xmlns:a="http://richfaces.org/a4j"
        xmlns:s="http://jboss.com/products/seam/taglib">
<html>
    <head>
      <meta http-equiv="Content-Type"
      content="text/html;charset=UTF-8"/>
      <title>AdvContactManager</title>
      <link rel="shortcut icon"
      href="#{request.contextPath}/favicon.ico"/>
      <a:loadStyle src="resource:///stylesheet/theme.xcss"/>
```

```
      <a:loadStyle src="/stylesheet/theme.css"/>
      <ui:insert name="head"/>
    </head>
    <body>
      <ui:include src="menu.xhtml">
      <ui:param name="projectName" value="AdvContactManager"/>
      </ui:include>
      <div class="body">
        <h:messages id="messages"
                    globalOnly="true"
                    styleClass="message"
                    errorClass="errormsg"
                    infoClass="infomsg"
                    warnClass="warnmsg"
                    rendered="#{showGlobalMessages != 'false'}"/>
        <ui:insert name="body"/>
      </div>
      <div class="footer">
      Powered by <a href="http://jboss.com/products/seam">Seam</a>.
      Generated by seam-gen.
      </div>
    </body>
  </html>
</f:view>
```

Let's discuss the page.

We can see the DOCTYPE declaration, which tells us the kind of document it is, and then the `<f:view>` tag with Facelets XML namespace declarations of the component libraries we are going to use. Note that in this page, we don't use RichFaces component (yet) and only the namespace for Ajax4Jsf components (`xmlns:a="http://richfaces.org/a4j"`) is written. This is because the `<a:loadStyle>` tag is used. If you want to use the other RichFaces components, you have to include the corresponding `xmlns` (the namespace required to be able to use every RichFaces component with the `rich` prefix) as follows:

```
xmlns:rich=http://richfaces.org/rich
```

We are going to insert it as we want to use RichFaces components in the `template.xhtml` page too.

Let's continue to analyze the page. Our document starts (we can see the `<html>`, `<head>`, `<meta>`, `<title>`, and `<link>` tags) after the `<f:view>` tag.

After those standard tags, we can see `<a:loadStyle>`, which is a very useful Ajax4Jsf component to render links to the `head` section of the page.

There is a Facelets component called `<ui:insert>`. We are not going to explain the Facelets framework in depth, all you have to know is that the component makes insertion points in order to insert code from other pages, which use this template. Therefore, it is very useful to put code into the `head` section from other pages.

We find the Facelets `<ui:include>` tag used to include another page called `menu.xhtml` in the `body` section. It is the top menu that we want to reuse for the entire application. We also pass `ui:param` inside the tag, which the included page can use (the parameter is the project name in this case).

Now we find a `div` element that contains the standard `<h:messages>` component, which we are going to replace with the corresponding RichFaces component.

Below the `h:messages` tag, we find the body Facelets insertion point that is used by other pages in order to insert specific content (we will see how it works in the following paragraphs).

At the end of the code, there is another `div` section, including some text with the JBoss Seam web site link.

Modifying the created project

For this example, we will just use one page and no menu, so let's edit the `template.xhtml` page and delete the section that includes the menu into every page:

```
<ui:include src="menu.xhtml">
  <ui:param name="projectName"
            value="AdvContactManager"/>
</ui:include>
```

If we want to, we can also personalize the footer by changing the text or deleting it.

We have to change the title of the page in the template to *Simple Contact Manager*.

Now open the `home.xhtml` file for editing, it comes with standard text presenting seam-gen. Let's delete the `h1` section and the `rich:panel` component to have an empty page.

Moreover, we can add the support for Ajx4JSF components by inserting the XML namespace at the top of the page. Now, the page looks like this:

```
<!DOCTYPE html PUBLIC "-//W3C//DTD XHTML 1.0 Transitional//EN"
http://www.w3.org/TR/xhtml1/DTD/xhtml1-transitional.dtd">

<ui:composition xmlns="http://www.w3.org/1999/xhtml"
    xmlns:s="http://jboss.com/products/seam/taglib"
    xmlns:ui="http://java.sun.com/jsf/facelets"
    xmlns:f="http://java.sun.com/jsf/core"
    xmlns:h="http://java.sun.com/jsf/html"
    xmlns:a4j="https://ajax4jsf.dev.java.net/ajax"
    xmlns:rich="http://richfaces.org/rich"
    template="layout/template.xhtml">

<ui:define name="body">
<!-- my code -->
</ui:define>

</ui:composition>
```

We still have to add the structure in order to render the form and the contact list. We will use a standard h:panelGrid with two columns for this purpose, so let's put the following code inside the body definition (replacing the `<!-- my code -->` comment):

```
<h3>Simple Contact Manager</h3>

<rich:separator height="1"
lineType="solid" width="100%"/>

<h:panelGrid columns="2" width="100%"
columnClasses="form-column, table-column">

<!-- Insert new contact form -->

<!-- Contact list -->

</h:panelGrid>
```

As you can see, we also added a header (h3) and a spacer between the header and h:panelGrid. We also used two CSS classes for the panel grid, but we have not defined them yet.

So, let's open the `theme.css` file inside the `stylesheet` folder. You can see some classes added by seam-gen, ignore them and add the following CSS code at the end of the file:

```
form-column {
   vertical-align: top;
   width: 20%;
}
table-column {
   vertical-align: top;
   width: 80%;
}
```

Those simple CSS classes define the width of the two columns and align the content on top.

The model

We have to store our contact information in a Java class. In this case, we don't have the database support and our data stays in memory. In the real application that we are going to develop in the next chapters we will have MySQL support.

Therefore, we will be using a simple **Plain Old Java Object (POJO)** to store the information we need. Let's create a new Java class called `ContactBean` in the `book.richfaces.scm` package (the one in the `src/main` folder) and insert the following code:

```
package book.richfaces.scm;
import java.util.Date;

public class ContactBean {
    private String name;
    private String surname;
    private String email;
    private Date birthdate;

    public ContactBean() {
    }

    public String getName() {
      return name;
    }

    public void setName(String name) {
      this.name = name;
    }

    public String getSurname() {
```

```
      return surname;
    }
    public void setSurname(String surname) {
      this.surname = surname;
    }
    public String getEmail() {
      return email;
    }
    public void setEmail(String email) {
      this.email = email;
    }
    public Date getBirthdate() {
      return birthdate;
    }
    public void setBirthdate(Date birthdate) {
      this.birthdate = birthdate;
    }
  }
```

As you can see, this is a simple Java class with private properties and public accessors and mutators.

The managed bean

In order to manage the actions of this simple example (such as inserting a new contact, deleting a contact, listing all contacts), we need a managed bean. We can use a standard JSF managed bean (so we have to configure the `faces-config.xml` file) or a Seam component, and we've chosen the second option because we don't have to configure anything while using a Seam component. We will just add an annotation to the class we are going to use (Seam simplifies JSF development a lot). Anyway, the code is simple and can be used as is for a standard JSF managed bean.

So, let's create a new Java class called `ContactsManager` in the `book.richfaces.scm` package (the one in `src/hot` folder). At first, the class is empty:

```
package book.richfaces.scm;

public class ContactsManager {
}
```

First of all, we need a place to save our contact list—a standard list of ContactBean instances. So, let's add the code to manage it:

```
package book.richfaces.scm;
import java.util.ArrayList;
import java.util.List;

public class ContactsManager {
    private List<ContactBean> contactsList;

    public List<ContactBean> getContactsList() {
      if (contactsList==null) {
        contactsList=new ArrayList<ContactBean>();
        }
        return contactsList;
    }

    public void setContactsList(List<ContactBean> contactsList) {
      this.contactsList = contactsList;
    }

}
```

It's a simple private property with a getter and a setter. The getter lazily initializes the contactsList property.

For inserting contacts, we create a new ContactBean instance to connect with the **Insert new contact** form and an action for inserting it into the list. Let's add the code we need inside the ContactsManager class:

```
private ContactBean newContact;
public ContactBean getNewContact() {
  if (newContact==null) {
    newContact=new ContactBean();
    }
    return newContact;
}

public void setNewContact(ContactBean newContact) {
  this.newContact = newContact;
}

public void insertContact() {
  getContactsList().add(0, getNewContact());
  setNewContact(null);
}
```

Again, we have the newContact property with the getter and the setter, and an insertContact action.

Making it a managed bean

As we have said, in order to make the class a managed bean, we can use the standard JSF way or the Seam way.

We'll show both of them now, so you can understand why using Seam is more simple.

Using the normal JSF way, we have to edit the `faces-config.xml` file to tell JSF that the `ContactsManager` class is a managed bean. We have to add the following code inside the `faces-config` element:

```
<managed-bean>
    <managed-bean-name>contactsManager</managed-bean-name>
    <managed-bean-class>
      com.test.manager.ContactsManager
    </managed-bean-class>
    <managed-bean-scope>session</managed-bean-scope>
</managed-bean>
```

Not a difficult code at all, but very verbose as we have to describe the class, its properties, and declare the scope (that is `session` in this case) of the class. Even if tools help us in doing this task, maintaining the `faces-config.xml` file remains difficult.

Using JBoss Seam, the only thing you have to do is to annotate the `ContactsManager` class, which becomes like this:

```
package book.richfaces.scm;
import java.util.ArrayList;
import java.util.List;
import org.jboss.seam.ScopeType;
import org.jboss.seam.annotations.Name;
import org.jboss.seam.annotations.Scope;

@Name("contactsManager")
@Scope(ScopeType.SESSION)
public class ContactsManager {

    // code...

}
```

In this case, we just added two annotations—one (the @Name) of them tells Seam that it is a Seam component (and also a managed bean) named contactsManager, and the other one (@Scope) tells it that the class has SESSION scope (so it will be kept in memory across the requests).

We don't need to modify the faces-config.xml file and describe every field of the class. Simple, isn't it? We are now ready to write the XHTML and connect it with the managed bean (we can refer to it in XHTML using its name, that is contactsManager).

The "Insert new contact" form

This is a form that asks the user for some data and inserts it into the contact list when the user clicks on the **Insert** button. All of this is done using Ajax calls!

All of the data validation is done in Ajax while entering the values for the **Name** and **Surname** fields, and after the button has been clicked for the other fields. But it's just our choice. Also, we can take advantage of Hibernate Validator annotations to set validators on fields, by using the RichFaces Ajax Validator support instead of the f:validation (we'll see how it's done in this section).

In order to show other Ajax functionalities, we also want the **Insert** button to change the caption while the user is typing their name and surname.

The next screenshot shows the final look that we want for the form:

The main box

In order to describe the box of the form, we use a `rich:panel` component with a header. Inside it, we put an `h:panelGrid` with one column to insert fields one below the other. Therefore, we have the form layout ready, just insert this code into the `home.xhtml` file (replace the `<!-- Insert new contact form -->` comment):

```
<rich:panel>
  <f:facet name="header">Insert new contact</f:facet>
  <h:form id="fInsertContact">
  <h:panelGrid columns="1">

    <!-- fields -->
  </h:panelGrid>
  </h:form>
</rich:panel>
```

We declared a simple panel with a header using the `"header"` facet to declare it. If the header is just text, we can also use the `header` attribute in this way:

```
<rich:panel header="Header text">
...
</rich:panel>
```

As you can see, a panel is simple to use and you can put whatever you want inside it. Also, it is fully customizable using the skinnability feature.

> **f:verbatim tag**
>
> It's important not to use `f:verbatim` for self-rendered containers, because it is a transient component and not saved in the JSF component tree.

The form fields

After declaring the panel, we have to put the fields inside, in order to connect them to the managed beans.

We have declared one managed bean called `contactsManager`, which contains an instance of `ContactBean` (the bean that represents a contact), other than all the methods to list, insert, and delete contacts. This is used for inserting a new contact called `newContact`, we are going to connect fields to this instance (that is inside the `contactsManager` bean).

Here is the code for describing the form fields, insert it in the place of the `<!--
fields -->` comment:

```
<h:outputLabel for="name" value="Name"/>
<h:inputText id="name"
             value="#{contactsManager.newContact.name}"
             required="true">
  <rich:beanValidator/>

  a4j:support event="onkeyup"
              timeout="200"
              ajaxSingle="true"
              reRender="insertButton"/>
</h:inputText>

<rich:message for="name" style="color: red;"/>

<h:outputLabel for="surname" value="Surname"/>
<h:inputText id="surname"
             value="#{contactsManager.newContact.surname}"
             required="true">
  <rich:beanValidator/>
  <a4j:support event="onkeyup" timeout="200"
               ajaxSingle="true" reRender="insertButton"/>
</h:inputText>

<rich:message for="surname" style="color: red;"/>

<h:outputLabel for="email" value="Email"/>
<h:inputText id="email"
             value="#{contactsManager.newContact.email}"
             required="true">
  <rich:beanValidator/>
</h:inputText>
<rich:message for="email" style="color: red;"/>

<h:outputLabel for="birthdate" value="Birthdate"/>
<rich:calendar id="birthdate"
               value="#{contactsManager.newContact.birthdate}"
               required="true">
  <rich:beanValidator/>
</rich:calendar>
<rich:message for="birthdate" style="color: red;"/>

<rich:spacer height="15"/>
<rich:separator height="1" lineType="dotted" width="100%"/>

<a4j:commandButton id="insertButton"
    action="#{contactsManager.insertContact}"
value="Insert #{contactsManager.newContact.name} #{contactsManager.
newContact.surname}"
reRender="fInsertContact"/>
```

As we can see, in the first block of code (in the `name` field) we have a standard JSF `h:outputLabel` for inserting the label of the input and a standard `h:inputText` connected to the `ContactBean` field using the `value` attribute.

After that, we used `rich:message` instead of the standard `h:message` component because it supports Ajax out of the box (and it offers more personalization too). See the next section for a better explanation.

Coming back to `h:inputText`, we can see two new tags—`rich:beanValidator` for Ajax field validation and `a4j:support` to update the **Insert** button caption while typing.

Using RichFaces message and messages components instead of the standard ones

By using a standard `h:message` or `h:messages` component, you don't get the Ajax JSF messaging support for JSF Ajax events and the messages are not shown after an Ajax event.

With the `rich:message` and `rich:messages` components, we don't have to care about that as they work with both Ajax and traditional JSF requests.

The basic usage is very simple and quite the same as the standard one:

```
<rich:message for="myComponentId" />
```

Making an Ajax version of the standard component is only a part of the work the RichFaces team has done on this component. In fact, they added a set of interesting features you can use to customize your application.

In fact, they provide a highly-customizable look and feel with CSS-based support. Also, you can customize every single part of the components by adding a facet for different kinds of messages (WARN, INFO, FATAL, ERROR), and customize the "marker" (for example, an icon) accordingly:

```
<rich:message for="myComponentId">
    <f:facet name="warnMarker">
        <h:graphicImage url="/images/warning.png"/>
    </f:facet>
    <f:facet name="errorMarker">
        <h:graphicImage url="/images/error.png"/>
    </f:facet>
    <f:facet name="passedMarker">
        <h:graphicImage url="/images/passed.png"/>
    </f:facet>
</rich:message>
```

Moreover, you can add a `passedLabel` text string that is shown when no error message appears.

Validating our field in a simple way

There are three JSF components that you can use for validation purposes. We will see them in more detail in Chapter 4, *The Application*. We've used `rich:beanValidator` here, because it uses the Hibernate Validator framework to read validation rules directly from the `ContactBean` field.

In this way, we don't have to write (and maintain!) the same validators in different input fields, which refer to the same input.

In our case, we can add Hibernate Validator annotations to the model class (`ContactBean`).

`rich:beanValidator` reads them and uses them to decide the validation strategy; the `ContactBean` class is now defined as follows:

```
public class ContactBean {
    private String name;
    private String surname;
    private String email;
    private Date birthdate;

    public ContactBean() {
    }

    @NotNull
    @Length(min = 3, max = 20)
    public String getName() {
        return name;
    }

    public void setName(String name) {
        this.name = name;
    }

    @NotNull
    @Length(min = 3, max = 20)
    public String getSurname() {
        return surname;
    }

    public void setSurname(String surname) {
        this.surname = surname;
    }

    @NotNull
    @Email
```

```
    public String getEmail() {
        return email;
    }
    public void setEmail(String email) {
        this.email = email;
    }
    @NotNull
    @Past
    public Date getBirthdate() {
        return birthdate;
    }
    public void setBirthdate(Date birthdate) {
        this.birthdate = birthdate;
    }
}
```

It is not the purpose of this book to explain how the Hibernate Validator framework works, but it is simple to understand from the example. If we look at the getName method, we can see the @NotNull and @Length annotations (the latter with two parameters). They tell rich:beanValidator that the field must not be null, and that it has a minimum length of two characters and a maximum length of 20 characters. In 99% of the applications, we just have to annotate validators for every field and we are done. Anyway, it is always possible to add another f:validator tag with rich:beanValidator in order to add specific validation rules.

If we look at the other fields of the ContactBean class, we can find other validators such as @Email and @Past. There are others that you can use and you can even create your own validators for a specific purpose.

Adding Ajax to standard JSF components: a4j:support

Coming back to the form code, after the validator tag, we can see another tag—a4j:support.

This is the most important Ajax component of the library and attaching it as a child adds Ajax capabilities to standard JSF components. The event attribute is used to define the JavaScript event that the Ajax request will be attached to (in this case, onkeyup that fires an event for every key the user types).

The timeout attribute describes the number of milliseconds (ms) to wait before firing the Ajax request. In this case, it is useful to avoid a lot of Ajax requests while the user is writing.

The ajaxSingle attribute tells the framework to just send the value of the field and not to submit the whole form (we just need the date to be inserted in the field, and the form data will be submitted by clicking on the **Insert** button).

Finally, the reRender attribute contains the id(s) of the JSF component to "reRender" after the Ajax request. In this case, we want to update the caption of the insertButton component, which contains the value of the field (contactsManager. newContact.name) updated by the Ajax request.

Another example is shown as follows:

```
<h:form>
    <h:inputText value="#{aBean.myText}">
        <a4j:support event="onblur" reRender="out1" />
    </h:inputText>
</h:form>

<h:outputText
    id="out1"
    value="#{aBean.myText}" />
```

After the user puts some text inside inputText and presses the *Tab* key or clicks outside the input field (JavaScript event onblur), a4j:support will update the myText property of the aBean bean with the typed text. Then it will update the outputText with id="out1".

The **Surname** field works like the **Name** field, unlike the **Email** field that doesn't contain the a4j:support tag and is validated (always using an Ajax request) when the user clicks on the **Insert** button (a4j:commandButton).

Calendar field

In the fourth field, we use the `rich:calendar` component to get the birth date of the contact. It is very simple to use, but it has a lot of optional fields and can become very powerful. It can be used to set the time too. It is fully customizable, shows a pop-up window, and it also works with manual input.

In the following screenshot, you can see how it appears when the user clicks on the icon on the right in order to select the date.

We will look at the use of this component in more depth in the following chapters.

Simple layout components: rich:separator and rich:spacer

Those are two simple, but very useful layout components. They can show a customizable line (such as solid, dotted, double, and so on) and a personalized (in size) empty block rendered as a transparent image, respectively.

The HTML result of inserting a `rich:separator` component with the `height` attribute set to `1`, the `width` attribute set to `100%`, and the `lineType` attribute set to `dotted` is as follows:

```
<div class="rich-separator " style="height: 1px; width: 100%;
background-image: url(/SimpleContactManager/a4j/g/3_2_2.SR1org.
richfaces.renderkit.html.images.SimpleSeparatorImage/DATB/
eAFjYNxa6sUIAATTAXc_); null;"></div>
```

Instead of using the `rich:separator` component, if you use a `rich:spacer` component with the `height` attribute set to `15`, you get this XHTML code:

```
<img class="rich-spacer " height="15" id="fInsertContact:j_id21"
src="/SimpleContactManager/a4j/g/3_2_2.SR1images/spacer.gif" width="1"
/>
```

Ajax command buttons: a4j:commandButton

The last component we can see in the form's field code is `a4j:commandButton`. It is the Ajax version of the standard JSF `h:commandButton` and it produces Ajax requests instead of standard ones, as well as having attributes to manage the Ajax options.

The most important one is the `reRender` attribute that tells the JavaScript Engine which area(s) of the page or component must be updated after an Ajax response.

It can re-render one or more components after an Ajax request. It accepts a `String` object (a component id or a comma-separated id list), `Set`, `Collection`, or `Array` (passed via the JSF EL).

In our code, it is used to call the action method (`contactsManager.insertContact`) that inserts the `newContact` bean into the contact list array, and then to re-render the form itself and the contact list `rich:dataTable`. The form might be re-rendered to clean fields (in fact, after insertion, the `contactsManager.insertContact` method clears the fields so we can insert another contact in a clean instance of `ContactBean`).

Also, as you can see, the value contains the inserted name and surname. Therefore, if the user writes *John* as the name and *Wilson* as the surname, the caption of the `a4j:commandButton` becomes "*Insert John Wilson*", and thanks to `a4j:support` (as we've seen in the previous paragraphs), it changes while the user is typing.

Here is another example:

```
<h:form>
  <a4j:commandButton value="update" action="#{myBean.
anOptionalAction}"
                     reRender="block1,text1"
</h:form>
<h:panelGroup id="block1">
...
</h:panelGroup>
<h:outputText id="text1" ... />
```

When the user clicks on the update button rendered by the `a4j:commandButton` tag, the RichFaces JavaScript Engine will make an Ajax request to the server and wait for the response. After that, it will update the `block1` and `text1` elements.

It has a lot of other useful attributes, which we'll see in the following chapters.

Ajax command links: a4j:commandLink

Another useful tag is `a4j:commandLink`, which is the Ajax version of `h:commandLink`. It works like `a4j:commandButton`, but renders a link (HTML A tag) instead of the `INPUT` element. It needs to stay inside the `h:form` tag.

The contact list

In order to show (and let the user delete) the contact list, we are going to use the RichFaces version of the classical `h:dataTable`. It works the same way, but it has very useful and simple-to-use enhanced features. It is enclosed in a `rich:panel` tag (this time without a header, because we are going to use the `header` facet of `rich:dataTable`).

We also will use `rich:datascoller` in order to add Ajax pagination to the `rich:dataTable` records and `a4j:commandLink` to add a button for every contact in the list.

You can see the final look in the next screenshot (the delete button is shown as an **X** icon in the last column of the table.)

Here is the code that you have to add to your `home.xhtml` page (replacing the `<!--Contact list -->` comment) in order to render the contact list:

```
<rich:panel>
  <h:form id="fContactsList">
    <rich:dataTable id="edtContactsList"
                    value="#{contactsManager.contactsList}"
      var="contact" rows="5" width="100%">
      <f:facet name="header">Contact List</f:facet>
      <rich:column sortBy="#{contact.name}"
                   filterBy="#{contact.name}">
        <f:facet name="header">Name</f:facet>
        <h:outputText value="#{contact.name}"/>
      </rich:column>
      <rich:column sortBy="#{contact.surname}"
                   filterBy="#{contact.surname}">
        <f:facet name="header">Surname</f:facet>
        <h:outputText value="#{contact.surname}"/>
```

```
        </rich:column>
        <rich:column sortBy="#{contact.email}"
                     filterBy="#{contact.email}">
          <f:facet name="header">Email</f:facet>
          <h:outputText value="#{contact.email}"/>
        </rich:column>
        <rich:column align="center">
          <f:facet name="header">Birthdate</f:facet>
          <h:outputText value="#{contact.birthdate}">
            <f:convertDateTime type="date" dateStyle="short"/>
          </h:outputText>
        </rich:column>
      </rich:dataTable>
      <h:outputText value="No contacts found"
       rendered="#{empty contactsManager.contactsList}"/>
      <rich:datascroller id="dsContactsList" for="edtContactsList"
                         renderIfSinglePage="false" />
    </h:form>
  </rich:panel>
```

As we can see, we've used a `rich:dataTable` tag as a normal `h:dataTable` tag (In fact, we've used the `var` value and the `rows` parameter respectively for setting the contact list array. The `rows` parameter is the request-scope variable to manage the current row object and the number of rows per page.).

We have also used the "rich" version of `h:column`, that is `rich:column`, in order to set up the filtering and sorting features for the **Name**, **Surname**, and **Email** fields. Enabling the column for basic sorting and filtering is very simple—just connect the `sortBy` and `filterBy` attributes of `rich:column` to the field that you want to sort (or filter).

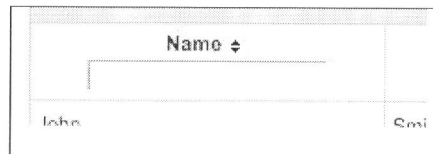

There is nothing new in the other code of the table.

We'll talk about the "No contacts found" value of `h:outputText` in the next chapter (talking about Ajax placeholders). After it, we inserted `rich:datascroller` and connected to the `rich:dataTable` using the `for` attribute. The `renderIfSinglePage` attribute does not render the datascroller until the table contains at least six records (one more than the `rows` attribute of `rich:dataTable`), which means two pages of data.

Re-rendering the contact list after adding a new contact

At this point, if we try to add a new contact, the contact list would not be updated. Why?

This is because we have to tell `insertButton` to update not only the form, but also the contact list after executing the action.

In order to do that, just modify the `reRender` property of `insertButton` by adding the `id` of the contact list form (`fContactList`), so the component now appears like this:

```
<a4j:commandButton
            id="insertButton"
            action="#{contactsManager.insertContact}"
            value="Insert #{contactsManager.newContact.name}
                    #{contactsManager.newContact.surname}"
            reRender="fContactsList,fInsertContact" />
```

Now it will also update the contact list that will show the just inserted contact.

Adding the delete button

We would like to add a delete button as the last column of the table. In order to do so, just insert this code after the `birthdate` column:

```
<rich:column width="50" align="center">
  <f:facet name="header">Delete</f:facet>
  <a4j:commandLink reRender="fContactsList"
                action="#{contactsManager.deleteContact}">
    <h:graphicImage style="border-width: 0px;"
                value="images/buttons/delete.gif" />
    <f:setPropertyActionListener value="#{contact}"
      target="#{contactsManager.contactToDelete}"/>
  </a4j:commandLink>
</rich:column>
```

We used `a4j:commandLink` and an image (but we should have used the `a4j:commandButton` with the `image` attribute set) to add the support to delete contacts.

This code is simple to understand. When the user clicks on the delete icon (it's a red-colored **X**), the `contact` variable (that points to the `ContactBean` instance for the selected table row) will be set into the `contactToDelete` property of the `contactsManager` bean. After that, the `contactsManager.deleteContact` action will be called and the instance will be removed from the contact list. Following the execution of the action, the RichFaces framework will re-render the contact list form (according to what is set into the `reRender` property of `a4j:commandLink`) showing the new list (without the deleted row).

Summary

In this chapter, you tasted the power of RichFaces components to build Ajax applications by developing a simple example.

You learned the basics of RichFaces step by step, from creating the project to editing the code, using very important components (such as `a4j:commandButton`, `a4j:commandLink`, `rich:dataTable`, and `rich:messages`) and their Ajax properties (for example, `reRender`).

In the next chapter, we will start building a real application (an Advanced Contact Manager) using the framework in depth.

4
The Application

In this chapter, we are going to start developing our rich web application!

We will explain all of the steps to build an empty project from scratch (using seam-gen), which supports all the technologies that we need in order to develop a "real" JSF application with Ajax support.

The aim of this book is not to be just a description of a technology, but we also want the reader to learn about the RichFaces framework while developing a real application, so that can be ready to develop an application of their own.

The application we have chosen is an Advanced Contact Manager with a lot of "rich" features that we will see in the next section.

After creating the project, we will start looking at and understanding the basic pages generated and the login box while doing some editing on them.

What we are going to develop?

The example we developed in Chapter 3, *First Steps* was basic. Now, in fact, we are going to develop a fully-featured advanced application for contact management.

During the development of every feature of the web application, we are going to use the RichFaces Ajax framework as much as possible. We will also use the rich components that it makes available to us.

The next image shows a simple mockup of the application we want to develop:

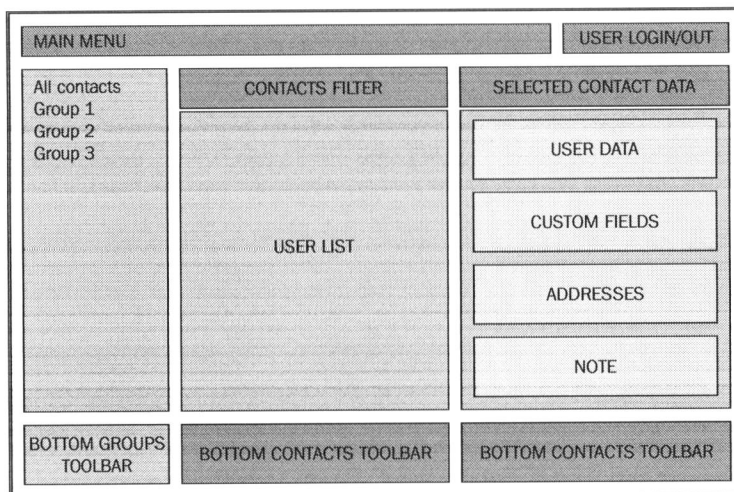

Features

Here is the description of the main features of the Advanced Contact Manager application.

Groups manager

Every contact can be put into one or more groups for better organization of your data. The contact group list appears inside a colored list with a tool tip showing the group description.

File uploads and notes

The user will be able to associate files (for example CV) and "rich text" notes to contacts. The file upload will allow the user to select more than one file at a time and add a description for each file using a wizard modal panel.

Simple search

A simple search will always be visible to the user. He/she will be able to search contacts, filtering them by name and surname.

User skin

Every user of the web application can choose his own skin and use it during the session.

Multilanguage

Our application is a real application. Therefore, even if it is not a RichFaces feature (but a JSF/Seam feature), it is going to support different languages.

The database: E-R diagram

This is the E-R (Entity-Relationship) diagram of the database that we are going to use:

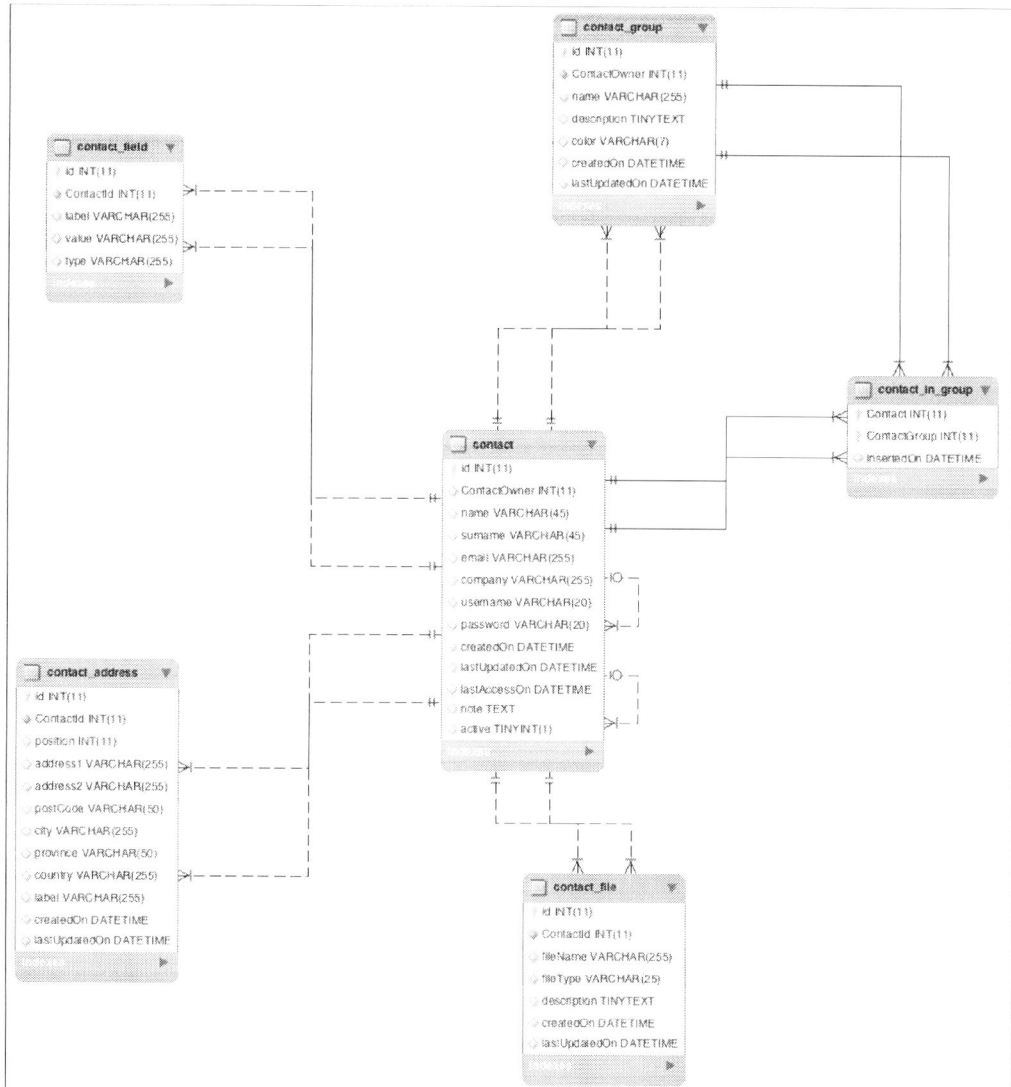

About the E-R diagram

An **Entity-Relationship (E-R)** diagram is, in short, used to represent a relational database. It describes the information that will be stored in the database in terms of the entities and connections between them (relationships).

An **entity** is an object (for example a person or a group) that can be uniquely identified and is independent (that is, it can "live" alone).

A **relationship** describes how two or more entities are related to each other.

Both entities and relationships can have attributes. To find more about ER diagrams, you can read `http://en.wikipedia.org/wiki/Entity-relationship_model`.

As you can see, it's quite simple—it is all based around the contact entity. Each contact can also be a user of the web application (having a username and a password set). Also, more fields can be associated with a different type of custom field (such as URL, email, and so on) and a label (home, work, and so on depending on the type). A contact can have one or more addresses associated with a label (such as home, work, and so on).

Users can create one or more groups of contacts with a different color for each one. Finally, a list of files (such as a CV or other) can be associated with each contact.

The database is ready; we can go on to create the project structure and the **Java Persistent API (JPA)** entities connected to the database tables.

What is JPA?

We have talked about JBoss Seam and Facelets, but this is the first time that we have talked about JPA. JPA is the acronym for Java Persistence API and it is the standard API for persistence and object/relational mapping for the Java (SE and EE) platform.

This is another must-know technology. It is very useful to manage (query, insert, update) persistent data connected to a DBMS in a simple way. The main concept here is the entity — it is a POJO that normally represents a table in a database, and every instance of it represents an individual row in the table.

To make an example, if you want to insert a new row in a database table, you have just to create an instance of the entity class that represents the table, then fill the fields of the entity with data, and call the persist method to insert a new row into the database. You don't have to write a single line of SQL (JPA is going to do that work for you). Also, when you query the database, you use a SQL-like language (called **Java Persistence Query Language (JPQL)**) and the result will be a list of objects(`java.util.list`) — these perfectly fit into a JSF application.

Connecting entities with tables is very simple using annotations (inside the class itself) or XML descriptor files.

There are some good implementations of the JPA. We are going to use the one from JBoss, which you may know — **Hibernate**. It was an ORM framework prior to the existence of JPA (that has got many ideas from it) and it's included in the project that seam-gen generates for us.

Importing the database

First of all, we have to create a new MySQL database called `advcm_db` and import the **Data Definition Language (DDL)** that creates the database structure we are going to use.

You can find the DDL SQL file at `http://www.packtpub.com/files/code/6880_Code.zip`

Seam-gen will read the database structure to generate the JPA entities for us. Let's see how to use this feature while creating the project.

Creating the project

The project creation is very similar to the one that we used for the example in Chapter 3, the only difference is that now we are going to connect our project to the MySQL DBMS. Therefore, we have to configure it in a proper way.

Open a terminal window and move into the JBoss Seam distribution directory, execute the following command from here, for Microsoft Windows and Unix/Linux/Mac OS X:

Microsoft Windows	Unix/Linux/Mac OS X
seam setup	./seam setup

After the welcome text, let's enter our new project configuration data (seam-gen will keep the old data, so you don't have to rewrite all the configuration information):

- Enter your Java project workspace (the directory that contains your Seam projects): This is the directory where we want to save our new project (it depends on our environment and preferences), it might be same as that of our example project.

- Enter your JBoss AS home directory: It is the directory where JBoss AS is installed.

- Enter the project name: Let's enter AdvContactManager.

- Do you want to use ICEfaces instead of RichFaces [n]: No. We want to use RichFaces, so just press *Enter*.

- Select a RichFaces skin [classic] (blueSky, [classic], deepMarine, DEFAULT, emeraldTown, japanCherry, ruby, wine): We can change it later, for now classic skin is okay, so just press *Enter*.

- Is this project deployed as an EAR (with EJB components) or a WAR (with no EJB support) [ear]: We would like a complete EAR application with EJB support, so just press *Enter*.

- Enter the Java package name for your session beans: Let's enter book. richfaces.advcm.

- Enter the Java package name for your entity beans: Again, let's enter book.richfaces.advcm.

- Enter the Java package name for your test cases: Let's enter book. richfaces.advcm.test.

- What kind of database are you using?: This time we want to use MySQL DBMS, so let's enter mysql.

- Enter the Hibernate dialect for your database: Let's enter org. hibernate.dialect.MySQLDialect.

- Enter the filesystem path to the JDBC driver jar: It must be a path to the MySQL JDBC driver JAR file (if you don't have it, download it from http://dev.mysql.com/downloads/connector/j/ (the actual version is 5.1.7)).

- Enter JDBC driver class for your database: Let's enter com.mysql.jdbc.Driver.

- Enter the JDBC URL for your database: If your MySQL DBMS is installed in your computer (localhost), enter jdbc:mysql://localhost/advcm_db. If not, specify a proper host instead of localhost.

- Enter database username: Insert the username to access the database.

- Enter database password: Insert the password to access the database.

- Enter the database schema name (it is OK to leave this blank): Leave it blank and press *Enter*.

- Enter the database catalog name (it is OK to leave this blank): Leave it blank and press *Enter*.

- Are you working with tables that already exist in the database?: Enter *y*.

- Do you want to drop and recreate the database tables and data in import.sql each time you deploy?: No, press *Enter*.

Okay, we've done the configuration, and we will see how to configure it for a MySQL DBMS connection in the next chapter (when we will start making the real application). For now it's okay to use the default answers.

We are ready to create the project using the following commands for Microsoft Windows and Unix/Linux/Mac OS X:

Microsoft Windows	Unix/Linux/Mac OS X
seam create-project	./seam create-project

Now let's create the JPA entities (our application data model) automatically using the following commands for Microsoft Windows and Unix/Linux/Mac OS X:

Microsoft Windows	Unix/Linux/Mac OS X
seam generate-model	./seam generate-model

If you are using the Eclipse IDE, you have to import the project into the workspace (we described how to do that in Chapter 2, *Getting Started*). With other IDEs (IntelliJ or NetBeans), you can just open it from the location in which you've told seam-gen to create it.

The class diagram

The next class diagram shows the JPA entity classes generated by seam-gen:

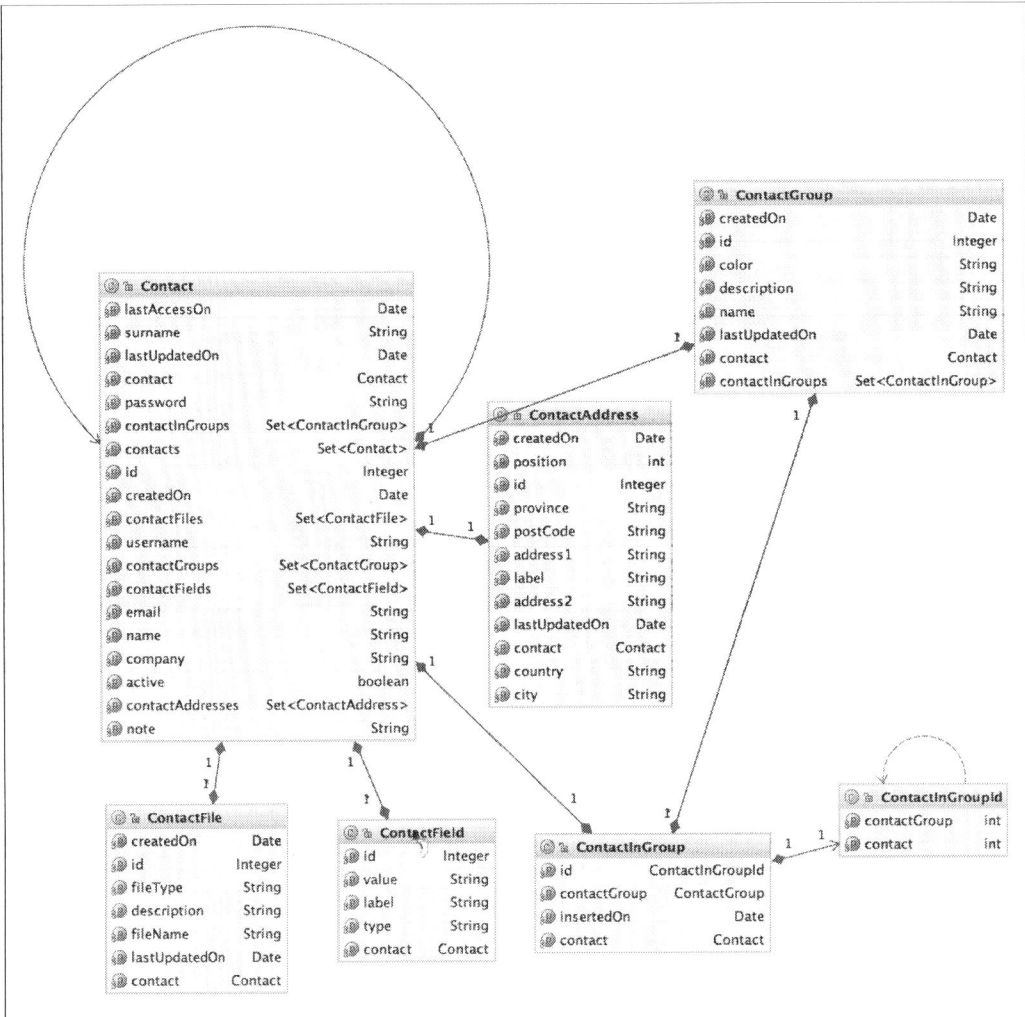

As you can see, it doesn't differ a lot from the E-R diagram—in fact, every class matches with the corresponding table in the database.

This is an example of the generated entity class (the `ContactGroup` entity). We've written some parts of the class, just to show some relevant JPA annotation:

```java
@Entity
@Table(name = "contact_group",
        catalog = "adv_contact_manager")
public class ContactGroup implements java.io.Serializable {
    private Integer id;
    private Contact contact;
    private String name;
    private Set<ContactInGroup> contactInGroups =
                        new HashSet<ContactInGroup>(0);

    // ... other fields, constructors, getters and setters ...

@Id
@GeneratedValue(strategy = IDENTITY)
@Column(name = "id", unique = true, nullable = false)
public Integer getId() {
    return this.id;
}

public void setId(Integer id) {
    this.id = id;
}

@ManyToOne(fetch = FetchType.LAZY)
@JoinColumn(name = "ContactOwner", nullable = false)
@NotNull
public Contact getContact() {
    return this.contact;
}

public void setContact(Contact contact) {
    this.contact = contact;
}

@Column(name = "name", nullable = false)
@NotNull
public String getName() {
    return this.name;
}

public void setName(String name) {
    this.name = name;
}
@OneToMany(cascade = CascadeType.ALL,
        fetch = FetchType.LAZY, mappedBy = "contactGroup")
```

```
    public Set<ContactInGroup> getContactInGroups() {
        return this.contactInGroups;
    }

    public void setContactInGroups(Set<ContactInGroup> contactInGroups) {
        this.contactInGroups = contactInGroups;
    }

}
```

It is just a normal class (with fields, getters, and setters) annotated by JPA annotations (we highlighted them) that connect the class and its fields with the corresponding table in the database. You can annotate fields or the getter (as in this case). In both cases, the annotation has the same effects.

@NotNull and @Length are Hibernate Validator annotations, which we have seen in Chapter 2. Seam-gen puts some basic Hibernate Validator annotations, but we need to complete them by editing the entity classes (we'll see an example in the next paragraph).

Another annotation you might know is the JPA @OneToMany—it manages the relationship with another entity class.

To make an example, the contactInGroups property returns all of the ContactInGroup instances that are connected to ContactGroup. In a simple way, if I have an instance of ContactGroup, I can get all the contacts in that group just by reading that property.

Some modification to the entities

Using JPA is convenient also because you have more features available such as Hibernate Validators (we have seen how they work in the first example) and other useful annotations that help us to write clean code.

Seam-gen does a lot of work for us, but like every automatic tool, it is not perfect and we would add features to the generated classes after the project generation.

In this case, we are adding more Hibernate Validators to our entity classes. Here are some useful built-in ones:

- @Length(min=, max=): Checks if the string length matches min and max values

- @Max(value=): Checks if the value is less than or equal to the max value

- @Min(value=): Checks if the value is more than or equal to the min value

- @NotNull: Checks if the value of the field is not null

- `@Email`: Checks whether the string conforms to the email address specification

- `@Range(min=, max=)`: Checks if the value is between the min and max values (included)

- `@Future`: Checks if the date is in the future

- `@Past`: Checks if the date is in the past

- `@Pattern(regex="regexp", flag=)`: Checks if the property matches the regular expression, given a match flag (see `java.util.regex.Pattern` for more information)

- `@Patterns( {@Pattern(...)} )`: Like `@Pattern`, but for multiple regular expressions

You can create your own validators in a simple way. Refer to the Hibernate Validator documentation for all the features of this framework.

Another useful feature we would like to add to our entities is represented by the `@PrePersist` and `@PreUpdate` annotations. If a method is annotated with one of these annotations, it will be called before persisting the instance into the database and before updating it.

Here is the added code for the entity class of the previous section (the `ContactGroup` entity):

```
/**
 * This method initializes the values before
 * the class is persisted
 */
@PrePersist
public void prePersist() {
        setCreatedOn(new Date());
        setLastUpdatedOn(new Date());
}


/**
 * This method initializes the values before
 * the class is updated
 */
@PreUpdate
public void preUpdate() {
        setLastUpdatedOn(new Date());
}
```

Here we used the @PrePersist and @PreUpdate annotations that enable us to automatically set the createdOn and lastUpdatedOn properties (using the setCreatedOn and setUpdatedOn methods) without having to do that every time we persist or update an entity. We will also use them to do something before the entity is persisted or updated.

> You can also use the @PreRemove annotation to annotate a method that will be called after deleting the corresponding instance of the entity class.

Editing the template page

For now, we will limit the editing of this page to transforming the h:messages component into the RichFaces one (rich:messages), which as we've seen, supports Ajax out of the box (rich:messages also has the same attribute as that of the JSF one, so we don't have to modify anything else).

In order to use it, we also have to add the RichFaces namespace we have seen. Therefore, this is how the template.xhtml page looks (some parts have been omitted because they are the same as before):

```
<f:view contentType="text/html"
        xmlns="http://www.w3.org/1999/xhtml"
        xmlns:ui="http://java.sun.com/jsf/facelets"
        xmlns:h="http://java.sun.com/jsf/html"
        xmlns:f="http://java.sun.com/jsf/core"
        xmlns:a="http://richfaces.org/a4j"
        xmlns:rich="http://richfaces.org/rich"
        xmlns:s="http://jboss.com/products/seam/taglib">
  <html>
    <head>
      ...
    </head>
    <body>
      <div class="body">
        <rich:messages id="messages"
                       globalOnly="true"
                       styleClass="message"
                       errorClass="errormsg"
                       infoClass="infomsg"
                       warnClass="warnmsg"
                       rendered="#{showGlobalMessages!='false'}"/>
        <ui:insert name="body"/>
      </div>
```

```
        ...
      </body>
   </html>
</f:view>
```

In the next chapter, we will add those functionalities to the template page, which we want to share across different pages.

> As you can see, the `rendered` attribute of the `rich:messages` component is controlled by the EL expression `#{showGlobalMessages!='false'}`. `showGlobalMessage` is a Facelets parameter that you can pass to the template (remember the `projectName` parameter passed to the menu?) in order to force it to not render the `rich:messages` component.

The menu page

This is a page included (as we have seen) in the template and it is a `rich:toolBar` with two `rich:toolBarGroup` instances (one on the left and one with right alignment):

```
<rich:toolBar
     xmlns="http://www.w3.org/1999/xhtml"
     xmlns:ui="http://java.sun.com/jsf/facelets"
     xmlns:h="http://java.sun.com/jsf/html"
     xmlns:f="http://java.sun.com/jsf/core"
     xmlns:s="http://jboss.com/products/seam/taglib"
     xmlns:rich="http://richfaces.org/rich">

     <rich:toolBarGroup>
         <h:outputText value="#{projectName}:"/>
         <s:link view="/home.xhtml" value="Home"
                          propagation="none"/>
     </rich:toolBarGroup>

     <rich:toolBarGroup location="right">
         <h:outputText
                          value="signed in as: #{identity.username}"
                          rendered="#{identity.loggedIn}"/>
         <s:link view="/login.xhtml" value="Login"
                          rendered="#{not identity.loggedIn}"
                          propagation="none"/>
         <s:link view="/home.xhtml" action="#{identity.logout}"
                          value="Logout" rendered="#{identity.
loggedIn}"
                          propagation="none"/>
     </rich:toolBarGroup>
</rich:toolBar>
```

After the `xmlns` declaration (used by Facelets), we can find the two groups with some texts and links inside. The group on the right contains the login link if the user is not logged in, and the user information and the logout link if the user is logged in.

Therefore, when no user is logged in, the page looks like:

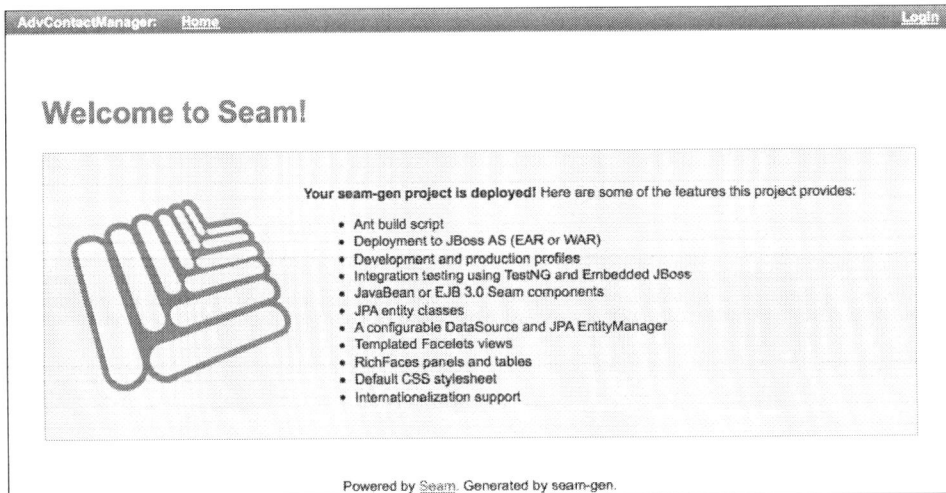

When a user is logged in, it appears as follows:

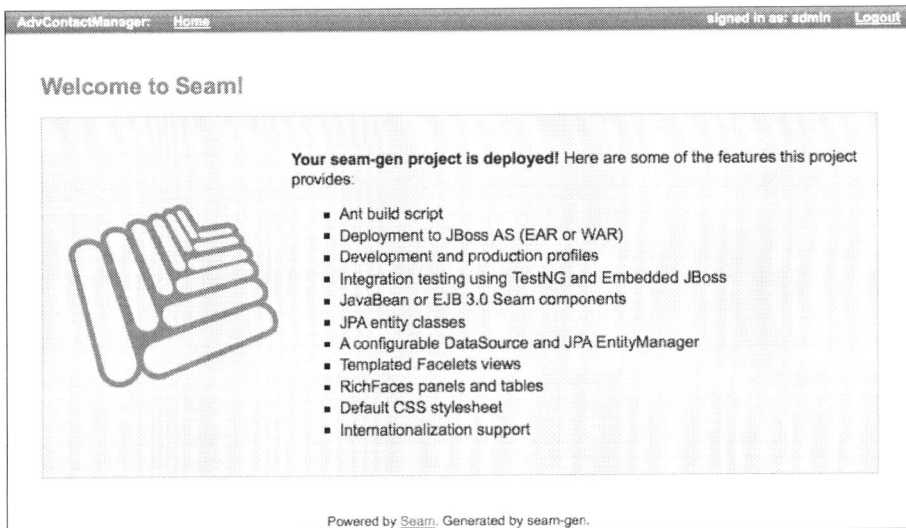

As you can see, the part on the righthand side of the menu bar changes according to the `identity.loggedIn` status of the variable.

The login page

Seam-gen generates a standard login page that we can personalize. It is called `login.xhtml` and you can find it in the `/view/` path. It uses the JBoss Seam authentication features, so we will extend it to include our login support code. Also, it uses the `template.xhtml` page that we have already seen.

Let's see the code:

```
<!DOCTYPE composition PUBLIC "-//W3C//DTD XHTML 1.0 Transitional//EN"
    "http://www.w3.org/TR/xhtml1/DTD/xhtml1-transitional.dtd">

<ui:composition xmlns="http://www.w3.org/1999/xhtml"
                xmlns:s="http://jboss.com/products/seam/taglib"
                xmlns:ui="http://java.sun.com/jsf/facelets"
                xmlns:f="http://java.sun.com/jsf/core"
                xmlns:h="http://java.sun.com/jsf/html"
                xmlns:rich="http://richfaces.org/rich"
                template="layout/template.xhtml">

  <ui:define name="body">
    <h:form id="login">

    <rich:panel>
      <f:facet name="header">Login</f:facet>

      <p>Please login here</p>

      <div class="dialog">
        <h:panelGrid columns="2" rowClasses="prop"
                     columnClasses="name,value">
          <h:outputLabel for="username">
                              Username
          </h:outputLabel>
            <h:inputText id="username"
                         value="#{credentials.username}"/>
          <h:outputLabel for="password">
                              Password
          </h:outputLabel>
          <h:inputSecret id="password"
                         value="#{credentials.password}"/>
          <h:outputLabel for="rememberMe">
                              Remember me
          </h:outputLabel>
          <h:selectBooleanCheckbox id="rememberMe"
                                   value="#{identity.rememberMe}"/>
        </h:panelGrid>
      </div>

      <p>
```

```
        <i>Note - </i>
You may login with the username 'admin' and a blank password.
      </p>
    </rich:panel>

      <div class="actionButtons">
        <h:commandButton value="Login"
                          action="#{identity.login}"/>
      </div>

    </h:form>

  </ui:define>
</ui:composition>
```

Again, we see DOCTYPE and the Facelets `ui:composition` component that wraps content to be included in another Facelet. As you can see, in fact, after the `xmlns` declarations, there is the `template` attribute that points to the `template.xhtml` page we have seen and uses it as a template.

Remember the body insertion point in `template.xhtml`? How do we insert code at that point?

The answer is simple—just use the `<ui:define>` tag and set the `name` attribute as one of the insertion points:

```
<ui:define name="body">
    <!-- this code will be inserted -->
</ui:define>
```

We can find it in our `login.xhtml` page. It includes the personalized part of the `login.xhtml` page, that is the one with the login form.

We can see the code to declare `<h:form>` and the `<rich:panel>` component inside it. It contains the inputs for username and password (and a **Remember me** checkbox). Below the panel, there is the standard JSF `h:commandButton` that calls the login action. We don't want an Ajax login, so it's okay to use a standard action component that will redirect to the home page after the login is complete.

All of those components point to a special Seam component called identity, which manages the login phase.

We are not going to edit this page a lot, the only thing we will do is delete the `Note` section, as we don't need it:

```
<p>
    <i>Note - </i> You may login with the username 'admin' and a blank
password.
</p>
```

This is how the login page appears:

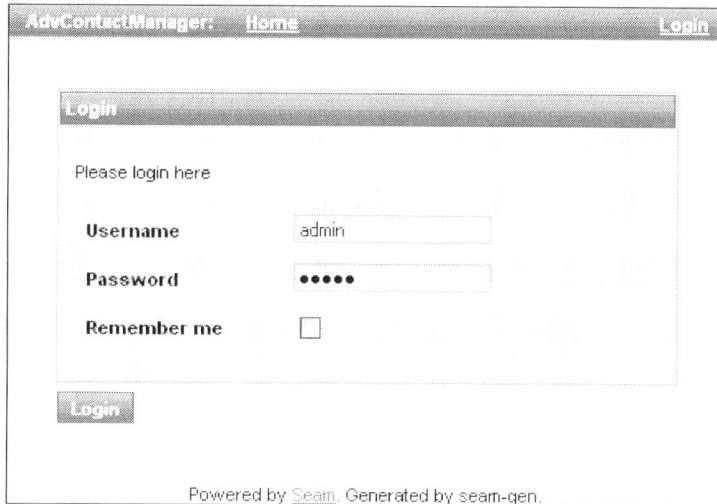

The home page

The home page (`home.xhtml`) is an empty page with a box that talks about Seam and seam-gen.

For now, we just delete the code for the box in order to obtain an empty page, which we will fill in the following chapters. The code is as follows:

```
<!DOCTYPE composition PUBLIC "-//W3C//DTD XHTML 1.0 Transitional//EN"
    "http://www.w3.org/TR/xhtml1/DTD/xhtml1-transitional.dtd">
<ui:composition xmlns="http://www.w3.org/1999/xhtml"
    xmlns:s="http://jboss.com/products/seam/taglib"
    xmlns:ui="http://java.sun.com/jsf/facelets"
    xmlns:f="http://java.sun.com/jsf/core"
    xmlns:h="http://java.sun.com/jsf/html"
    xmlns:rich="http://richfaces.org/rich"
    template="layout/template.xhtml">
  <ui:define name="body">
  </ui:define>
</ui:composition>
```

And this is how it appears (you can see the menu bar that comes from the template):

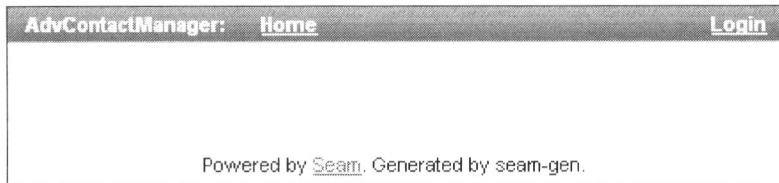

AdvContactManager: **Home**   **Login**

Powered by Seam. Generated by seam-gen.

Summary

In this chapter, we created the basics of our project by having a look at the side technologies that we might know, in order to build good applications while being more productive and fast.

We've had a look at a seam-gen generated project and its included support for Ajax and rich components (with RichFaces). Also, we looked at templating (with Facelets) and JBoss Seam authentication. We've also started doing a little customization of the entities (by adding the Hibernate Validator annotations) and the XHTML code.

In the next chapter, we'll go deeper into developing the application using RichFaces components.

5
Making the Application Structure

In this chapter, we are going to develop the structure and the login/logout/ registration pages of our application. We will see step by step how to implement every feature in an effective way using the latest technology in Java Enterprise.

Skinnability and dynamic skin change

As we've said in Chapter 1, *What is RichFaces?*, skinnability is a feature of the RichFaces framework that gives us control over the look of our application and its components.

In fact, it is very important to have a consistent user interface in a real application. This is not a simple task when you have to integrate a different set of components or give the user the ability to choose his/her preferred skin without the need of copying and pasting values between CSS files for every skin.

RichFaces helps us to manage all those things by extending the capabilities of the CSS technology in order to make our lives easier.

Selecting the application skin

A very important feature is the skin parameters—with them you can define a value and reuse it in CSS selectors. Those values are associated to a particular skin, so to change them you have just to define and select another skin.

A skin is simply a properties file containing skin parameters and values, so to add a skin, just create a file of the format `<skin_name>.skin.properties` (or copy and change the existing ones that you can find in the `richfaces-impl-xxx.jar` file, inside the `/META-INF/skins/` folder) and put it in `/META-INF/skins/` or another folder in the classpath.

We'll see it in depth in Chapter 10, *Advanced techniques*; we are going to use the built-in ones for now.

In order to choose a default skin for your project, you have to specify its name in the `org.richfaces.SKIN` context parameter of `web.xml`:

```
<context-param>
    <param-name>org.richfaces.SKIN</param-name>
    <param-value>skin_name</param-value>
</context-param>
```

You can select another skin at runtime too, we'll see how later.

RichFaces built-in skins (simple skins that use just skin parameters personalization described previously) are:

- DEFAULT
- plain
- emeraldTown
- blueSky
- wine
- japanCherry
- ruby
- classic
- deepMarine

Those skins contain parameters used by the RichFaces framework in order to customize the look and feel of the component.

A special mention for the `plain` skin—it has no parameters and is used in projects that have their own CSS styles.

RichFaces skinnability also allows you to associate custom renders to a new skin in order to render standard and custom JSF components with the same style.

User-selected application skin

Until now we have talked about setting just one application-wide skin to use, without the possibility for the user to change it.

Doing that is very simple and needs a couple of managed beans and some configuration. We want to add support for user-selected skins in our application—so first of all, let's choose the default skin and the supported ones as application parameters.

Passing application parameters using components.xml

In every application, there are some configuration parameters that might not be put and compiled with the code, as they are related to the server to which they are deployed (a directory in which to save files, mail connection parameters, and so on) and you can just edit a text file to modify them without the need of recompiling the Java code.

In a standard JSF application, you would use `context-param` of `web.xml` in order to pass parameters to the application and add the parameter to the `web.xml` file in this way:

```
<web-app>
..
  <context-param>
    <param-name>firstParameter</param-name>
    <param-value>27</param-value>
  </context-param>
  <context-param>
    <param-name>secondParameter</param-name>
    <param-value>myOtherValue</param-value>
  </context-param>
...
</web-app>
```

Then, from the bean, you would have to access the external context to get it; you can do that using this code:

```
String strParam=FacesContext.getCurrentInstance()
        .getExternalContext()
        .getInitParameter("firstParameter");
```

As you can see, this is not integrated with JSF and not so convenient.

You can also use `faces-config.xml` and the `managedBeans` declaration to pass parameters, but there is a simpler way.

As we are using JBoss Seam, in fact, we can take advantage of the XML capabilities of the framework about instantiating `managedBean` (or, better, Seam components) and setting their properties, all by using the `components.xml` configuration file.

In our case, we would like to configure the default skin name and the list of the other skins that the user can select. In order to do that, let's start creating the bean that will manage those parameters: `AppOptions`.

First create a package called `book.richfaces.advcm.options`. Inside it, create a class called `AppOptions` that looks like this:

```java
package book.richfaces.advcm.options;
import org.jboss.seam.ScopeType;
import org.jboss.seam.annotations.Name;
import org.jboss.seam.annotations.Scope;
import org.jboss.seam.annotations.Startup;
import org.jboss.seam.annotations.Synchronized;
import java.util.List;
@Name("AppOptions")
@Scope(ScopeType.APPLICATION)
@Startup
@Synchronized
public class AppOptions {
    private String defaultSkin;
    private List<String> availableSkins;
    public String getDefaultSkin() {
        return defaultSkin;
    }
    public void setDefaultSkin(String defaultSkin) {
        this.defaultSkin = defaultSkin;
    }
    public List<String> getAvailableSkins() {
        return availableSkins;
    }
    public void setAvailableSkins(List<String> availableSkins)
    {
        this.availableSkins = availableSkins;
    }
}
```

As you can see, we declared a managed bean/Seam component called `appOptions` that is created at the application startup (we do that using the `@Startup` annotation) and has `APPLICATION` scope (and because of this, it is synchronized using the corresponding annotation). It has two properties with their getter and setter— `defaultSkin` contains the name of the skin that will be used by default (if the user didn't select a personal one, we'll see it later) and `availableSkins` is the list of all the supported skins.

Now, how to pass our own values?

Just edit the `components.xml` file and add the following section:

```
<component name="appOptions">
    <property name="defaultSkin">wine</property>
    <property name="availableSkins">
        <value>blueSky</value>
        <value>classic</value>
        <value>ruby</value>
        <value>wine</value>
        <value>deepMarine</value>
        <value>emeraldTown</value>
        <value>japanCherry</value>
    </property>
</component>
```

We are telling the JBoss Seam framework that it has to set the `defaultSkin` property of the `appOptions` component to `wine` and `availableSkins` with the listed values (notice that it is a list (`java.util.List`) of values).

Even if we use Integer properties, Seam will automatically convert them while setting them into the bean.

Making skin selection user-dependent

We want it so that every user can decide what application skin to work with, so this parameter differs from user to user. In few words, we have to use session-scoped parameters.

In order to do so, we have to create a session-scoped bean that contains the user options; let's put it into the same package of `AppOptions` (`book.richfaces.advcm.options`) and create a class called `UserOptions` that looks like this:

```
package book.richfaces.advcm.options;

import book.richfaces.advcm.Contact;
import org.jboss.seam.ScopeType;
```

```
import org.jboss.seam.annotations.In;
import org.jboss.seam.annotations.Logger;
import org.jboss.seam.annotations.Name;
import org.jboss.seam.annotations.Scope;
import org.jboss.seam.log.Log;

@Name("userOptions")
@Scope(ScopeType.SESSION)
public class UserOptions {

    @In
    AppOptions appOptions;

    private String skin;

    public String getSkin() {
        if (skin==null) {
            skin=appOptions.getDefaultSkin();
        }
        return skin;
    }

    public void setSkin(String skin) {
        this.skin = skin;
    }
}
```

This is a session-bean scoped Seam component called `userOptions`. As you can see, we inject (using the `@In` annotation) the `appOptions` component in order to get the default skin, if the user hasn't selected his/her own favorite one (so the `skin` property is `null`).

After that, we just need to set the `org.richfaces.SKIN` parameter with the skin property of the bean we have just created (`userOptions`). In this way, the `application` skin for the user will depend on the skin property of the userOptions component.

In order to do that, let's edit `web.xml` and change the value of the `org.richfaces.SKIN` parameter to make it look like this:

```
<context-param>
    <param-name>org.richfaces.SKIN</param-name>
    <param-value>#{userOptions.skin}</param-value>
</context-param>
```

The last step is to make it possible for the user to select the preferred skin. In order to do that, we will use the simple `h:selectOneMenu` component, which is bound to the `userOptions.skin` property.

In order to add it, let's open the `/view/layout/template.xhtml` file and add the following code before the footer `div`:

```
<div class="rightFooter">
    <h:form>
        <h:outputText value="Choose skin:"/>
        <h:selectOneMenu value="#{userOptions.skin}">
            <s:selectItems
                           value="#{appOptions.availableSkins}"
                           var="skin"
                           label="#{skin}"
                           itemValue="#{skin}"/>
        </h:selectOneMenu>
        <h:commandButton value="Change skin"/>
    </h:form>
</div>
```

In order to fill `h:selectOneMenu`, we use `s:selectItems`.

The seam component enhances the standard `f:selectItems` by adding the possibility to use other types (`string` in this case) for the list instead of only the `SelectItem` type. It is also very useful to list entity beans lists without the need of converting them into `SelectItem` lists (we will use this feature in the following chapters).

You might have noticed that we are using the non-Ajax `h:commandButton` in this case, because we want to refresh the whole page after skin changing.

The last thing we have to do is to add the `rightFooter` class to our CSS file in order to make the menu on the righthand side of the bottom. Just open `/view/stylesheet/theme.css` and enter the following code:

```
rightFooter {
    text-align: right;
    font-size: 11px;
    float: right;
}
```

Done, now we can make the application look how we like it!

Standard controls skinning

RichFaces unifies the application appearance by skinning the standard HTML elements the same way that it does with the other components of the library.

There are two levels of skinning:

- Standard: Used to customize basic style properties, it works with Internet Explorer 6 and 7 (in `BackCompat` mode), Opera, and Safari
- Extended: For advanced skinning support, it works with Mozilla FireFox and Internet Explorer 7 (in standards-compliant mode)

We'll see how to manage it in Chapter 10.

XCSS and Plug-n-Skin

With RichFaces, you can use XML-formatted CSS (XCSS) in order to use all the power of the skinnability feature: you can dynamically create a CSS file by mixing skin parameters, CSS, and external resources such as class-defined gradients (we'll see an example later).

In XCSS, you can use `u:selector` and `u:style` for composing the styles to be converted in CSS:

```
<u:selector name=".rich-name, .mystyle, .otherstyle">
    <u:style name="color" skin="generalTextColor" />
    <u:style name="border-color" skin="panelBorderColor" />
    <u:style name="border-width" value="1px" />
</u:selector>
```

The above code is transformed to the following in CSS:

```
.rich-name, .mystyle, .otherstyle {
   color: #000000;
   border-color: #BED6F8;
   border-width: 1px;
}
```

XCSS is used a lot in the Plug-n-Skin skinnability feature.

With Plug-n-Skin, you can develop a new customized skin using all the possibilities we have seen so far, create a jar file, and "plug" it into the `application/WEB-INF/lib/` directory.

In order to select the new skin, just change the value of the `org.richfaces.SKIN` context parameter with the name of the new skin.

For creating the new skin, you have to import the template using Maven, and then edit it to customize the skin. Inside the template, there are also ready-to-use gradient classes that you can use in XCSS:

```
<u:selector name=".rich-calendar-week">
    <u:style name="background-position" value="0% 50%" />
    <u:style name="background-image">
    <f:resource
      f:key="org.richfaces.renderkit.html.CustomizeableGradient">
      <f:attribute name="valign" value="middle" />
      <f:attribute name="gradientHeight" value="20px" />
      <f:attribute
                 name="baseColor"
                 skin="calendarWeekBackgroundColor" />
    </f:resource>
    </u:style>
    <u:style name="border-color" skin="newBorder" />
</u:selector>
```

As you can see from the example, we can use the CSS values (as for `background-position`), dynamic resources (as for `background-image`), and skin parameters (as for `border-color`).

> **What is Maven?**
>
> Maven is a very useful tool that helps developers to maintain their project and library dependences. It is more powerful than Apache Ant and can be used for building automation.
>
> In order to install Maven, just go to the download section of its web site (`http://maven.apache.org/download.html`) and grab the latest version of the `bin` package, unzip it, and follow the simple instructions you find inside the `README.txt` file.
>
> We will use it to configure a new Ajax JSF component using the CDK (see Chapter 11, *Component Development Kit*).

We are going to see this in depth in Chapter 10. In the meantime, we just want to put a gradient to our footer—in order to do that, let's open the `theme.xcss` page that you find in the `/view/stylesheet/` directory and add the following code:

```
<u:selector name=".footer">
    <u:style name="background-image">
        <f:resource
f:key="org.richfaces.renderkit.html.images.SliderFieldGradient"/>
    </u:style>
</u:selector>
```

We are just using a Java class for rendering a gradient according to the colors of the skin; we can use built-in resources (as in this case) or build our own ones.

Adding built-in plug'n'skin skins

There are three plug 'n' skin examples available, which have been developed by the RichFaces team. We can download them from the **Download** section of the RichFaces web site at `http://www.jboss.org/jbossrichfaces/downloads/`.

These examples are:

- `darkX-X.Y.Z.GA.jar`
- `glassX-X.Y.Z.GA.jar`
- `lagunaX-X.Y.Z.GA.jar`

If you want to use them as skins, just download them and copy them into the classpath, so that they are available to be selected by name as the other skins.

If you want to use one of these skins, just download the `jar` file, copy it into the classpath (for example the `/lib` folder) and then set the `org.richfaces.SKIN` context parameter with the name of the skin.

```
darkX*.jar
glassX*.jar
laguna*.jar
```

Now, the `jar` files will be included into the `/WEB-INF/lib/` directory and be available for use.

In order to let the user also choose these skins, just add the skin name into the `availableSkins` list. Let's edit `components.xml` and add the three values. In the end, it will look like this:

```xml
<component name="appOptions">
    <property name="defaultSkin">wine</property>
    <property name="availableSkins">
        <value>laguna</value>
        <value>darkX</value>
        <value>glassX</value>
        <value>blueSky</value>
        <value>classic</value>
        <value>ruby</value>
        <value>wine</value>
        <value>deepMarine</value>
        <value>emeraldTown</value>
        <value>japanCherry</value>
    </property>
</component>
```

Now the user will see them in the skin selection menu.

Some examples

Here are some examples of skin changing for the login page. The first screenshot is using the **wine** skin, which turns the look and feel of RichFaces components to green:

The second screenshot is using a light-blue skin called **blueSky**:

The third screenshot shows a pink version using the **japanCherry** built-in skin:

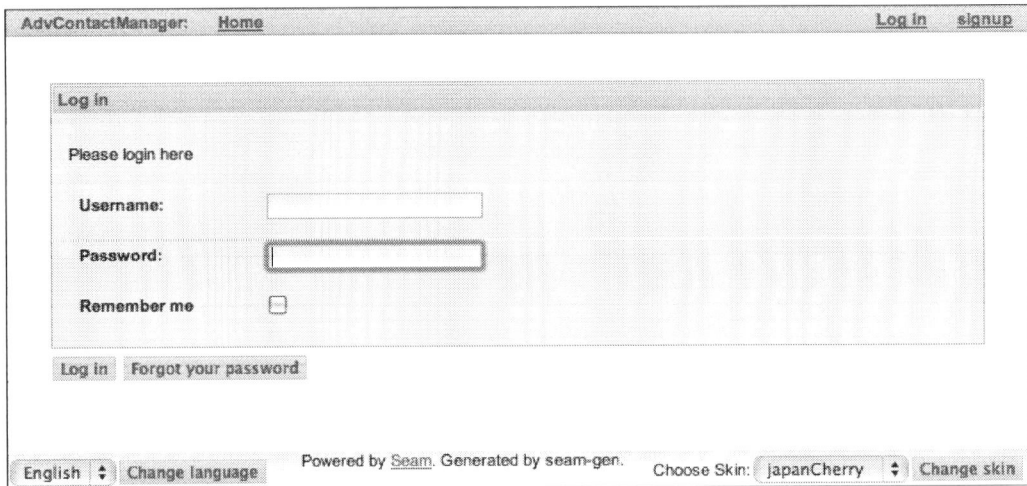

Notice that the gradient for the footer changes according to the skin.

Internationalization

Internationalization (i18n) is not a RichFaces feature. So, we will briefly describe it, as we are going to support different locales in our application (as for every real, well-made one).

In order to internationalize text strings, we can use message bundles for every language we would like to support; those bundles are normal properties files that contain the localized version of a string message. For example, if we want to write a "Hello World!" string in a different language, we have to define a label (for example, `helloWorld`) and use it inside the message bundles.

Let's configure our application for i18n and then make an example for changing the menu bar.

Configuration

Our seam-gen project is configured for i18n. In fact, if you look inside the `/view/resources/WEB-INF/faces-config.xml` file, you will find a section configuring supported locales and the default one:

```
<application>
    <locale-config>
        <default-locale>en</default-locale>
        <supported-locale>bg</supported-locale>
        <supported-locale>de</supported-locale>
        <supported-locale>en</supported-locale>
        <supported-locale>fr</supported-locale>
        <supported-locale>it</supported-locale>
        <supported-locale>tr</supported-locale>
    </locale-config>
    ...
</application>
```

For now, we just want to support two locales (English and Italian), so we can just remove the other ones.

For every locale, we have an associated message bundle file that you can find in the `resource` directory — it is called `messages_<locale>.properties`.

Therefore, for the English locale (with `en` code), we will have `messages_en.properties` and so on — you will find the label with the associated translation inside it; we will see how to use them soon.

Configuring the locale using components.xml

Although the standard JSF way to configure the locales using `faces-config.xml` works with JBoss Seam, it gives another way to do it using `components.xml`.

In order to use the "Seam way", just delete the locale configuration from the `faces-config.xml` file and add the following code to `components.xml`:

```
<?xml version="1.0" encoding="UTF-8"?>
<components
...other xmlns...
xmlns:international="http://jboss.com/products/seam/
international"xmlns:xsi="http://www.w3.org/2001/
XMLSchema-instance"
xsi:schemaLocation=
...other locations...
http://jboss.com/products/seam/international
http://jboss.com/products/seam/international-2.1.xsd>
...other configuration...
<international:locale-config
                default-locale="en"
                supported-locales="en it"/>
</components>
```

There are other features you can enable using Seam to configure i18n, refer to the Seam documentation for more information.

Internationalize strings

Now that we have configured everything, we can start using i18n for every string we write. As an example, let's edit the `/view/layout/menu.xhtml` file.

Now it looks like this:

```
<rich:toolBar
            xmlns="http://www.w3.org/1999/xhtml"
            xmlns:ui="http://java.sun.com/jsf/facelets"
            xmlns:h="http://java.sun.com/jsf/html"
            xmlns:f="http://java.sun.com/jsf/core"
            xmlns:s="http://jboss.com/products/seam/taglib"
            xmlns:rich="http://richfaces.org/rich">
  <rich:toolBarGroup>
    <h:outputText value="#{projectName}:"/>
      <s:link view="/home.xhtml"
              value="Home"
              propagation="none"/>
  </rich:toolBarGroup>

  <rich:toolBarGroup location="right">
    <h:outputText
              value="#{loggedUser.name} #{loggedUser.surname}"
              rendered="#{identity.loggedIn}"/>
    <s:link view="/login.xhtml"
            value="Login"
            rendered="#{not identity.loggedIn}"
            propagation="none"/>
    <s:link view="/home.xhtml"
            action="#{identity.logout}"
            value="Logout"
            rendered="#{identity.loggedIn}"
            propagation="none" />
  </rich:toolBarGroup>
</rich:toolBar>
```

As you can see, the highlighted lines show that we have the English translation hardcoded into the XHTML—this way they can't be changed.

If we want to support i18n, we have to add the label and the respective translation into the messages bundle files—let's edit `/resource/messages_en.properties` and add the following lines:

```
home=Home
login=Log in
logout=Log out
```

Then, let's edit the `/resource/messages_it.properties` file and add the following lines:

```
home=Pagina principale
login=Accedi
logout=Esci
```

In order to display the localized string in JBoss Seam, we can just use the built-in `messages` property in either of the following two ways:

```
<h:outputText value="#{messages.helloWorld}"/>
<h:outputText value="#{messages['helloWorld']}"/>
```

Therefore, in our case, the menu will look like this:

```
<rich:toolBar
            xmlns="http://www.w3.org/1999/xhtml"
            xmlns:ui="http://java.sun.com/jsf/facelets"
            xmlns:h="http://java.sun.com/jsf/html"
            xmlns:f="http://java.sun.com/jsf/core"
            xmlns:s="http://jboss.com/products/seam/taglib"
            xmlns:rich="http://richfaces.org/rich">
  <rich:toolBarGroup>
    <h:outputText value="#{projectName}:"/>
    <s:link view="/home.xhtml" value="#{messages.home}"
            propagation="none"/>
  </rich:toolBarGroup>

  <rich:toolBarGroup location="right">
    <h:outputText value="#{loggedUser.name} #{loggedUser.surname}"
                rendered="#{identity.loggedIn}"/>

    <s:link view="/login.xhtml" value="#{messages.login}"
            rendered="#{not identity.loggedIn}" propagation="none"/>
    <s:link view="/home.xhtml" action="#{identity.logout}"
            value="#{messages.logout}" rendered="#{identity.loggedIn}"
            propagation="none" />
  </rich:toolBarGroup>
</rich:toolBar>
```

We can also use the EL expression inside the resource bundle, in this way:

```
hello=Hello, #{loggedUser.name} #{loggedUser.surname}
```

User-selected language

As for the skin, we want the user to be able to change the default locale using a menu. In order to do that, we use built-in Seam components that make our task trivial.

Let's open the `layout/template.xhtml` file again and add this code before the footer `div`:

```
<div class="leftFooter">
  <h:form>
    <h:selectOneMenu value="#{localeSelector.localeString}">
      <f:selectItems value="#{localeSelector.supportedLocales}"/>
    </h:selectOneMenu>
    <h:commandButton action="#{localeSelector.select}"
                     value="#{messages['changeLanguage']}"/>
  </h:form>
</div>
```

We are using the `localeSelector` Seam component to get the supported locales list and select the preferred one.

Again, we are using the non-Ajax version of the `commandButton` component because we want the page to be completely reloaded in order to reflect the new selected locale.

We have also to add the new class to the `/view/stylesheet/theme.css` file, shown as follows:

```
.leftFooter {
    text-align: left;
    font-size: 11px;
     float: left;
}
```

And we need to add the `changeLanguage` label for the button into the message bundles.

In order to do that, let's open the `/resources/messages_en.properties` file and add the following line:

```
changeLanguage=Change language
```

Now let's open the `/resources/messages_it.properties` file and add the Italian translation for the same label, shown as follows:

```
changeLanguage=Cambia lingua
```

We have to internationalize the "change skin" button and all of the other strings used into the application we have; this repetitive task (that consists of editing the two files as explained for the `changeLanguage` label) is left as an exercise for the reader.

> **Default language**
>
> The selected language (if the user didn't make a choice) for a Seam application is the one sent by the browser in the HTTP headers, if the application accepts that language. If not, the default locale is selected.

Persist the selected locale using a cookie

JBoss Seam makes it simple to persist the selected locale in a cookie—just add the following line into the `components.xml` file:

```
<international:locale-selector cookie-enabled="true"/>
```

For more information on other features, refer to the Seam framework documentation at `http://seamframework.org/Documentation`.

Menu bar using rich:toolBar component

In the previous section, we modified `/view/layout/menu.xhtml` in order to add i18n support to our menu buttons. Now we are going to see in depth how the `rich:toolBar` component works and how we can use it.

This component is very important for a web site application and can be customized in different ways. Also, it can be used in different ways—it can be used as a tool bar, a menu bar, or both.

Inside the bar, you can put any content (such as a link, menu, image, `h:inputText` for searching, login form, and so on.). You can also make groups and align them to the righthand or lefthand side, dividing them with built-in or customized separators.

Here is an example including all those things we've talked about:

This is the code we used to make the example, as shown in the previous screenshot:

```
<rich:toolBar itemSeparator="square">
    <rich:toolBarGroup>
        <s:link view="/home.xhtml"
                                value="#{messages['home']}" />
    </rich:toolBarGroup>

    <rich:toolBarGroup>
        <s:link view="/core/users/profile.xhtml"
                value="#{messages['profile']}">
            </s:link>
        <h:form>
            <rich:dropDownMenu value="#{messages['Inbox']}">
                <rich:menuItem submitMode="none">
                    <s:link value="#{messages['messageInbox']}" />
                </rich:menuItem>

                <rich:menuSeparator/>

                <rich:menuItem submitMode="none">
                    <s:link value="#{messages['newMessage']}" />
                </rich:menuItem>
            </rich:dropDownMenu>
        </h:form>
    </rich:toolBarGroup>
    <rich:toolBarGroup location="right">
        <h:form id="loginTopForm">
            <h:outputLabel value="#{messages['username']} "
                            for="plUsername" />
            <h:inputText id="plUsername"
                        value="#{identity.username}" />

            <h:outputLabel value="#{messages['password']} "
                            for="plPassword" />
            <h:inputSecret id="plPassword"
                        value="#{identity.password}" />
            <h:commandButton value="#{messages['login']}"
                            action="#{identity.login}" />
            <s:button value="#{messages['forgotPwdQuestion']}"
                    view="/resetPassword.xhtml" />
        </h:form>
        <s:button view="/core/login/register.xhtml"
                value="#{messages['signUp']}" />
        <s:link view="/contact.xhtml"
                value="#{messages['contact']}" />
    </rich:toolBarGroup>

    <rich:toolBarGroup location="right">
```

```
<h:form>
  <h:inputText value="#{searchHelper.query}"/>
  <h:commandButton action="#{searchHelper.search}"
                   value="#{messages['search']}"/>
</h:form>
</rich:toolBarGroup>
</rich:toolBar>
```

The components that are of interest to us have been highlighted—`rich:toolbar` and `rich:toolbarGroup`.

Using the first one, you can declare a tool bar and sets of attributes such as `itemSeparator` (In this case it is `square`, but you can set it as `none`, `line`, `disc`, and `grid`—the default value is `none`) and `separatorClass` in order to customize it. Also, you can set the `height` and `width`, `style` and `styleClass` attributes; you can set the `contentClass` and `contentStyle` attributes for the item inside it.

In order to add a custom separator, you can set the separator image in the `itemSeparator` attribute as `itemSeparator="/mySeparatorImage.png"`, or use a facet like this:

```
<f:facet name="itemSeparator">
    <!-- my separator -->
</f:facet>
```

Remember that you can place any content inside the facet, but only one child. If you have more than one component to insert, you have to enclose it in `h:panelGroup`.

The other component is `rich:toolBarGroup`—it is very useful to group any content and style it. Also, you can decide whether to put that group on the lefthand side or the righthand side of the tool bar in a very simple and effective way.

Making the login work

Our application comes with login/logout support, but it obviously must be personalized by making the authentication method check whether the username and password passed are associated with a user.

In order to do that, let's edit the `book.richfaces.advcm.modules.login.Authenticator` class to make it look like this:

```
package book.richfaces.advcm.modules.login;

@Name("authenticator")
public class Authenticator
{
```

```
@Logger
private Log log;

@In Credentials credentials;

@In (create=true)
EntityManager entityManager;

@Out (scope=ScopeType.SESSION, required = false)
Contact loggedUser;

public boolean authenticate()
{
    log.debug("authenticating {0}", credentials.getUsername());

    try {
    // Try to find the user from username and password
        String query = "select c from Contact c where
          c.username = :username and c.password = :password
          and c.active=1";

        loggedUser = (Contact)entityManager.createQuery(query)
        .setParameter("username",credentials.getUsername())
        .setParameter("password",credentials.getPassword())
        .getSingleResult();

    // Update the lastAccessOn field
        // with the current date
        loggedUser.setLastAccessOn(new Date());

        // Save the changes on db
        entityManager.merge(loggedUser);

        // The login is successful
        return true;
        } catch (NoResultException e) {
        // No logged user
        loggedUser = null;

        // The login is failed
        return false;
        }
    }
}
```

The authenticate() method executes a JPA query to check if a user with the given username and password (stored in the credentials component) exists. If so, it updates the lastAccessOn date property of the entity and returns true, otherwise it returns false.

The `loggedUser` property is annotated with the `@Out` property. It means that after the execution of the `authenticate()` method, if the user instance exists, it will be outjected into the session context in order to be used by other components. It is necessary to set `required = false`, because if the authentication fails, no instance will be outjected.

Finally, notice the use of the Seam standard logger for the purpose of debugging.

User registration

We have to let the user register into the platform using a registration page. This page might ask for user information and might have a captcha to avoid automatic registrations.

The fields we are going to ask the user to complete are:

- Username
- Password
- Name
- Surname
- Email
- Company

Creating the page structure

Let's start creating the registration page—create a folder called `/user` inside the `/view/` directory. Create a blank page (use `home.xhtml` as a model page) called `register.xhtml` inside it and open it for editing.

Let's put a form and a panel inside the body definition using this code:

```
<ui:define name="body">
  <h:form id="login">
    <rich:panel>
      <f:facet name="header">
        <h:outputText value="#{messages['registration']}" />
      </f:facet>
        <!-- code -->
    </rich:panel>
  </h:form>
</ui:define>
```

As you can see, we defined a form and we put inside it a panel with an internationalized title.

Let's define the `registration` label in our messages bundle:

Let's open `/resources/messages_en.properties` and add the following line:

```
registration=Registration
```

Now let's do the same thing for the Italian messages bundle file at `/resources/messages_it.properties`:

```
registration=Registrazione
```

Creating the support bean

In order to support the registration feature, we have to create a bean that can hold the entity to be inserted as a property and persist it into the database.

Let's create a new class called `RegistrationHelper` in the `book.richfaces.advcm.modules.login` package, by using the following code:

```
package book.richfaces.advcm.modules.login;

@Name("registrationHelper")
public class RegistrationHelper {
    @In (create=true)
    EntityManager entityManager;

    @In
    FacesMessages facesMessages;

    private Contact newUser;

    public void signUp() {
    // Save the user and send the emails
        try {
        entityManager.persist(getNewUser());

        facesMessages.add(Severity.INFO,
          "#{messages['userRegisteredThanks']}");

         } catch (NoResultException e) {
             facesMessages.add(Severity.ERROR,
             "#{messages['emailNotFound']}");
        }
    }
```

```
    public void setNewUser(Contact newUser) {
    this.newUser = newUser;
    }

    public Contact getNewUser() {
    if (newUser==null) {
      newUser=new Contact();
    // The user is active without confirming
  // the email address (for now)
      newUser.setActive(true);
        }
      return newUser;
    }
  }
```

You can use the newUser property (highlighted in the above code), which we are using in the form (we'll see how in a minute), the signUp() action method that persists the user to the database, and the facesMessages component to alert the user about the action adding a JSF global messages component (notice the use of the messages object for i18n).

Another highlight is the newUser property getter called getNewUser() — it lazily initializes the newUser property the first time it is accessed, by creating a new instance (while it is still null) and setting the default values for its properties (in this case just the active one).

Creating the form fields and action buttons

Now we are ready to create all the form fields and the action buttons inside the panel. Let's come back to the register.xhtml file and insert the following code by replacing the <!-- code --> comment. Let's start explaining the first field, the others have the same mechanism:

```
<h:panelGrid columns="3" rowClasses="prop"
            columnClasses="name,value,validatormsg">

  <h:outputLabel for="usernameRegistration">
                #{messages['username']}:
  </h:outputLabel>

  <h:inputText
              id="usernameRegistration"
              value="#{registrationHelper.newUser.username}">
  </h:inputText>
  <rich:message for="usernameRegistration"
                styleClass="messagesingle"
                errorClass="errormsg"
```

```
                    infoClass="infomsg"
                    warnClass="warnmsg">
  </rich:message>

...

  </h:panelGrid>
```

The code is standard JSF code, so it is very simple to understand. We use a three-column h:panelGrid to put the label, the input field, and the rich:message component respectively for validation text; the input field value is the property of the Contact instance called newUser, which we've created inside the registrationHelper bean.

We added a new CSS class (validatormsg) besides the ones defined by seam-gen (name and value) and new ones for the validators style; just open the theme.css file and add the following code:

```
.validatormsg {
    padding: 5px;
}
.messagesingle {

}
.errormsg {
    color: red;
    background: url(../img/msgerror.png) no-repeat left center;
    padding-top: 1px;
    padding-left: 20px;
    margin-left: 3px;
}
.warningmsg {
    color: blue;
    background: url(../img/msgwarn.png) no-repeat left center;
    padding-top: 1px;
    padding-left: 20px;
    margin-left: 3px;
}
.infomsg {
    color: yellow;
    background: url(../img/msginfo.png) no-repeat left center;
    padding-top: 1px;
    padding-left: 20px;
    margin-left: 3px;
}
```

We just added a bit of internal space to better show the validation text and customized it with an icon for the different kind of validation messages (info, warning, and error).

Now let's add the other fields inside h:panelGrid:

```
<h:outputLabel for="passwordRegistration">
                #{messages['password']}:
</h:outputLabel>
<h:inputSecret
                id="passwordRegistration"
                value="#{registrationHelper.newUser.password}"/>
<rich:message for="passwordRegistration" styleClass="messagesingle"
    errorClass="errormsg" infoClass="infomsg" warnClass="warnmsg">
</rich:message>



<h:outputLabel for="nameRegistration">
                #{messages['name']}:
</h:outputLabel>
<h:inputText id="nameRegistration"
                value="#{registrationHelper.newUser.name}"/>
<rich:message for="nameRegistration" styleClass="messagesingle"
                errorClass="errormsg" infoClass="infomsg"
                warnClass="warnmsg">
</rich:message>



<h:outputLabel for="surnameRegistration">
                #{messages['surname']}:
</h:outputLabel>
<h:inputText id="surnameRegistration"
                value="#{registrationHelper.newUser.surname}"/>
<rich:message for="surnameRegistration" styleClass="messagesingle"
                errorClass="errormsg" infoClass="infomsg"
                warnClass="warnmsg">
</rich:message>
<h:outputLabel for="emailRegistration">
                #{messages['email']}:
</h:outputLabel>
<h:inputText
                id="emailRegistration"
                value="#{registrationHelper.newUser.email}"/>
<rich:message for="emailRegistration" styleClass="messagesingle"
                errorClass="errormsg" infoClass="infomsg"
                warnClass="warnmsg">
</rich:message>
```

```
<h:outputLabel for="companyRegistration">
                #{messages['company']}:
</h:outputLabel>
<h:inputText
                id="companyRegistration"
                value="#{registrationHelper.newUser.company}" />
<rich:message for="companyRegistration" styleClass="messagesingle"
                errorClass="errormsg" infoClass="infomsg"
                warnClass="warnmsg">
</rich:message>
```

We now have to add the action button to confirm the sign up, by adding the following code right after the panel:

```
<div class="actionButtons">
  <a:commandButton id="registerBtn" value="#{messages['signUp']}"
                action="#{registrationHelper.signUp}">
    <s:defaultAction />
  </a:commandButton>
</div>
```

The button calls the `signUp` method inside the `registrationHelper` bean that persists the entity instance into the database.

We also used the `s:defaultAction` Seam component that calls the action when the *Enter* key is pressed (it is very useful when there is more then one action button) in a field of the form.

Adding the validation rules

We still have to add the support for bean validation—in fact, we want to annotate the `Contact` entity with the Hibernate Validator validation annotation and tell JSF to use it instead of rewriting all the rules using the standard `f:validateXYZ` component (we have seen it in the first example).

So, let's open the `Contact.java` file and add a bit of the Hibernate Validator annotations we have covered in Chapter 3, *First Steps*. Therefore, now we will just see what we've added in this case by highlighting the important parts:

```
@Column(name = "name", length = 45)
@Length(min=3, max = 45)
public String getName() { ... }


@Column(name = "surname", length = 45)
@Length(min=3, max = 45)
public String getSurname() { ... }
```

```
@Column(name = "username", nullable = false, length = 20)
@NotNull
@Length(min=5, max = 20)
public String getUsername() { ... }

@Column(name = "password", nullable = false, length = 20)
@NotNull
@Length(min=5, max = 20)
public String getPassword() { ... }

@Column(name = "email", nullable = false)
@NotNull
@Email
public String getEmail() { ... }
```

We can put the `rich:beanValidator` component inside every input component in order to use Hibernate validators such as the JSF ones. In this case, we would have many inputs in the form, so we prefer to use another RichFaces component—`rich:graphValidator`.

Using `rich:graphValidator` we can add validation support to more than one field at a time, just by including them inside the tag. In our case, surround `h:panelGrid` with the `rich:graphValidator` tag and we're done!

So, let's open the `register.xhtml` page and do that:

```
<rich:graphValidator>
  <h:panelGrid columns="3" rowClasses="prop"
               columnClasses="name,value,validatormsg">

        <!-- fields -->
  </h:panelGrid>
</rich:graphValidator>
```

Simple, isn't it? Instead of adding a single `rich:beanValidator` for every input field, we surround all of the fields with `rich:graphValidator`, thereby obtaining the same result.

Adding the sign up link to the menu bar

In order to make the registration accessible, we have to add a link to the menu bar. Let's open the `/view/layout/menu.xhtml` file and add the following code before the logout link:

```
<s:link view="/user/register.xhtml" value="#{messages.signup}"
        rendered="#{not identity.loggedIn}" propagation="none" />
```

This is just an internationalized link that is visible when the user is not logged in and redirects to the `register.xhtml` page without propagating the conversation.

Validating the password against another "Rewrite password" field

Another common use case we see in web sites is the "Rewrite password" field that checks if the rewritten password is same as the one in the password field (to avoid user mistakes while writing it).

In order to do that, we are going to add another field under the password field and use a Seam validator called `s:validateEquality`, as shown in the following code:

```
<h:outputLabel for="rewritePasswordRegistration">
               #{messages['rewritePassword']}:
</h:outputLabel>
<h:inputSecret id="rewritePasswordRegistration">
   <s:validateEquality for="passwordRegistration"
                       messageId="validateNotSamePassword"
                       operator="equal" />
</h:inputSecret>
<rich:message for="rewritePasswordRegistration"
              styleClass="messagesingle" errorClass="errormsg"
              infoClass="infomsg" warnClass="warnmsg">
</rich:message>
```

We don't even need to set the value for `h:inputSecret`, because we are using it only for validation.

Making your own validators

It's true that we can use Hibernate, JSF, and Seam validators. However, a lot of the time, we can have the need of creating our own ones, which work for particular use cases. In that case, we would want to check whether the inserted username exists or not, and that the user is not using *reserved names* in place of the username. Let's start from the latter one.

First of all, we have to configure a list of reserved names; we can use `appOptions` components to do that and pass the list via `component.xml` (as we've seen for the available skins list). Let's open the `AppOptions` class and add the following code:

```
private List<String> reservedWords;

public void setReservedWords(List<String> reservedWords) {
    this.reservedWords = reservedWords;
}

public List<String> getReservedWords() {
    return reservedWords;
}
```

It is just a property (`reservedWords`) with getter and setter.

Now let's open `components.xml` and edit the `appOptions` component section, by adding the reserved names to the list as shown in the following code:

```
<component name="appOptions">
  <property name="defaultSkin">wine</property>
  <property name="availableSkins">
    <value>laguna</value>
    <value>darkX</value>
    <value>glassX</value>
    <value>blueSky</value>
    <value>classic</value>
    <value>ruby</value>
    <value>wine</value>
    <value>deepMarine</value>
    <value>emeraldTown</value>
    <value>japanCherry</value>
  </property>
  <property name="reservedWords">
    <value>guest</value>
    <value>admin</value>
    <value>editor</value>
    <value>root</value>
    <value>anonymous</value>
  </property>
</component>
```

The highlighted code fills the `reservedWord` property with the list of words, which the users can't use as usernames.

Now the list is configured and ready, so let's create our validator—let's create a new class called `ValidateReservedWords` inside the `book.richfaces.advcm.validators` package.

Let's start making it a JSF validator by adding the right annotations (for Seam) and making it implement `javax.faces.validator.Validator`:

```
@Name("reservedWordValidator")
@BypassInterceptors
@Validator
public class ValidateReservedWords
                  implements javax.faces.validator.Validator {

...

}
```

You don't have to register it in the `faces-config.xml` file as Seam is doing it for us (because of the `@Validator` annotation). Now let's implement the required methods:

```
public void validate(FacesContext facesContext,
                     UIComponent uiComponent, Object o)
                     throws ValidatorException {
    AppOptions appOptions = (AppOptions) Component.
                     getInstance("appOptions");
    boolean valid = isReservedWords(appOptions.getReservedWords(),
                     (String) o);
  if (!valid)
    {
      throws new ValidatorException(FacesMessages.
          createFacesMessage(FacesMessage.SEVERITY_ERROR, "snet.
          validator.reservedWord", "#{messages['javax.faces.component.
          UIInput.REQUIRED']}", o));
    }
}
protected boolean isReservedWords(List<String> reservedWords,
                        String word) {
    for (String resWord : reservedWords) {
      if (word.compareToIgnoreCase(resWord) == 0) {
        return false;
        }
    }
    return true;
}
```

This code needs some explanation—the `validate` method must throw a `ValidatorException` if the value is not validated, because we need the list of reserved words we want in order to access the `appOptions` component. We can't do this by injecting it because of the `@BypassInterceptors` annotation in the class. In this way, Seam can't inject the value before accessing it, so we have to get it using the `static` method (`(AppOptions)Component.getInstance("appOptions")`). As you can see, it is not very complex, but it's important to know why we are doing this.

Now that the validator is ready, we can use it inside the registration form—let's open the `/view/user/register.xhtml` file and add the code inside the username `h:inputText` component:

```
<h:inputText id="usernameRegistration"
             value="#{registrationHelper.newUser.username}">
  <f:validator validatorId="reservedWordValidator" />
</h:inputText>
```

We are using the standard `f:validator` tag for passing the name of our validator; now it is integrated with the other validators attached to the input components by `rich:graphValidator`.

The other validator we would like to use is to check the username existence in order to allow only non-existent usernames to be registered. In order to do that, let's create our validator called `ValidateUsernameExistence` in the same package and with the same structure of the one we've seen:

```
@Name("usernameExistenceValidator")
@BypassInterceptors
@Validator
public class ValidateUsernameExistence
        implements javax.faces.validator.Validator {

  public void validate(FacesContext facesContext,
                       UIComponent uiComponent, Object )
        throws ValidatorException {

        boolean usernameExists = usernameExists((String) );
        if (usernameExists) {
          throw new ValidatorException(FacesMessages.
          createFacesMessage(FacesMessage.SEVERITY_ERROR,
          "snet.validator.usernameExists",
          "#{messages['snet.validator.usernameExists']}",));
        }
  }

  protected boolean usernameExists(String username) {
    EntityManager em = (EntityManager) Component.
                getInstance("entityManager");
```

```
        if (username != null) {
          try {
          String query = "select c from Contact c
            where c.username = :username";
            List<Contact> actorsFound = (List<Contact>)
            em.createQuery(query).setParameter("username", username)
            .getResultList();
        if (actorsFound.size() > 0) {
            return true;
        }   else {
          return false;
              }
          } catch (NoResultException e)
            {
             // not found
             return false;
            }
          }
          return false;
      }
  }
```

Also, in this case we are *getting* the entityManager component using the Component.getInstance("entityManager") static method, after which we will use it as usual to make a JPA query and see if the username is used by another user.

Let's add the validator to the username h:inputText in register.xhtml:

```
<h:inputText id="usernameRegistration"
            value="#{registrationHelper.newUser.username}">
  <f:validator validatorId="usernameExistenceValidator" />
  <f:validator validatorId="reservedWordValidator" />
</h:inputText>
```

As you can see, implementing you r own JSF validators is very simple and powerful!

Using a captcha

Captchas are very useful and can avoid, in most cases, automatic registrations by asking to rewrite text or, as in our case, to resolve a simple math calculation.

JBoss Seam supports it out of the box, so we can just add a bit of code to integrate it. Let's add the following code after the "Company" field:

```
<h:outputLabel for="verifyCaptcha">
  #{messages['captcha']}:
</h:outputLabel>
<h:panelGroup id="verifyCaptchaPnl">
```

```
<h:graphicImage id="verifyCaptchaImg"
                value="/seam/resource/captcha?f=#{currentDate.time}"
                height="20" width="70" styleClass="captchaImage" />
    <h:inputText id="verifyCaptcha" value="#{captcha.response}"
                required="true" size="4">
    </h:inputText>
</h:panelGroup>
<rich:message for="verifyCaptcha" styleClass="messagesingle"
                errorClass="errormsg" infoClass="infomsg"
                warnClass="warnmsg">
</rich:message>
```

We use the standard captcha resource and the captcha Seam component in order to show and verify the response.

After every try of submitting the form, you have to re-render the captcha in order to show the new value if the user inserted a wrong one. For doing that, just use the reRender attribute of the form command button, like this:

```
<div class="actionButtons">
    <a:commandButton id="registerBtn" value="#{messages['signUp']}"
                action="#{registrationHelper.signUp}"
                reRender="verifyCaptchaImg">
    <s:defaultAction />
    </a:commandButton>
</div>
```

Here is a screenshot displaying how our captcha looks:

Verification code: 33 + 48 =

The date trick

You might have noticed that we used the f parameter with the captcha image resource; the value of the parameter is the actual date. We use that to avoid browser caching of the captcha image. By using this trick, the image will be always updated.

Resetting the captcha

The captcha response is reset only in case of wrong answers, so it is very important to manually reset the captcha after a successful registration (if not, the same response will be used again). In order to do that, let's edit the `signUp()` method of `RegistrationHelper` class, adding the following code after the `entityManager.persist(getNewUser());` call:

```
// Empty the captcha
Captcha.instance().setResponse(null);
Captcha.instance().init();
```

Automatic login after registration

In our registration use case, the user is immediately active after the registration. Therefore, it would be good if he/she would be logged in automatically after the registration task.

In order to do that, we just have to inject the `identity` and the `credentials` Seam components (the ones that we've used in the login form), log in from inside the registration bean, and add this code to the `RegistrationHelper` class:

```
@Name("registrationHelper")
public class RegistrationHelper {

    ...

    @In
    Credentials credentials;

    @In
    Identity identity;

    ...

  public void signUp() {
        // Save the user and send the emails
        try {

...

    // Execute the login
        credentials.setUsername(...credentials.
        setPassword(getNewUser().getPassword());
                            identity.login();
      } catch (NoResultException e) {
        facesMessages.add(Severity.ERROR,"#{messages['emailNotFound']
}");
```

```
        }
     }
     ...
  }
```

As you can see, we set the user and password in the `credentials` component and then call `indentity.login()` — exactly as the login form does!

We also want that after the login, the user should be redirected to the home page; there are different ways to do so. We would like to show the navigation features of JBoss Seam: let's create a new file in the `/view/user/` directory (where the `register.xhtml` file is located) and call it `register.page.xml` — this file defines the page option for `register.xhtml`.

Open the file and add the following code:

```xml
<?xml version="1.0" encoding="UTF-8"?>
<page xmlns="http://jboss.com/products/seam/pages"
      xmlns:xsi="http://www.w3.org/2001/XMLSchema-instance"
      xsi:schemaLocation="http://jboss.com/products/seam/pages
      http://jboss.com/products/seam/pages-2.1.xsd">
  <navigation from-action="#{registrationHelper.signUp}">
    <rule if="#{identity.loggedIn}">
      <redirect view-id="/home.xhtml" />
    </rule>
  </navigation>
</page>
```

We've highlighted the navigation rule, which says that when a user clicks on the signup command button of the registration form, if the login after the registration is successful, he/she must be redirected to the `home.xhtml` page — very simple and powerful!

Sending the confirmation emails

Another feature we would like our application to support (as every real application does) is that of email sending after registration, in order to inform the user that the registration was successful, and the administrator that a new user registered.

This task has nothing to do with the RichFaces framework, but we are briefly touching on it to show how to do it in our application. Refer to the Seam documentation in order to get information about all of its functionalities.

Let's start adding the email support to our project—open `components.xml` and add the following code:

```
<components
        ...
        xmlns:mail=http://jboss.com/products/seam/mail
        ...
        xsi:schemaLocation="...http://jboss.com/products/seam/mail
        http://jboss.com/products/seam/mail-2.1.xsd... ">
        <mail:mail-session host="localhost" port="25"
                        username="test" password="test" />

</components>
```

The `mail-session` tag attributes contain the data of the SMTP mail server, which we want to use for sending email (this depends on your server). There are other options you can set in order to support different types of SMTP server and authentication; refer to the JBoss Seam documentation to find out more.

Our project is now ready to send emails—we have to create the email template for the two kinds of emails we want to send after registration.

Let's start with the model for the email directed to the user—create a new directory called `/view/mailTemplates/` inside the `view/` directory. Inside this directory, let's create an `xhtml` file called `newRegistrationForUser.xhtml` and insert the following code:

```
<m:message xmlns="http://www.w3.org/1999/xhtml"
    xmlns:m="http://jboss.com/products/seam/mail"
    xmlns:h="http://java.sun.com/jsf/html">

    <m:from name="Advanced Contact Manager administration">
            info@mydomain.com
    </m:from>

    <m:to name="#{registrationHelper.newUser.name}
                #{registrationHelper.newUser.surname}">
                #{registrationHelper.newUser.email}
    </m:to>

    <m:subject>
        #{messages['thankYouForRegistrationMailSubject']}
    </m:subject>

    <m:body>
        <p>
            <h:outputText
                value="#{messages['thankYouForRegistrationMailDear']}:
            #{registrationHelper.newUser.name} #{registrationHelper.
                                        newUser.surname}," />
```

```
      <br/>
      <h:outputText
        value="#{messages['thankYouForRegistrationMailText']}" />
       <br/>
      <h:outputText value="#{messages['mailStaffSignature']}" />
      <br/>
    </p>
  </m:body>
</m:message>
```

As you can see, this is a normal XHTML page with special tags for emails: you can use m:from, m:to, m:subject, and m:body in order to compose the email. You can access the Seam components (in this case, we get the registering user's information from the registrationHelper bean) and also use the message bundles for i18n!

Let's create the email template to inform the administrator about the new registered user, and call the file newRegistrationForAdmin.xhtml:

```
<m:message xmlns="http://www.w3.org/1999/xhtml"
            xmlns:m="http://jboss.com/products/seam/mail"
            xmlns:h="http://java.sun.com/jsf/html">

  <m:from name="Advanced Contact Manager administration">
          info@mydomain.com
  </m:from>

  <m:to name="Advanced Contact Manager administration ">
     info@mydomain.com
  </m:to>

  <m:subject>New user registration!</m:subject>

  <m:body>
       <p>A new user has registered!<br/>
       <h:outputText value="#{messages['name']}:
         #{registrationHelper.newUser.name}" /><br/>
       <h:outputText value="#{messages['surname']}:
         #{registrationHelper.newUser.surname}" /><br/>
<h:outputText value="#{messages['email']}: #{registrationHelper.
newUser.email}" /><br/>
       </p>
  </m:body>
</m:message>
```

In this case, we don't need to use i18n for strings, because the email is only for administrators.

It's also very simple to send them: let's open the RegistrationHelper class again, and add the following code:

```
@Name("registrationHelper")
public class RegistrationHelper {

    . . .

    @In (create=true)
    Renderer renderer;

    . . .

    public void signUp() {
        // Save the user and send the emails
      try {
                    . . .

    renderer.render("/mailTemplates/newRegistrationForAdmin.xhtml");

    renderer.render("/mailTemplates/newRegistrationForUser.xhtml");
                . . .
        } catch (NoResultException e) {
            facesMessages.add(Severity.ERROR,
            "#{messages['emailNotFound']}");
        }
    }

    . . .

}
```

We just have to make one call to render the email page and then send it.

Screenshot

Here is the final version of our registration form with some validation messages shown as follows (we tried to sign up without entering the data):

Reset password box

Another use case that our application is going to support is the one that lets the user reset his/her password. This is a simplified use case, so the user must insert the username. Then the application just resets the password and sends an email with the new password to the account owner.

We are doing all the stuff we have talked about by now in this chapter, so we will be fast explaining what to do in order to add this support to our application.

First of all, let's create a support bean called `ResetPwdHelper` in the `book.richfaces.advcm.modules.login` package using this code:

```
@Name("resetPwdHelper")
public class ResetPwdHelper {

    @In (create=true)
    Renderer renderer;

    @In (create=true)
    EntityManager entityManager;

    @In
```

```
FacesMessages facesMessages;

private String newPassword;

private String username;

public void reset() {
        try {
        String query = "select c from Contact c
        where c.username = :username";
          Contact actor = (Contact)(entityManager.createQuery(query)
                        .setParameter("username", getUsername())
                        .getSingleResult());

          // Saving the new password (will be used
                   // by the email template)
          setNewPassword(PasswordUtils.getRandomPassword());

          // Updating the entity
          actor.setPassword(getNewPassword());

          // Saving it
          entityManager.merge(actor);


          // Sending the email
         renderer.render("/mailTemplates/resetPasswordMail.xhtml");

          facesMessages.add(Severity.INFO,
          "#{messages['newPasswordSent']}");

          // Empty the data
          setUsername(null);
          setNewPassword(null);
          } catch (NoResultException e) {
          facesMessages.addToControl("username",Severity.ERROR,
          "#{messages['usernameNotFound']}");
       }
}

public String getNewPassword() {
        return newPassword;
}

public void setNewPassword(String forgotPwdNewPassword) {
        this.newPassword = forgotPwdNewPassword;
}

@NotNull
public String getUsername() {
        return username;
}
```

```
    public void setUsername(String email) {
            this.username = email;
    }

}
```

The `username` property is the one that the user will fill from the form (notice that we used the `@NotNull` Hibernate Validator annotation in order to inform JSF that the property must not be empty); the `reset()` method retrieves the user with that username, changes the password, and informs him/her by sending an email with the new password.

Let's create the form—create a file called `resetPassword.xhtml` inside the `/view/user/` directory of our project (use `home.xhtml` as a template). Add the following code for the form inside the body definition:

```
<h:form id="login">
  <rich:panel>
    <f:facet name="header">
            #{messages['forgotUsername']}
    </f:facet>

    <div class="dialog">
      <h:panelGrid columns="3" rowClasses="prop"
                   columnClasses="name,value,validatormsg">
        <h:outputLabel for="email">
                     #{messages['email']}:
        </h:outputLabel>
        <h:inputText id="email"
                     value="#{forgotUsernameHelper.email}">
          <rich:beanValidator />
        </h:inputText>
        <rich:message for="email"
                      styleClass="messagesingle"
                      errorClass="errormsg"
                      infoClass="infomsg"
                      warnClass="warnmsg">
        </rich:message>
      </h:panelGrid>
    </div>
  </rich:panel>

  <div class="actionButtons">
    <a:commandButton value="#{messages['sendUsername']}"
                     action="#{forgotUsernameHelper.sendUsername}"
```

```
                              reRender="email">
      <s:defaultAction />
      </a:commandButton>
    </div>
  </h:form>
```

In this case, we have just the username field, so we use `rich:beanValidator` in the registration form instead of `rich:graphValidator` that we've seen. After this field, there is also an internationalized link for users who forgot their username (we'll see this in the next section).

You may also have noticed that now we are using an Ajax `commandButton`, which just re-renders the username field to empty it after the execution of the action (if you see the `reset()` method in the support bean, we empty the data after sending the email).

The last missing piece is the email template that the user will receive: let's create a file called `resetPasswordMail.xhtml` inside the `/view/mailTemplates/` directory and open it.

Let's add the following code to it:

```
<m:message xmlns="http://www.w3.org/1999/xhtml"
           xmlns:m="http://jboss.com/products/seam/mail"
           xmlns:h="http://java.sun.com/jsf/html">
  <m:from name="Advanced Contact Manager administration">
          info@mydomain.com </m:from>
  <m:to name="#{resetPwdHelper.email}">
              #{resetPwdHelper.email}
  </m:to>
  <m:subject>#{messages['resetPwdMailSubject']}</m:subject>
  <m:body>
    <p>
      <h:outputText value="#{messages['resetPwdMailContent']}" />
    <br/><br/>
      <h:outputText value="#{messages['resetPwdMailPwdLabel']}: " />
      <h:outputText value="#{resetPwdHelper.resetPwdNewPassword}"
                    style="font-weight: bold;" />
    </p>
  </m:body>
</m:message>
```

We're done! We've created an internationalized email for our user, and here is a screenshot of the panel created:

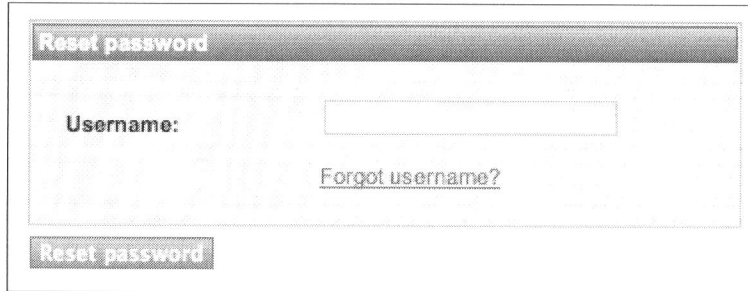

Forgot username box

If a user can't remember even the username, he/she just has to access this page and insert their email, and he/she will receive an email with the username information.

This feature is very similar to the reset password one, so we will just present the code to be added along with a few comments.

First, add another support bean called `ForgotUsernameHelper` to the `book.richfaces.advcm.modules.login` package using the following code:

```
@Name("forgotUsernameHelper")
public class ForgotUsernameHelper {

    @In(create = true)
    Renderer renderer;

    @In(create = true)
    EntityManager entityManager;

    @In
    FacesMessages facesMessages;

    private String usernameFound;
    private String email;

    public void sendUsername() {
        try {
            String query = "select c from Contact c
                            where c.email =:email";
            Contact actor = (Contact) (entityManager.
                                createQuery(query).
            setParameter("email", getEmail()).getSingleResult());
            // Saving the username (it will be used into the
```

```
                              // email)
              setUsernameFound(actor.getUsername());
              // Sending the email
              renderer.render("/mailTemplates/forgotUsernameMail.xhtml");

              facesMessages.add(Severity.INFO,
              "#{messages['newUsernameSent']}");

              // Empty the data
              setEmail(null);
              setUsernameFound(null);
          } catch (NoResultException e) {
              facesMessages.addToControl("email", Severity.ERROR,
                                 "#{messages['emailNotFound']}");
          }
      }

      @NotNull
      @Email
      public String getEmail() {
          return email;
      }
      public void setEmail(String email) {
          this.email = email;
      }
      public String getUsernameFound() {
          return usernameFound;
      }
      public void setUsernameFound(String forgotPwdNewPassword) {
          this.usernameFound = forgotPwdNewPassword;
      }
  }
```

This code is the same as that for `ResetPwdHelper` (the reset password feature)—we just get an email and not the username. Therefore, we also added the Hibernate validator `@Email` annotation in order to inform JSF that this might be a well-formed email address.

Now let's create the `forgotUsername.xhtml` page inside the `/view/user/` directory (use `home.xhtml` as the template) and add the following code inside its body definition:

```
<h:form id="login">
  <rich:panel>
    <f:facet name="header">
      #{messages['forgotUsername']}
    </f:facet>
```

```
<div class="dialog">
  <h:panelGrid columns="3" rowClasses="prop"
               columnClasses="name,value,validatormsg">
    <h:outputLabel for="email"> #{messages['email']}:
    </h:outputLabel>
    <h:inputText id="email" value="#{forgotUsernameHelper.email}">
       <rich:beanValidator />
    </h:inputText>
    <rich:message for="email" styleClass="messagesingle"
                  errorClass="errormsg" infoClass="infomsg"
                  warnClass="warnmsg">
    </rich:message>
  </h:panelGrid>
</div>
</rich:panel>

<div class="actionButtons">
  <a:commandButton value="#{messages['sendUsername']}"
                   action="#{forgotUsernameHelper.sendUsername}"
                   reRender="email">
    <s:defaultAction />
  </a:commandButton>
</div>
</h:form>
```

Also, in this case, the code is very similar to the one we've seen for the resetPassword.xhtml page.

Now the email template: let's add a new file called forgotUsernameMail.xhtml into the /view/mailTemplates/ directory. Open this new file and add the following code:

```
<m:message xmlns="http://www.w3.org/1999/xhtml"
           xmlns:m="http://jboss.com/products/seam/mail"
           xmlns:h="http://java.sun.com/jsf/html">

  <m:from name="Advanced Contact Manager administration">
         info@mydomain.com
  </m:from>

  <m:to name="#{forgotUsernameHelper.email}">
      #{forgotUsernameHelper.email}
  </m:to>
  <m:subject> #{messages['forgotUsernameMailSubject']} </m:subject>

  <m:body>
    <p>
```

```
      <h:outputText
        value="#{messages['forgotUsernameMailContent']}" />
    <br/><br/>
      <h:outputText
        value="#{messages['forgotUsernameMailUsernameLabel']}: "/>
      <h:outputText value="#{forgotUsernameHelper.
        forgotUsernameNewPassword}" style="font-weight: bold;" />
    </p>
  </m:body>

</m:message>
```

Nothing new here too—we have created a new feature in a very simple way! Here is the screenshot:

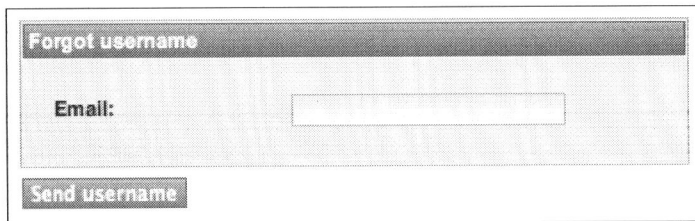

URL rewriting: making it simple and powerful

Another very important feature we would like to support is the URL rewriting—this is very useful to make simple URLs for both SEO optimization and users.

Seam gives very good support for this by just adding the support to the components.xml file:

```
<components ...>

...

<web:rewrite-filter view-mapping="*.seam"/>

...

</components>
```

Now you have to tell, for every page, how to rewrite it: you can do both by using pages.xml file or a single <page_name>.page.xml file for every page.

We are going to use the single page approach: let's create a file called `home.page.xml` inside the `/view/` directory and insert the following code into it:

```
<?xml version="1.0" encoding="UTF-8"?>
<page xmlns="http://jboss.com/products/seam/pages"
      xmlns:xsi="http://www.w3.org/2001/XMLSchema-instance"
      xsi:schemaLocation="http://jboss.com/products/seam/pages
      http://jboss.com/products/seam/pages-2.1.xsd"
      login-required="true">

  <rewrite pattern="/home" />
</page>
```

Apart from the page definition, you can see that the tag to define the rewrite pattern is highlighted—you don't have to change anything to view the links, for example in the menu points to the `.xhtml` page, then Seam will rewrite it in the right way: try it yourself!

Another useful feature is that we can use `param` inside the pattern. We'll see it in more detail in the next chapter, for now let's see a simple example:

```
<?xml version="1.0" encoding="UTF-8"?>
<page xmlns="http://jboss.com/products/seam/pages"
      xmlns:xsi="http://www.w3.org/2001/XMLSchema-instance"
      xsi:schemaLocation="http://jboss.com/products/seam/pages
      http://jboss.com/products/seam/pages-2.1.xsd"
      login-required="true">
<param name="userId" required="true" />

<rewrite pattern="/myPage-{myParam}" />
</page>
```

As you can see, we can include `param` inside the pattern and Seam will make it work automatically; very simple!

We will see more concrete use cases of `param` in rewrite patterns in the following chapters.

The insertion of URL rewrite patterns for every page that we have created till now is left as an exercise for the reader.

Summary

In this chapter, we created the login and registration system of the web site, looking at all the features that a real application might have.

Those feature includes i18n and skin management, registration page, login box, forgot username, reset password, captcha, email sending, and URL rewriting—the base is ready and we can move on to making the logic specific for the type of web application we want to develop.

6
Making the Contacts List and Detail

In this chapter, we are going to develop the contacts management feature of our application, which includes listing, adding, editing, and deleting contacts—all of this the Ajax way!

Moreover, we are going to learn new concepts about the RichFaces component framework and Ajax support.

The main layout

Let's start preparing the space for the core features of the application. As you've seen in Chapter 4, *The Application*, we want a three-column layout for groups, contacts list, and contact detail. Let's open the `home.xhtml` file and add a three-column panel grid inside the body:

```
<h:panelGrid columns="3"
             width="100%"
             columnClasses="main-group-column, main-contacts-list-
column, main-contact-detail-column">
</h:panelGrid>
```

We are using three new CSS classes (one for every column). Let's open the `/view/stylesheet/theme.css` file and add the following code:

```
.main-group-column {
    width: 20%;
    vertical-align: top;
}

.main-contacts-list-column {
```

```
    width: 40%;
    vertical-align: top;
}
.main-contact-detail-column {
    width: 40%;
    vertical-align: top;
}
```

The main columns are ready; now we want to split the content of every column in a separate file (so we don't have a large and difficult file to read) by using the Facelets templating capabilities—let's create a new folder inside the /view folder called main, and let's create the following empty files inside it:

- contactsGroups.xhtml

- contactsList.xhtml

- contactEdit.xhtml

- contactView.xhtml

Now let's open them and put the standard code for an empty (included) file:

```
<!DOCTYPE composition PUBLIC "-//W3C//DTD XHTML 1.0 Transitional//EN"
        "http://www.w3.org/TR/xhtml1/DTD/xhtml1-transitional.dtd">
<ui:composition xmlns="http://www.w3.org/1999/xhtml"
                xmlns:s="http://jboss.com/products/seam/taglib"
                xmlns:ui="http://java.sun.com/jsf/facelets"
                xmlns:f="http://java.sun.com/jsf/core"
                xmlns:h="http://java.sun.com/jsf/html"
                xmlns:rich="http://richfaces.org/rich"
                xmlns:a="http://richfaces.org/a4j">
<!-- my code here -->
</ui:composition>
```

Now, we have all of the pieces ready to be included into the home.xhtml file, let's open it and start adding the first column inside h:panelGrid:

```
<a:outputPanel id="contactsGroups">
  <ui:include src="main/contactsGroups.xhtml"/>
</a:outputPanel>
```

As you can see, we surrounded the include with an a:outputPanel that will be used as a placeholder for the re-rendering purpose.

Include a Facelets tag (ui:include) into the a:outputPanel that we used in order to include the page at that point.

Ajax placeholders

A very important concept to keep in mind while developing is that the Ajax framework can't add or delete, but can only replace existing elements in the page. For this reason, if you want to append some code, you need to use a placeholder.

RichFaces has a component that can be used as a placeholder—`a4j:outputPanel`.

Inside `a4j:outputPanel`, you can put other components that use the "rendered" attribute in order to decide if they are visible or not. When you want to re-render all the included components, just re-render the `outputPanel`, and all will work without any problem.

Here is a non-working code snippet:

```
<h:form>
    <h:inputText value="#{aBean.myText}">
            <a4j:support event="onkeyup" reRender="out1" />
    </h:inputText>
</h:form>

<h:outputText
    id="out1"
    value="#{aBean.myText}"
    rendered="#{not empty aBean.myText}"/>
```

This code seems the same as that of the `a4j:support` example, but it won't work.

The problem is that we added the rendered attribute to `outputText`, so initially, `out1` will not be rendered (because the text property is initially empty and `rendered` will be equal to `false`). After the Ajax response, the JavaScript Engine will not find the `out1` element (it is not in the page because of `rendered="false"`), and it will not be able to update it (remember that you can't add or delete elements, only replace them).

It is very simple to make the code work:

```
<h:form>
  <h:inputText value="#{aBean.myText}">
    <a4j:support event="onkeyup" reRender="out2" />
  </h:inputText>
</h:form>
<a4j:outputPanel id="out2">
  <h:outputText
    id="out1"
    rendered="#{not empty aBean.myText}"
    value="#{aBean.myText}" />
</a4j:outputPanel>
```

As you can see, you just have to put the `out1` component inside `a4j:outputPanel` (called `out2`) and tell `a4j:support` to re-render `out2` instead of `out1`.

Initially, `out2` will be rendered but empty (because `out1` will not be rendered). After the Ajax response, the empty `out2` will be replaced with markup elements that also contain the `out1` component (that is now visible, because the `myText` property is not empty after the Ajax update and the `rendered` property is `true`).

A very important concept to keep in mind while developing is that the Ajax framework can't add or delete, but can only replace existing elements of the page. For this reason, if you want to append some code, you need to use a placeholder.

> In the contact list example of Chapter 3, *First Steps*, we didn't use a placeholder for the "No contact found" `h:outputText`, because the Ajax action components (such as the "delete" button) re-render the surrounding `fContactsList` form that acts as a placeholder in this case.

The groups box

This box will contain all the contacts groups, so the user will be able to organize contacts in different groups in a better way.

We will not implement the group box features in this chapter. Therefore, by now the group column is just a `rich:panel` with a link to refresh the contact list.

Let's open the `contactsGroups.xhtml` file and insert the following code:

```
<h:form>
    <rich:panel>
        <f:facet name="header">
          <h:outputText value="#{messages['groups']}" />
        </f:facet>
        <h:panelGrid columns="1">
          <a:commandLink value="#{messages['allContacts']}"
                        ajaxSingle="true"
                        reRender="contactsList">
            <f:setPropertyActionListener value="#{null}"
              target="#{homeContactsListHelper.contactsList}" />
          </a:commandLink>
        </h:panelGrid>
    </rich:panel>
</h:form>
```

As you can see, we've put a three-column h:panelGrid (to be used in the future) and a:commandLink, which just sets the contactsList property of the homeContactListHelper bean (that we will see in the next section) to null, in order to make the list be read again. At the end of the Ajax interaction, it will re-render the contactsList column in order to show the new data.

Also, notice that we are still supporting i18n for every text using the messages property; the task to fill the messages_XX.properties file is left as an exercise for the user.

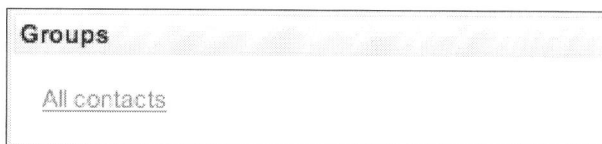

```
Groups

All contacts
```

The contacts list

The second column inside h:panelGrid of home.xhtml looks like:

```
<a:outputPanel id="contactsList">
  <ui:include src="main/contactsList.xhtml"/>
</a:outputPanel>
```

As for groups, we used a placeholder surrounding the ui:include tag.

Now let's focus on creating the data table—open the /view/main/contactsList.xhtml file and add the first snippet of code for dataTable:

```
<h:form>
  <rich:dataTable id="contactsTable"
                  reRender="contactsTableDS"
                  rows="20"
                  value="#{homeContactsListHelper.contactsList}"
                  var="contact">
    <rich:column width="45%">
      <h:outputText value="#{contact.name}"/>
    </rich:column>
    <rich:column width="45%">
      <h:outputText value="#{contact.surname}"/>
    </rich:column>
      <f:facet name="footer">
        <rich:datascroller id="contactsTableDS"
                           for="contactsTable"
```

```
                              renderIfSinglePage="false"/>
        </f:facet>
    </rich:dataTable>
        <h:outputText value="#{messages['noContactsInList']}"
        rendered="#{homeContactsListHelper.contactsList.size()==0}"/>
    </h:form>
```

We just added the `rich:dataTable` component with some columns and an Ajax data scroller at the end.

Differences between h:dataTable and rich: dataTable

RichFaces provides its own version of `h:dataTable`, which contains more features and is better integrated with the RichFaces framework.

The first important additional feature, in fact, is the skinnability support following the RichFaces standards.

Other features are row and column spans support (we will discuss it in the *Columns and column groups* section), out-of-the-box filter and sorting (discussed in the *Filtering and sorting* section), more JavaScript event handlers (such as `onRowClick`, `onRowContextMenu`, `onRowDblClick`, and so on) and the `reRender` attribute.

Like other data iteration components of the RichFaces framework, it also supports the partial-row update (see Chapter 10, *Advanced Techniques* for more information).

Data pagination

Implementing Ajax data pagination using RichFaces is really simple—just decide how many rows must be shown in every page by setting the `rows` attribute of `dataTable` (in our case, we've chosen 20 rows per page), and then "attach" the `rich:datascroller` component to it by filling the `for` attribute with the `dataTable` id:

```
    <rich:datascroller id="contactsTableDS"
                       for="contactsTable"
                       renderIfSinglePage="false"/>
```

Here you can see another very useful attribute (`renderIfSinglePage`) that makes the component hidden when there is just a single page in the list (it means the list contains a number of items that is less than or equal to the value of the `rows` attribute).

A thing to keep in mind is that the `rich:datascroller` component must stay inside a form component (`h:form` or `a:form`) in order to work.

Customizing `rich:datascroller` is possible not only by using CSS classes (as usual), but also by personalizing our own parts using the following facets:

- pages
- controlsSeparator
- first, first_disabled
- last, last_disabled
- next, next_disabled
- previous, previous_disabled
- fastforward, fastforward_disabled
- fastrewind, fastrewinf_disabled

Here is an example with some customized facets (using strings):

```
<rich:datascroller id="contactsTableDS" for="contactsTable" renderIfSi
nglePage="false">
    <f:facet name="first">
        <h:outputText value="First" />
    </f:facet>
    <f:facet name="last">
        <h:outputText value="Last" />
    </f:facet>
</rich:datascroller>
```

Here is the result:

You can use an image (or another component) instead of text, in order to create your own customized scroller.

Another interesting example is:

```
<rich:datascroller id="contactsTableDS" for="contactsTable"
                    renderIfSinglePage="false">
  <f:facet name="first">
    <h:outputText value="First"/>
```

```
    </f:facet>
    <f:facet name="last">
      <h:outputText value="Last"/>
    </f:facet>
    <f:attribute name="pageIndexVar"
                 value="pageIndexVar"/>
    <f:attribute name="pagesVar" value="pagesVar"/>
    <f:facet name="pages">
      <h:panelGroup>
        <h:outputText value="Page #{pageIndexVar} / #{pagesVar}"/>
      </h:panelGroup>
    </f:facet>
  </rich:datascroller>
```

The result is:

First « Page 2 / 3 » Last

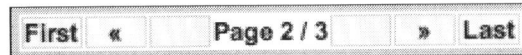

By setting the pageIndexVar and pagesVar attributes, we are able to use them in an outputText component, as we've done in the example.

A useful attribute of the component is maxPages that sets the maximum number of page links (the numbers in the middle), which the scroller shows—therefore, we can control the size of it.

The page attribute could be bound to a property of a bean, in order to switch to a page giving the number—a simple use-case could be using an inputText and a commandButton, in order to let the client insert the page number that he/she wants to go to.

Here is the code that shows how to implement it:

```
<rich:datascroller
    for="contactsList" maxPages="20" fastControls="hide"
    page="#{customDataScrollerExampleHelper.scrollerPage}"
pagesVar="pages"
    id="ds">
  <f:facet name="first">
      <h:outputText value="First" />
  </f:facet>
  <f:facet name="first_disabled">
      <h:outputText value="First" />
  </f:facet>
  <f:facet name="last">
      <h:outputText value="Last" />
```

```
        </f:facet>
        <f:facet name="last_disabled">
            <h:outputText value="Last" />
        </f:facet>
        <f:facet name="previous">
            <h:outputText value="Previous" />
        </f:facet>
        <f:facet name="previous_disabled">
            <h:outputText value="Previous" />
        </f:facet>
        <f:facet name="next">
            <h:outputText value="Next" />
        </f:facet>
        <f:facet name="next_disabled">
            <h:outputText value="Next" />
        </f:facet>
        <f:facet name="pages">
            <h:panelGroup>
                <h:outputText value="Page "/>
                <h:inputText
                    value="#{customDataScrollerExampleHelper.
                    scrollerPage}"
                    size="4">
                    <f:validateLongRange minimum="0" />
                    <a:support event="onkeyup" timeout="500"
                    oncomplete="#{rich:component('ds')}.
                    switchToPage(this.value)" />
                </h:inputText>
                <h:outputText value=" of #{pages}"/>
            </h:panelGroup>
        </f:facet>
    </rich:datascroller>
```

As you can see, besides customizing the text of the **First**, **Last**, **Previous**, and **Next** sections, we defined a `pages` facet by inserting `h:inputText` connected with an integer value inside a backing bean. We also added the `a:support` tag, in order to trim the page change after the `keyup` event is completed. We've also set the `timeout` attribute, in order to call the server every 500 ms and not every time the user types.

You can see a screenshot of the feature here:

All contacts	
Name	**Surname**
⇕	⇕
Carrie-Anne	Moss
Hugo	Weaving
First Previous Page 2 of 3 Next Last	

Adding the column headers

Now we would like to add a header for every column of the `dataTable`; the simplest way is to just put a facet inside the `rich:column` component, this way:

```
<rich:column>
  <f:facet name="header">
    <h:outputText value="my header" />
  </f:facet>
    . . .
</rich:column>
```

This method also works for the standard `h:dataTable` component—RichFaces enhances the table heading capabilities by allowing grouping, using the `rich:columnGroup` component.

Therefore, coming back to our application, we can put the following code inside the `rich:dataTable` tag in order to define the header of the `dataTable`:

```
<rich:dataTable ... >
  <f:facet name="header">
    <rich:columnGroup>
      <rich:column colspan="2">
        <h:outputText value="Contacts"/>
      </rich:column>
      <rich:column breakBefore="true">
        <h:outputText value="Name"/>
      </rich:column>
      <rich:column>
        <h:outputText value="Surname"/>
      </rich:column>
    </rich:columnGroup>
  </f:facet>
    . . .
```

And the result will be as follows:

	Contacts	
Name		Surname

Columns and column groups

Using the RichFaces version is also very convenient for extending the `dataTable` behavior on row rendering.

Let's take a simplified version (without `header`, `footer`, and `datascroller`) of the `contactsList` table:

```
<rich:dataTable id="contactsTable"
                value="#{homeContactsListHelper.contactsList}"
                var="contact">
   <rich:column>
     <h:outputText value="#{contact.name}"/>
   </rich:column>
   <rich:column>
     <h:outputText value="#{contact.surname}"/>
   </rich:column>
   <rich:column>
     <a:commandButton image="/img/view.png" />
   </rich:column>
</rich:dataTable>
```

It is a normal `dataTable` and looks like:

Marcus	Chong	
Laurence	Fishburne	
Carrie-Anne	Moss	
Hugo	Weaving	
Keanu	Reeves	

Now let's do a little editing by adding the two attributes— span and breakBefore:

```
<rich:dataTable id="contactsTable"
                value="#{homeContactsListHelper.contactsList}"
                var="contact">
    <rich:column colspan="2">
        <h:outputText value="#{contact.name}"/>
    </rich:column>
    <rich:column breakBefore="true">
        <h:outputText value="#{contact.surname}"/>
    </rich:column>
    <rich:column>
        <a:commandButton image="/img/view.png" />
    </rich:column>
</rich:dataTable>
```

With the above attributes, it looks like:

Marcus	
Chong	🔍
Laurence	
Fishburne	🔍
Carrie-Anne	
Moss	🔍
Hugo	
Weaving	🔍
Keanu	
Reeves	🔍

What has happened?

We've told to the first column to "span" (you might know the meaning because it's a standard html table column attribute) two columns and the second one to "break before" rendering it, in the sense of closing the row (putting the HTML </tr> tag).

So, the first column fills the space of two columns and the second one is rendered in another row; simple, isn't it?

You can also use the rowSpan attribute in order to span rows instead of columns, as for standard HTML tables.

We can have the same result using a `rich:columnGroup` component instead of the `breakBefore` attribute, as in the following example:

```
<rich:dataTable id="contactsTable"
                value="#{homeContactsListHelper.contactsList}"
                var="contact">
   <rich:column colspan="2">
     <h:outputText value="#{contact.name}"/>
   </rich:column>
   <rich:columnGroup>
     <rich:column>
       <h:outputText value="#{contact.surname}"/>
     </rich:column>
     <rich:column>
       <a:commandButton image="/img/view.png"/>
     </rich:column>
   </rich:columnGroup>
</rich:dataTable>
```

As we can see, the result is exactly the same.

Another use of `rich:column` and `rich:columnGroup` is to define a complex table header as we have done in our application, as shown in the previous section.

`rich:column` contains very useful attributes other than span, `breakBefore`, and the filtering and sorting attributes (that we are going to see in the next section), which we don't find in the standard `h:column` component.

For example, in our application, we used the `width` attribute in order to set the width for every column without using a CSS class just for that.

Out-of-the-box filtering and sorting

Another important feature that we've seen in a simple example in Chapter 3 is the out-of-the-box filtering and sorting support that the `rich:dataTable` component offers.

In order to add this feature to our table, let's just edit the `rich:column` tags for name and surname, as shown in the following code:

```
<rich:column width="45%"
             sortBy="#{contact.name}"
             filterBy="#{contact.name}">
   <h:outputText value="#{contact.name}"/>
</rich:column>
```

```
<rich:column width="45%"
            sortBy="#{contact.surname}"
            filterBy="#{contact.surname}">
  <h:outputText value="#{contact.surname}"/>
</rich:column>
```

You will have a working sort and filter feature for your table just by adding these two attributes!

Contacts	
Name	**Surname**
⬍	⬍
Marcus	Chong
Laurence	Fishburne
Carrie-Anne	Moss
Hugo	Weaving
Keanu	Reeves

In Chapter 10, we will explain a more customized way to manage filtering and sorting.

The bottom toolbar

We need a toolbar at the bottom of the table that will contain action buttons for different kinds of action (we will add the button to add a new contact in the next section).

We have seen the rich:toolbar component in the Chapter 5, *Making the Application Structure*, so just add this code after the code for rich:datascroller:

```
<rich:toolBar>
  <rich:toolBarGroup>
  <!-- my action buttons here -->
  </rich:toolBarGroup>
</rich:toolBar>
```

The backing bean

We've seen the connection of the table with a backing bean called homeContactsListHelper—let's create it!

Let's create a new package called `main` inside `book.richfaces.advcm.modules`, and create a new class called `HomeContactsListHelper` inside it.

The Seam component is very simple, as it has just to retrieve the contacts list from the database (groups are not managed by now)—it might look like the following:

```
@Name("homeContactsListHelper")
@Scope(ScopeType.CONVERSATION)
public class HomeContactsListHelper {
  @In(create=true)
  EntityManager entityManager;

  @In(required = true)
  Contact loggedUser;

  private List<Contact> contactsList;

    public List<Contact> getContactsList() {
      if (contactsList ==null) {
        // Creating the query
        String query="from Contact c where c.contact.id=:fatherId";
        // Getting the contacts list
        contactsList = (List<Contact>)
        entityManager.createQuery(query)
                    .setParameter("fatherId",
                     loggedUser.getId())
                    .getResultList();
      }
    return contactsList;
  }

    public void setContactsList(List<Contact> contactsList) {
      this.contactsList = contactsList;
    }
}
```

To summarize—the `@Name` annotation defines the name of the Seam component/JSF backing bean, `@Scope` defines the scope of the component, we inject (using the `@In` annotation) the `entityManager` component (to query the database using JPA) and the contact instance referring to the logged user, who we outjected during the login phase.

In addition, the bean has a property called `contactsList` that is lazy initialized into the `getContactsList()` method by querying the database.

As we are using the conversation scope, we would like to start the conversation when entering the home page. There are different ways to do this—in our case, let's open the `/view/home.page.xml` file and add the following content:

```
<begin-conversation join="true" />
```

So, now when the user navigates to the home page, a new conversation is created if there is none. If not, the existing one would be kept (`join="true"`).

The contact detail

For the third column, we would like to show three different statuses:

- The "No contact selected" message when no contact is selected (so the property is null)
- A view-only box when we are not in the edit mode (the property `selectedContactEditing` is set to `false`)
- An edit box when we are in the edit mode (the property `selectedContactEditing` is set to `true`)

So, let's open the `home.xhtml` page and insert the third column inside the panel grid with the three statuses:

```
<a:outputPanel id="contactDetail">
  <a:outputPanel rendered="#{homeSelectedContactHelper.
                  selectedContact==null}">
    <rich:panel>
        <h:outputText
                   value="#{messages['noContactSelected']}"/>
    </rich:panel>
  </a:outputPanel>

  <a:outputPanel
        rendered="#{homeSelectedContactHelper.
                  selectedContact!=null and
                  homeSelectedContactHelper.
                  selectedContactEditing==false}">
      <ui:include src="main/contactView.xhtml"/>
  </a:outputPanel>
```

```
<a:outputPanel
          rendered="#{homeSelectedContactHelper.
               selectedContact!=null and
               homeSelectedContactHelper.
               selectedContactEditing==true}">
  <ui:include src="main/contactEdit.xhtml"/>
</a:outputPanel>
</a:outputPanel>
```

Here, we have put the main `a:outputPanel` as the main placeholder, and inside it we put three more instances of `a:outputPanel` (one for every state) with the rendered attribute in order to decide which one to show.

The first one just shows a message when `homeSelectedContactHelper.selectedContact` is set to `null`:

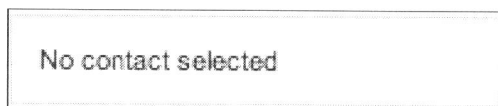

No contact selected

The second instance of `a:outputPanel` will include the `main/contactView.xhtml` file only if `homeSelectedContactHelper.selectedContact` is not `null`, and we are not in editing mode (so `homeSelectedContactHelper.selectedContactEditing` is set to `false`); the third one will be shown only if `homeSelectedContactHelper.selectedContact` is not `null`, and we are in the `edit` mode (that is `homeSelectedContactHelper.selectedContactEditing` is equal to `true`).

Before starting to write the include sections, let's see how the main bean for the selected contact would look, and connect it with the data table for selecting the contact from it.

The support bean

Let's create a new class called `HomeSelectedContactHelper` inside the `book.richfaces.advcm.modules.main` package; the class might look like this:

```
@Name("homeSelectedContactHelper")
@Scope(ScopeType.CONVERSATION)
public class HomeSelectedContactHelper {

    @In(create = true)
    EntityManager entityManager;

    @In(required = true)
    Contact loggedUser;
```

```
    @In
    FacesMessages facesMessages;

    // My code here
}
```

This is a standard JBoss Seam component as we've seen in the other chapters; now let's add our properties.

The bean that we are going to use for view and edit features is very simple to understand—it just contains two properties (namely `selectedContact` and `selectedContactEditing`) and some action methods to manage them.

Let's add the properties to our class:

```
private Contact selectedContact;

private Boolean selectedContactEditing;

public Contact getSelectedContact() {
    return selectedContact;
}

public void setSelectedContact(Contact selectedContact) {
    this.selectedContact = selectedContact;
}

public Boolean getSelectedContactEditing() {
    return selectedContactEditing;
}

public void setSelectedContactEditing(Boolean selectedContactEditing)
{
    this.selectedContactEditing = selectedContactEditing;
}
```

As you can see, we just added two properties with standard the getter and setter.

Let's now see the action methods:

```
public void createNewEmptyContactInstance() {
    setSelectedContact(new Contact());
}

public void insertNewContact() {
    // Attaching the owner of the contact
    getSelectedContact().setContact(loggedUser);

    entityManager.persist(getSelectedContact());
```

```
        facesMessages.addFromResourceBundle(StatusMessage.Severity.INFO,
    "contactAdded");
    }

    public void saveContactData() {
        entityManager.merge(getSelectedContact());

        facesMessages.addFromResourceBundle(StatusMessage.Severity.INFO,
    "contactSaved");
    }

    public void deleteSelectedContact() {
        entityManager.remove(getSelectedContact());

        // De-selecting the current contact
        setSelectedContact(null);
        setSelectedContactEditing(null);

        facesMessages.addFromResourceBundle(StatusMessage.Severity.INFO,
    "contactDeleted");
    }

    public boolean isSelectedContactManaged() {
        return getSelectedContact() != null && entityManager.contains(getS
    electedContact());
    }
```

It's not difficult to understand what they do, however, in order to be clear, we are going to describe what each method does.

The method `createNewEmptyContactInstance()` simply sets the `selectedContact` property with a new instance of the `Contact` class—it will be called by the "add contact" button.

After the user has clicked on the "add contact" button and inserted the contact data, he/she has to persist this new instance of data into the database. It is done by the `insertNewContact()` method, called when he/she clicks on the **Insert** button.

If the user edits a contact and clicks on the "Save" button, the `saveContactData()` method will be called, in order to store the modifications into the database.

As for saving, the `deleteSelectedContact()` method will be called by the "Delete" button, in order to remove the instance from the database.

A special mention for the `isSelectedContactManaged()` method — it is used to determine if the `selectedContact` property contains a bean that exists in the database (so, I'm editing it), or a new instance not yet persisted to the database. We use it especially in rendered properties, in order to determine which component to show (you will see this in the next section).

Selecting the contact from the contacts list

We will use the contacts list in order to decide which contact must be shown in the detail view.

The simple way is to add a new column into the `dataTable`, and put a command button (or link) to select the bean in order to visualize the detail view.

Let's open the `contactsList.xhtml` file and add another column as follows:

```
<rich:column width="10%" style="text-align: center">
    <a:commandButton image="/img/view.png"
                                        reRender="contactDetail">
        <f:setPropertyActionListener value="#{contact}"
    target="#{homeSelectedContactHelper.selectedContact}"/>
        <f:setPropertyActionListener value="#{false}"
    target="#{homeSelectedContactHelper.selectedContactEditing}"/>
    </a:commandButton>
</rich:column>
```

Inside the column, we added the `a:commandButton` component (that shows an image instead of the standard text) that doesn't call any action — it uses the `f:setPropertyAction` method to set the `homeSelectedContactHelper.selectedContact` value to `contact` (the row value of the `dataTable`), and to tell to show the view box and not the edit one (setting `homeSelectedContactHelper.selectedContactEditing` to `false`).

After the Ajax call, it will re-render the `contactDetail` box in order to reflect the change.

Also, the header must be changed to reflect the column add:

```
<rich:dataTable ... >
    <f:facet name="header">
        <rich:columnGroup>
            <rich:column colspan="3">
                <h:outputText value="Contacts"/>
            </rich:column>
            <rich:column breakBefore="true">
```

```
            <h:outputText value="Name"/>
        </rich:column>
        <rich:column>
            <h:outputText value="Surname"/>
        </rich:column>
        <rich:column>
            <rich:spacer/>
        </rich:column>
    </rich:columnGroup>
</f:facet>
...
```

We incremented the `colspan` attribute value and added a new (empty) column header.

The new contacts list will look like the following screenshot:

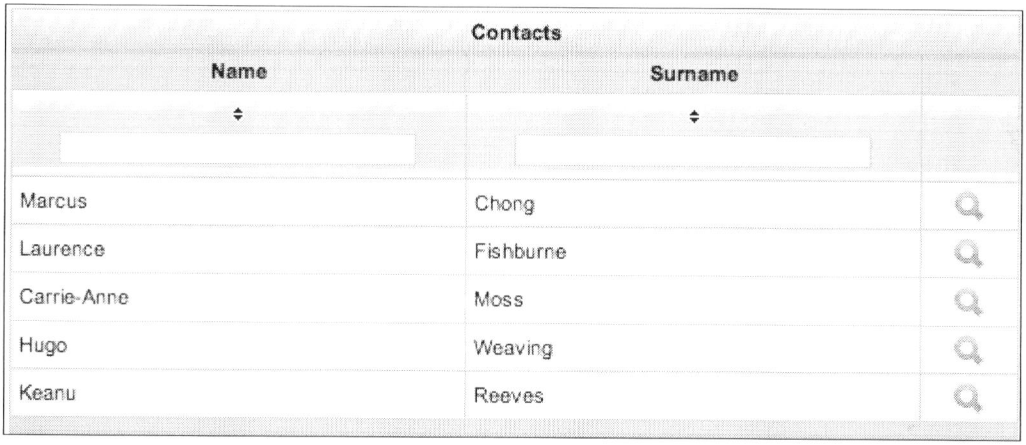

Contacts		
Name	**Surname**	
⇕	⇕	
Marcus	Chong	🔍
Laurence	Fishburne	🔍
Carrie-Anne	Moss	🔍
Hugo	Weaving	🔍
Keanu	Reeves	🔍

Adding a new contact

Another feature we would like to add to the contacts list is the "Add contact" button. In order to do that, we are going to use the empty toolbar we put in the first section of the chapter.

Let's add a new action button into the `rich:toolBar` component:

```
<a:commandButton image="/img/addcontact.png"
                 reRender="contactDetail"
action="#{homeSelectedContactHelper.createNewEmptyContactInstance}">
  <f:setPropertyActionListener value="#{true}"
target="#{homeSelectedContactHelper.selectedContactEditing}"/>
</a:commandButton>
```

This button will call the `homeSelectedContactHelper.`
`createNewEmptyContactInstance()` action method in order to create
and select an empty instance and will set `homeSelectedContactHelper.`
`selectedContactEditing` to `true` in order to start the editing; after those Ajax
calls, it will re-render the `contactDetail` box to reflect the changes.

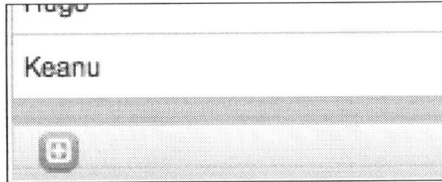

Viewing contact detail

We are ready to implement the view contact detail box; just open the `/view/main/`
`contactView.xhtml` file and add the following code:

```
<h:form>
    <rich:panel>
        <f:facet name="header">
            <h:outputText
                value="#{homeSelectedContactHelper.selectedContact.name}
                    #{homeSelectedContactHelper.selectedContact.surname}"/>
        </f:facet>
        <h:panelGrid columns="2" rowClasses="prop"
                    columnClasses="name,value">
            <h:outputText value="#{messages['name']}:"/>
            <h:outputText
                value="#{homeSelectedContactHelper.selectedContact.name}"/>
            <h:outputText value="#{messages['surname']}:"/>
            <h:outputText
         value="#{homeSelectedContactHelper.selectedContact.surname}"/>

            <h:outputText value="#{messages['company']}:"/>
            <h:outputText
         value="#{homeSelectedContactHelper.selectedContact.company}"/>

            <h:outputText value="#{messages['email']}:"/>
            <h:outputText
            value="#{homeSelectedContactHelper.selectedContact.email}"/>
        </h:panelGrid>
    </rich:panel>

    <rich:toolBar>
        <rich:toolBarGroup>
```

```
            <a:commandLink ajaxSingle="true"
                        reRender="contactDetail"
                        styleClass="image-command-link">
            <f:setPropertyActionListener value="#{true}"
        target="#{homeSelectedContactHelper.selectedContactEditing}"/>

            <h:graphicImage value="/img/edit.png" />
            <h:outputText value="#{messages['edit']}" />

            </a:commandLink>
        </rich:toolBarGroup>
      </rich:toolBar>
    </h:form>
```

The first part is just `rich:panel` containing `h:panelGrid` with the fields' detail. In the second part of the code, we put `rich:toolBar` containing a command link (with an image and a text) that activates the edit mode — it, in fact, just sets the `homeSelectedContactHelper.selectedContactEditing` property to `true` and re-renders `contactDetail` in order to make it appear in the edit box.

We also added a new CSS class into the `/view/stylesheet/theme.css` file to manage the layout of command links with images:

```
.image-command-link {
    text-decoration: none;
}

.image-command-link img {
    vertical-align: middle;
    padding-right: 3px;
}
```

The view box looks like:

We are now ready to develop the edit box.

Editing contact detail

When in the edit mode, the content of the `/view/main/contactEdit.xhtml` file will be shown in the contact detail box—let's open it for editing.

Let's add the code for creating the main panel:

```
<h:form>
  <rich:panel>
    <f:facet name="header">
      <h:panelGroup>
        <h:outputText
            value="#{homeSelectedContactHelper.selectedContact.name}
#{homeSelectedContactHelper.selectedContact.surname}"
rendered="#{homeSelectedContactHelper.selectedContactManaged}"/>

        <h:outputText
            value="#{messages['newContact']}"
rendered="#{!homeSelectedContactHelper.selectedContactManaged}"/>
      </h:panelGroup>
    </f:facet>

    <!-- my code here -->

  </rich:panel>

  <!-- my code here -->

</h:form>
```

This is a standard `rich:panel` with a customized header—it has two `h:outputText` components that will be shown depending on the rendered attribute (whether it's a new contact or not).

> **More than one component inside f:facet**
>
> Remember that `f:facet` must have only one child, so, to put more than one component, you have to use a surrounding one like `h:panelGroup` or something similar.

Inside the panel, we are going to put `h:panelGrid` containing the components for data editing:

```
<rich:graphValidator>
  <h:panelGrid columns="3" rowClasses="prop"
                columnClasses="name,value,validatormsg">
    <h:outputLabel for="scName"
                   value="#{messages['name']}:"/>
    <h:inputText id="scName"
          value="#{homeSelectedContactHelper.selectedContact.name}"/>
    <rich:message for="scName" styleClass="messagesingle"
                  errorClass="errormsg"
                  infoClass="infomsg"
                  warnClass="warnmsg"/>

    <h:outputLabel for="scSurname"
                   value="#{messages['surname']}:"/>
    <h:inputText id="scSurname"
      value="#{homeSelectedContactHelper.selectedContact.surname}"/>
    <rich:message for="scSurname"
                    styleClass="messagesingle"
                    errorClass="errormsg"
                    infoClass="infomsg"
                    warnClass="warnmsg"/>

    <h:outputLabel for="scCompany"
                   value="#{messages['company']}:"/>
    <h:inputText id="scCompany"
      value="#{homeSelectedContactHelper.selectedContact.company}"/>
    <rich:message for="scCompany"
                    styleClass="messagesingle"
                    errorClass="errormsg"
                    infoClass="infomsg"
                    warnClass="warnmsg"/>
    <h:outputLabel for="scEmail"
                   value="#{messages['email']}:"/>
    <h:inputText id="scEmail"
        value="#{homeSelectedContactHelper.selectedContact.email}"/>
    <rich:message for="scEmail" styleClass="messagesingle"
                  errorClass="errormsg"
                  infoClass="infomsg"
                  warnClass="warnmsg"/>
  </h:panelGrid>
<rich:graphValidator>
```

Nothing complicated here, we've just used `h:outputLabel`, `h:inputText`, and `rich:message` for every `Contact` property to be edited; it appears as follows:

The button toolbar

At the end of the panel, we would like to put the toolbar containing the action buttons for inserting, saving, canceling, and deleting the selected contact shown.

In order to do that, let's insert the following code after the `rich:panel` closing tag (and before the `h:form` closing tag):

```
<rich:toolBar>
    <rich:toolBarGroup>

<!-- my action buttons here -->

    </rich:toolBarGroup>
</rich:toolBar>
```

Let's start inserting the insert action buttons for a new contact:

```
<a:commandLink reRender="contactsList,contactDetail"
action="#{homeSelectedContactHelper.insertNewContact}"
rendered="#{!homeSelectedCon  tactHelper.selectedContactManaged}"
styleClass="image-command-link">

    <f:setPropertyActionListener value="#{null}"
                target="#{homeContactsListHelper.contactsList}"/>

    <h:graphicImage value="/img/insert.png"/>
    <h:outputText value="#{messages['insert']}"/>
</a:commandLink>
```

This button persists the new contact into the database (by calling the
`homeSelectedContactHelper.insertNewContact()` method) and, using `f:setPropertyActionListener`, it sets the `contactsList` property to null, so the list
will be read again from the database (reflecting the changes)—after that, it re-renders
the list and the detail box to reflect the changes.

Let's see the button code to cancel the insertion:

```
<a:commandLink ajaxSingle="true" reRender="contactDetail"
               rendered="#{!homeSelectedContactHelper.
                               selectedContactManaged}"
               styleClass="image-command-link">

    <f:setPropertyActionListener
               value="#{false}"
               target="#{homeSelectedContactHelper.
               selectedContactEditing}"/>

    <f:setPropertyActionListener
               value="#{null}"
               target="#{homeSelectedContactHelper.
               selectedContact}"/>

    <h:graphicImage value="/img/cancel.png"/>
    <h:outputText value="#{messages['cancel']}"/>
</a:commandLink>
```

This button doesn't call any action method, but it only sets the `selectedContact`
property to null and the `selectedContactEditing` property to false to "cancel"
the insertion action.

We highlighted the `ajaxSingle` property — this is a very important feature used to
avoid the form submission when the button is clicked (so, in this case, when the user
clicks on the **Cancel** button, the form data is not submitted with the Ajax request).
We will see it more in depth at the end of the section.

The other button we are going to add is the **Save** button:

```
<a:commandLink reRender="contactsList,contactDetail"
               action="#{homeSelectedContactHelper.saveContactData}"
           rendered="#{homeSelectedContactHelper.selectedContactManaged}"
           styleClass="image-command-link">

    <f:setPropertyActionListener value="#{false}"
        target="#{homeSelectedContactHelper.selectedContactEditing}"/>
```

```
    <f:setPropertyActionListener value="#{null}"
        target="#{homeContactsListHelper.contactsList}"/>

    <h:graphicImage value="/img/save.png"/>
    <h:outputText value="#{messages['save']}"/>
</a:commandLink>
```

It simply saves the property modification, sets the contact list property to null, (so, it will be read again from the database) and, sets the edit mode to false (so, the contact detail will be shown).

The Cancel button for an existing contact is almost the same as the one for new contacts:

```
<a:commandLink ajaxSingle="true" reRender="contactDetail"
        rendered="#{homeSelectedContactHelper.selectedContactManaged}"
        styleClass="image-command-link">

    <f:setPropertyActionListener value="#{false}"
target="#{homeSelectedContactHelper.selectedContactEditing}"/>

    <h:graphicImage value="/img/cancel.png"/>
    <h:outputText value="#{messages['cancel']}"/>
</a:commandLink>
```

The only difference is that it doesn't set the `selectedContact` to null as we would like to see the contact in view mode after canceling the editing.

The last button we are going to insert is the one for deletion:

```
<a:commandLink ajaxSingle="true" reRender="contactDetail,contactsList"
        action="#{homeSelectedContactHelper.deleteSelectedContact}"
        rendered="#{homeSelectedContactHelper.selectedContactManaged}"
        styleClass="image-command-link">

    <f:setPropertyActionListener value="#{null}"
        target="#{homeContactsListHelper.contactsList}"/>

    <h:graphicImage value="/img/delete.png"/>
    <h:outputText value="#{messages['delete']}"/>
</a:commandLink>
```

It calls the `homeSelectedContactHelper.deleteSelectedContact()` method that sets to null the `selectedContact` and the `selectedContactEditing` (it is a different way to do what we've done for the other action buttons using `f:setPropertyListener` components). It then sets to null the `contactsList` property and re-renders the `contactList` and the `contactDetail` boxes.

Here is a screenshot of the edit box with the toolbar:

The ajaxSingle and the process attributes

The `ajaxSingle` property is very useful to control the form submission when `ajaxSingle` is set to `true`—the form is not submitted and, just the Ajax component data is sent.

This attribute is available in every Ajax action component and we can use it to call an action from a button, skipping the form validation (like the JSF immediate property does), or to send the value of just an input into a form without validation and submitting the other ones.

The second use case can be used, for example, when we need an input menu that dynamically changes the value of other inputs without submitting the entire form:

```
<h:form>
  <!-- other input controls -->
  <h:selectOneMenu id="country"
                   value="#{myBean.selectedCountry}">
    <f:selectItems value="#{myBean.myCountries}">
    <a:support event="onchange" ajaxSingle="true"
            reRender="city" />
  </h:selectOneMenu>
  <h:selectOneMenu id="city"
                   value="#{myBean.selectedCity}">
```

```
      <f:selectItems value="#{myBean.myCities}">
    </h:selectOneMenu>
    <!-- other input controls -->
  </h:form>
```

In this example, every time the user selects a new country, the value is submitted to the bean that recalculates the `myCities` property for the new country, after that the city menu will be re-rendered to show the new cities.

All that without submitting the form or blocking the changes because of some validation problem.

What if you would like to send more than one value, but still not the entire form?

We can use Ajax regions (we will see in the next sections), or we can use the process attribute. It contains a list of components to process while submitting the Ajax action:

```
<h:form>
  <!-- other input controls -->
  <h:inputText id="input1" ... />
  <h:selectOneMenu id="country"
                   value="#{myBean.selectedCountry}">
    <f:selectItems value="#{myBean.myCountries}">
    <a:support event="onchange"
               ajaxSingle="true"
               process="input2, input3"
               reRender="city" />
  </h:selectOneMenu>
  <h:inputText id="input2" ... />
  <h:inputText id="input3" ... />
  <h:selectOneMenu id="city"
                   value="#{myBean.selectedCity}">
    <f:selectItems value="#{myBean.myCities}">
    </h:selectOneMenu>
    <!-- other input controls -->
  </h:form>
```

In this example, we also wanted to submit the `input2` and the `input3` values together with the new country, because they are useful for retrieving the new cities list—just by setting the process attribute with the id list and during the submission, they will be processed. Thus `input1` will not be sent.

Also, for action components such as buttons, you can decide what to send using the `ajaxSingle` and process attributes.

Form submission and processing

We speak about form "submission" to simplify the concept and make things more understandable. In reality, for every request, all of the form is submitted, but only the selected components (using `ajaxSingle` and/or process attributes) will be "processed". By "processed" we mean "pass through" the JSF phases (decoding, conversion, validation, and model updating).

More Ajax!

For every contact, we would like to add more customizable fields, so let's use the `ContactField` entity connected to every `Contact` instance.

First of all, let's create a support bean called `HomeSelectedContactOtherFieldsHelper` inside the `book.richfaces.advcm. modules.main` package.

It might look like this:

```
@Name("homeSelectedContactOtherFieldsHelper")
@Scope(ScopeType.CONVERSATION)
public class HomeSelectedContactOtherFieldsHelper {

    @In(create = true)
    EntityManager entityManager;

    @In(required = true)
    Contact loggedUser;

    @In
    FacesMessages facesMessages;
    @In(required = true)
    HomeSelectedContactHelper homeSelectedContactHelper;

    // my code
}
```

A notable thing is highlighted—we injected the `homeSelectedContactHelper` component, because to get the list of the customized fields from the database, we need the contact owner. We also set the required attribute to true, because this bean can't live without the existence of `homeSelectedContactHelper` in the context.

Now, let's add the property containing the list of personalized fields for the selected contact:

```
private List<ContactField> contactFieldsList;

public List<ContactField> getContactFieldsList() {
    if (contactFieldsList == null) {
        // Getting the list of all the contact fields
        String query = "from ContactField cf where cf.contact.id=:
idContactOwner order by cf.id";
        contactFieldsList = (List<ContactField>)
        entityManager.createQuery(query)
        .setParameter("idContactOwner",
        homeSelectedContactHelper.getSelectedContact()
        .getId()).getResultList();
    }
    return contactFieldsList;
}

public void setContactFieldsList(List<ContactField>
                                 contactFieldsList) {
    this.contactFieldsList = contactFieldsList;
}
```

As you can see, it is a normal property lazy initialized using the getter. This queries the database to retrieve the list of customized fields for the selected contact.

We have to put into the bean some other method useful to manage the customized field (adding and deleting field to and from the database), let's add those methods:

```
public void createNewContactFieldInstance() {
    // Adding the new instance as last field
       (for inserting a new field)
    getContactFieldsList().add(new ContactField());
}

public void persistNewContactField(ContactField field) {
    // Attaching the owner of the contact
    field.setContact(homeSelectedContactHelper.getSelectedContact());

    entityManager.persist(field);
}

public void deleteContactField(ContactField field) {
    // If it is in the database, delete it
    if (isContactFieldManaged(field)) {
```

```
            entityManager.remove(field);
        }

        // Removing the field from the list
        getContactFieldsList().remove(field);
    }

    public boolean isContactFieldManaged(ContactField field) {
        return field != null && entityManager.contains(field);
    }
```

The `createNewContactFieldInstance()` method will just add a new (not yet persisted), empty instance of the `ContactField` class into the list.

After the user has filled the values in, he/she will press a button that calls the `persistNewContactField()` method to save the new data into the database.

In order to delete it, we are going to use the `deleteContactField()` method, and to determine if an instance is persisted into the database or not, we are going to use the `isContactFieldManaged()` method.

Now, let's open the `/view/main/contactView.xhtml` file and add the code to show the personalized fields after `h:panelGrid`— i shows the standard ones:

```
<a:repeat value="#{homeSelectedContactOtherFieldsHelper.
contactFieldsList}" var="field">
    <h:panelGrid columns="2" rowClasses="prop"
                 columnClasses="name,value">
        <h:outputText value="#{field.type} (#{field.label}):"/>
        <h:outputText value="#{field.value}"/>
    </h:panelGrid>
</a:repeat>
```

We are using a new RichFaces data iteration component that permits us to iterate over a collection and put the data we want (the `rich:dataTable` component would instead create a table for the elements list).

In our case, the `h:panelGrid` block will be repeated for every element of the collection (so for every customized field).

Now, let's open the `/view/main/contactEdit.xhtml` file and add the code for editing the customized fields into the list:

```
<a:region>
  <a:outputPanel id="otherFieldsList">
    <a:repeat value="#{homeSelectedContactOtherFieldsHelper.
                                        contactFieldsList}"
```

```
            var="field">
<h:panelGrid columns="3" rowClasses="prop"
              columnClasses="name,value,validatormsg">
  <h:panelGroup>
    <h:inputText id="scOtherFieldType"
                 value="#{field.type}"
                 required="true" size="5">
      <a:support event="onblur"
                 ajaxSingle="true"/>
    </h:inputText>

    <h:outputText value=" ("/>
    <h:inputText id="scOtherFieldLabel"
                 value="#{field.label}"
                 size="5">
      <a:support event="onblur"
                 ajaxSingle="true"/>
    </h:inputText>
    <h:outputText value=")"/><br/>
    <rich:message for="scOtherFieldType"
                 styleClass="messagesingle"
                 errorClass="errormsg"
                 infoClass="infomsg"
                 warnClass="warnmsg"/>
  </h:panelGroup>

  <h:panelGroup>
    <h:inputText id="scOtherFieldValue"
                 value="#{field.value}"
                 required="true">
      <a:support event="onblur"
                ajaxSingle="true"/>
    </h:inputText><br/>
    <rich:message for="scOtherFieldValue"
                 styleClass="messagesingle"
                 errorClass="errormsg"
                 infoClass="infomsg"
                 warnClass="warnmsg"/>
  </h:panelGroup>

  <h:panelGroup>
    <a:commandButton image="/img/add.png"
      reRender="otherFieldsList"
      action="#{homeSelectedContactOtherFieldsHelper.
```

```
                                persistNewContactField(field)}"
                rendered="#{!homeSelectedContactOtherFieldsHelper.
                                isContactFieldManaged(field)}">
            </a:commandButton>

            <a:commandButton image="/img/remove.png"
                reRender="otherFieldsList" ajaxSingle="true"
                action="#{homeSelectedContactOtherFieldsHelper.
                                deleteContactField(field)}">
            </a:commandButton>
        </h:panelGroup>
    </h:panelGrid>
</a:repeat>

<a:commandLink reRender="otherFieldsList"
                ajaxSingle="true"
                action="#{homeSelectedContactOtherFieldsHelper.
                createNewContactFieldInstance}"
                rendered="#{homeSelectedContactHelper.
                            selectedContactManaged}"
                styleClass="image-command-link">
    <h:graphicImage value="/img/add.png"/>
    <h:outputText value="#{messages['addNewField']}"/>
</a:commandLink>
    </a:outputPanel>
</a:region>
```

The code looks very similar to the one in the view box, except for the action buttons (to add a new instance, persist, save, or delete) and, for the presence of the surrounding tag a:region (highlighted). This is very important in order to make sure the form works correctly; we will see why in the next section.

Also, notice that every input component has the a:support tag as a child that will update the bean with the edited value at the onblur event (which means that every time you switch the focus to another component, the value of the last one is submitted). So, if you delete or add a field, you will now loose the edited values for other fields. It is also used for Ajax validation, as the user is informed that the value is not valid when it moves the cursor to another input.

Here is a screenshot with the new feature in the edit box:

Ajax containers

While developing a web application with RichFaces, it's very useful to know how to use Ajax containers (such as the `a:region` component) in order to optimize Ajax requests.

In this section, we'll discuss about the `a:region` component.

It is a very important component of the framework—it can define Ajax areas to limit the part of the component tree to be processed during an Ajax request.

Regions can be nested during an Ajax request and the closest one will be used.

By setting to `true` the `a:region` attribute called `regionRenderOnly`, you can use this component to limit the elements' update—In this way, in fact, only the components inside the region can be updated.

Another important attribute is `selfRendered`; setting this to true tells the framework to render the response basing on component tree without referring to the page code — it is faster, but all of the transient elements that are not saved in the tree (such as `f:verbatim` or HTML code written directly without using JSF components) will be lost at the first refresh, so you can't use them in this case.

To summarize, it is very useful to control the rendering process and optimize it, in order to limit the elements of a form to send during an Ajax request without validation problems, to show different indicators for Ajax status.

Example of using `a:region`:

```
<h:form>
    <a:region>
            <h:inputText id="it1" value="#{aBean.text1}">
                    <a:support event="onkeyup" reRender="text1" />
            </h:inputText>
            <h:inputText id="it2" value="#{aBean.text2}" />
    </a:region>

    <h:inputText id="it3" value="#{aBean.text3}" />

    <a:commandButton
            action="#{aBean.saveTexts}"
            reRender="text1,text2" />
</h:form>

<h:outputText id="text1" value="#{aBean.text1}" />

<h:outputText id="text2" value="#{aBean.text2}" />
```

In this example, while the user is typing in the `text1` value of `inputText`, `a:support` sends an Ajax request containing only the `it1` and `it2` values of `inputText`.

In this case, in fact, `a:region` limits the components sent by every Ajax request originated from inside the region. So, the Ajax request will only update `aBean.text1` and `aBean.text2`.

> Wrapping only a component inside an Ajax region is the equivalent of using the `ajaxSingle` property set to `true`.

If the user clicks on the `a:commandButton aBean.text1`, the `aBean.text2` and `aBean.text3` values will be updated by the Ajax request.

Coming back to our application, as all the customized fields are inside the same form component, we surround each one with the `a:region` tag. In this way, the single field is submitted regardless of the other ones.

For example, without using `a:region`, if the user empties the name input value and then tries to insert a new customized field, the process will fail because the name input is not validated. If we use the `a:region` component, the name field will not be processed and a new field will be inserted.

Now that we know how to use the `a:region` tag, we can combine it with `ajaxSingle` and `process` in order to decide what to send at every request, and to better optimize Ajax interactions into the application.

Data iteration using RichFaces

All RichFaces data iteration components share the same working way of the standard `h:dataTable`. So, once you know how to use it, you are able to use all of them without any problem.

Let's have a look again at a simple version of the `rich:dataTable` we've used for the contacts list:

```
<rich:dataTable
        value="#{homeContactsListHelper.contactsList}"
        var="contact">
    <rich:column>
        <h:outputText value="#{contact.name}"/>
    </rich:column>
    <rich:column>
        <h:outputText value="#{contact.surname}"/>
    </rich:column>
</rich:dataTable>
```

The result of this code is simply predictable—a table with two columns, one for the name and the other one for the surname.

Now, let's suppose I don't want the table format but a list of contacts, all I have to do is to use the `rich:dataList` component the same way as the `rich:dataTable` one:

```
<rich:dataList value="#{homeContactsListHelper.contactsList}"
                        var="contact">
    <h:outputText value="#{contact.name} #{contact.surname}"/>
</rich:dataList>
```

For every element, it will render a list of contacts as follows:

- Marcus Chong
- Laurence Fishburne
- Carrie-Anne Moss
- Hugo Weaving
- Keanu Reeves

Exactly the same mechanism enables you to use the `rich:dataOrderingList` and `rich:dataDefinitionList` components.

A special mention for `rich:dataGrid` that has few differences:

```
<rich:dataGrid value="#{homeContactsListHelper.contactsList}"
               var="contact"
               columns="3">
   <h:outputText
               value="#{contact.name} #{contact.surname}"/>
</rich:dataGrid>
```

As you can see, we had to set the `columns` attribute to tell when to break the row and start a new one. Here is the result:

Marcus Chong	Laurence Fishburne	Carrie-Anne Moss
Hugo Weaving	Keanu Reeves	

You can put any component you want inside it:

```
<rich:dataGrid value="#{homeContactsListHelper.contactsList}"
               var="contact"
               columns="3">
   <rich:panel>
   <f:facet name="header">
        <h:outputText value="Contact" />
    </f:facet>
    <h:outputText
               value="#{contact.name} #{contact.surname}"/>
   </rich:panel>
</rich:dataGrid>
```

And the result is:

Data pagination with data iteration components

As for h:dataTable (and rich:dataTable), you can attach datascroller to every data iteration component the same way you did for your dataTable:

```
<h:form>
    <rich:dataList id="contactsList"
                   value="#{homeContactsListHelper.contactsList}"
                   var="contact"
                   rows="3">
    <h:outputText value="#{contact.name} #{contact.surname}"/>
    </rich:dataList>
    <rich:datascroller for="contactsList" />
</h:form>
```

Just remember to put the datascroller into form, set the for attribute, and set the rows attribute for one of the data iteration components.

The result is as follows:

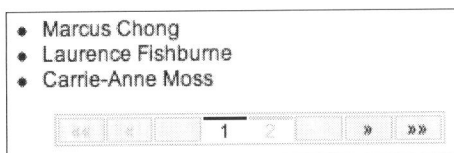

Also, in this case, there is a little exception for the `rich:dataGrid` component, as it doesn't have the `rows` attribute, but the corresponding one is `elements` (you can figure out why). Therefore, our example will be:

```
<h:form>
  <rich:dataGrid id="contactsGrid"
                  value="#{homeContactsListHelper.contactsList}"
                  var="contact"
                  columns="3"
                  elements="3">
    <rich:panel>
      <f:facet name="header">
        <h:outputText value="Contact" />
      </f:facet>
        <h:outputText
                  value="#{contact.name} #{contact.surname}"/>
    </rich:panel>
  </rich:dataGrid>
  <rich:datascroller for="contactsGrid" />
</h:form>
```

And the result would appear as follows:

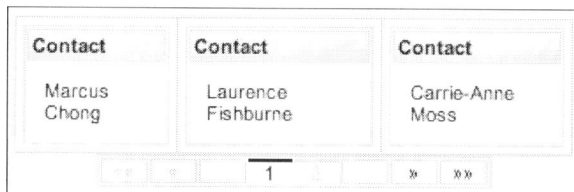

Addresses management

Another piece we would like to implement is addresses management using the `ContactAddress` entity. This is the same working mechanism as the customized field, so it is left as an exercise for the reader.

However, you can find the developed feature in the source code of the application.

Some screenshots

Here, we present some screenshots of the application with all the features we've seen uptil now.

We can see the **Contacts** list with a contact selected:

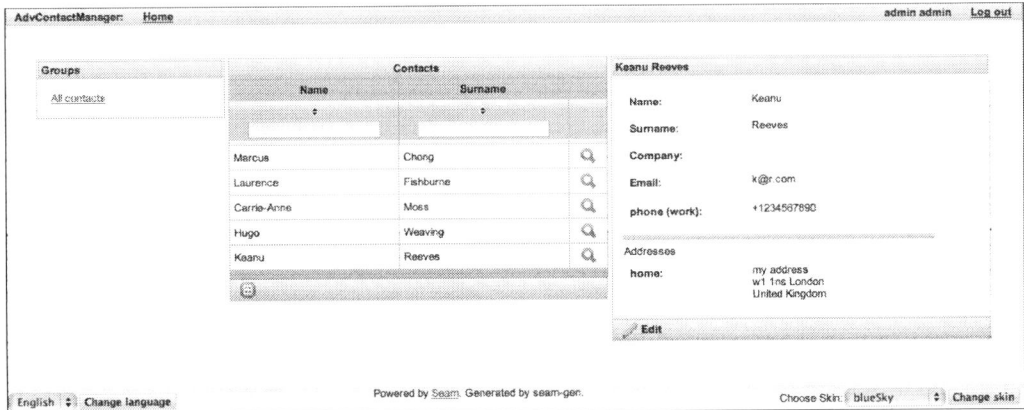

The contact editing form (you can notice the buttons to add/delete more fields and addresses) appears as follows:

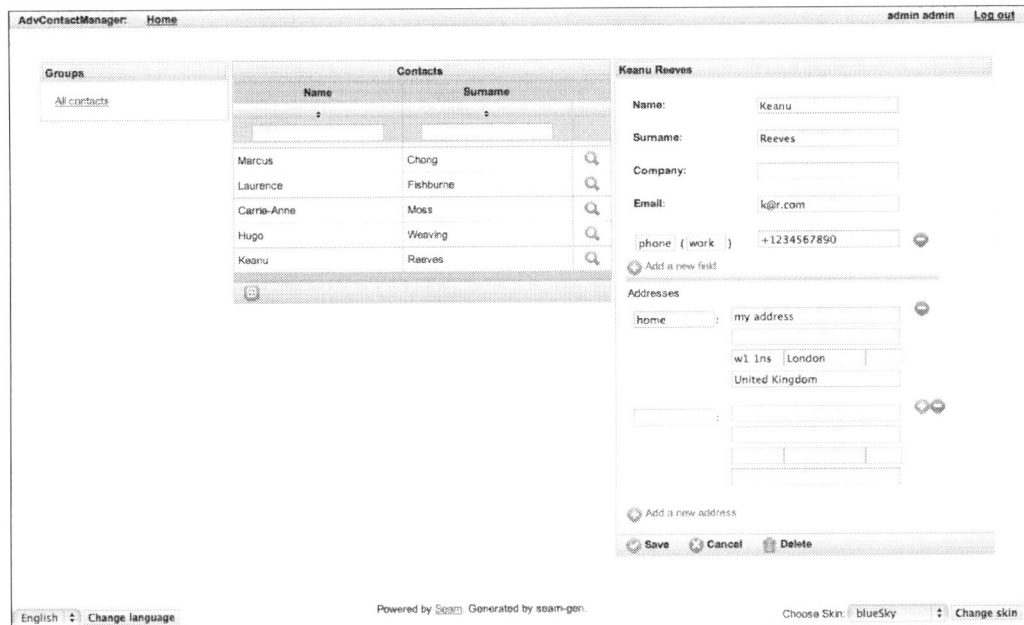

And finally, you can see the add contact form:

Summary

In this chapter, we've developed the core feature of our application—contact management. We have learned about Ajax interaction and containers and about new Ajax components that RichFaces offers.

In the next chapter, we'll be developing new features of the Advanced Contact Manager and discovering new RichFaces components and patterns.

7

Finishing the Application

We have almost finished our application! In this chapter, we are going to develop a side feature that would be very useful for us to learn how to use other RichFaces components in a real world application.

We are going to see many cool features that we can reuse in our application with few changes.

Taking a note of every contact

For every contact we have in our Address Book, we want to be able to add a short note about them. This can be very useful in a lot of scenarios and it's really easy to implement!

A richer editor

We are going to use the `rich:editor` component of the RichFaces framework. It creates a WYSIWYG editor based on the TinyMCE JavaScript (`http://tinymce.moxiecode.com`). This component is very easy to use, but at the same time can be completely customized and extended using the TinyMCE plugins.

In order to connect the editor to the `note` property of the `Contact` entity, let's just open the `/view/main/contactEdit.xhtml` file and insert the following code, just between the closing `</a:region>` and `</rich:graphValidator>` tags, before the bottom `rich:toolBar`:

```
<rich:spacer height="10"/>
<rich:separator width="320px"/>
<rich:spacer height="15"/>
<h:outputText value="#{messages['note']}"/>
<rich:editor value="#{homeSelectedContactHelper.selectedContact.note}"
             width="320" height="150"/>
```

The first part is just to create a separator and the label, the most important part is the highlighted one—we've just bound the `rich:editor` to the `note` property, and defined two attributes (`width` and `height`) to control the dimension of the edit area.

The result is pretty nice:

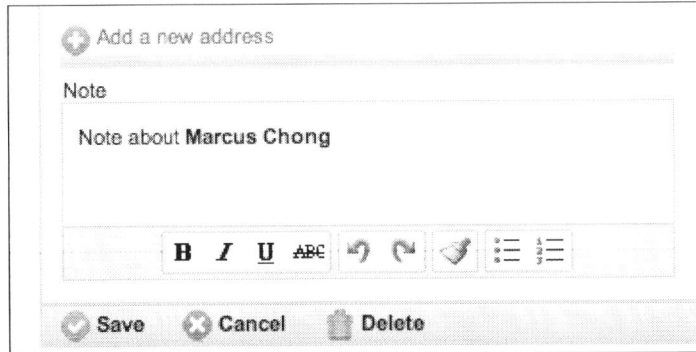

By default, the editor theme used is the `simple` one, so we have a limited set of control into the button bar, let's try to set the `advanced` theme, this way:

```
<rich:editor value="#{homeSelectedContactHelper.selectedContact.note}"
            theme="advanced" width="320" height="150"/>
```

The result is:

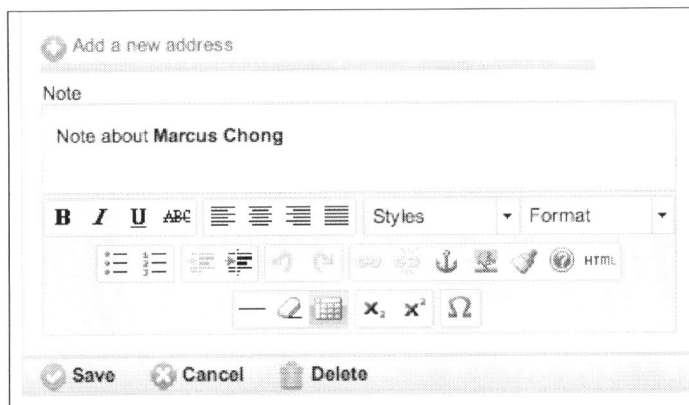

Customization capabilities are not limited to just setting the theme, we can also decide to add more buttons (from external plug-ins for example) or to change the disposition.

In the next sample code, we are going to show the basis of customization, adding the paste plugin and relative buttons, and setting the toolbar's position to the top side:

```
<rich:editor
        value="#{homeSelectedContactHelper.selectedContact.note}
        width="320" height="150" theme="advanced" plugins="paste">
    <f:param name="theme_advanced_buttons1" value="cut,copy,paste,
                                    pasteword,|,bold,italic,underline"/>
    <f:param name="theme_advanced_toolbar_location" value="top"/>
    <f:param name="theme_advanced_toolbar_align" value="left"/>
</rich:editor>
```

This is the result:

Notice that the toolbars are now on the top and the first one has a different button as we decided (paste and pasteword buttons come from the paste plugin we add).

Using the f:param tag, you can configure every TinyMCE option (read the TinyMCE documentation for more information) as we've seen—the option goes inside the name attribute and the option value goes into the value attribute.

Let's group our contacts

It would be very useful to group our contacts and have different lists of contacts to quickly search for one or the other.

In order to do that, we are going to implement the group feature—basically, you can add as many groups as you want and every contact can stay in one or more groups. Every group has a color and a description. Let's see how to implement it!

Listing, adding, and removing groups

We are going to use the first box that, until now, contained just the All contacts link, In order to do that, let's open the /view/main/contactsGroup.xhtml and start writing the main table containing the All contacts link and the other group links.

Let's replace the <h:panelGrid>...</h:panelGrid> code with this one:

```
<table width="100%" border="0">
  <tr>
    <td width="14" align="center">
      <h:graphicImage value="/img/right_arrow_small.png"
        rendered="#{homeContactsListHelper.groupFilter==null}"/>
    </td>
    <td colspan="3">
      <h:graphicImage value="/img/contact_small.png"/>
        <a:commandLink value="#{messages['allContacts']}"
                       ajaxSingle="true"
                       style="margin-left: 5px;"
                       reRender="contactsList, contactsGroups">
        <f:setPropertyActionListener value="#{null}"
          target="#{homeContactsListHelper.contactsList}"/>
        </a:commandLink>
    </td>
  </tr>
</table>
```

In this case, we didn't use the rich:dataTable component because we are mixing a standard link with a list (the groups list) that doesn't contain the All contacts link—so, if you want to have a unique table containing both, you have to do it this way. Thanks to Facelets it is possible to mix normal XHTML code without any kind of problem.

As you can see in the code, we are also referring to the groupFilter property of homeContactsListHelper that is used to show the group contents in the contact list. All the contacts will be shown only if groupFilter is null, and that's why we set it to null in the All contacts link.

Moreover, the first column of the table contains a small arrow that will be visible when the groupFilter property is null (so that all contacts are shown).

In order to implement this, let's open the `HomeContactsListHelper` class and add the new property:

```
private ContactGroup groupFilter;

public ContactGroup getGroupFilter() {
    return groupFilter;
}

public void setGroupFilter(ContactGroup groupFilter) {
    this.groupFilter = groupFilter;
}
```

Now let's change the `getContactList()` method to make it using the new property:

```
public List<Contact> getContactsList() {
    if (contactsList == null) {
        // Creating the query
        String queryString;
        if (getGroupFilter() == null) {
            queryString = "from Contact c where c.contact.id=:
fatherId";
        } else {
            queryString = "select cig.contact from ContactInGroup cig
where cig.id.contactGroup=:groupFilterId";
        }

        // Creating the query
        Query query = entityManager.createQuery(queryString);

        if (getGroupFilter() == null) {
            query = query.setParameter("fatherId", loggedUser.
getId());
        } else {
            query = query.setParameter("groupFilterId",
getGroupFilter().getId());
        }
        // Getting the contacts list
        contactsList = (List<Contact>) query.getResultList();
    }
    return contactsList;
}
```

Also, we want to show that the contacts list table is filter changing the table header text and color (according to the current filtered group color).

Let's open the `contactsList.xhtml` file and edit the header of the `dataTable` to look this way:

```
<f:facet name="header">
  <rich:columnGroup>
    <rich:column colspan="3">
      <h:outputText value="#{messages['allContacts']}"
        rendered="#{homeContactsListHelper.groupFilter==null}"/>
      <h:outputText value="#{messages['contactsInGroup']}:
                    #{homeContactsListHelper.groupFilter.name}"
                    style="color: #{homeContactsListHelper.
                    groupFilter.color};margin-left: 5px;"
                    rendered="#{homeContactsListHelper.
                    groupFilter!=null}"/>
    </rich:column>
    <rich:column breakBefore="true">
      <h:outputText value="#{messages['name']}"/>
    </rich:column>
    <rich:column>
      <h:outputText value="#{messages['surname']}"/>
    </rich:column>
    <rich:column>
      <rich:spacer/>
    </rich:column>
  </rich:columnGroup>
</f:facet>
```

We have the logic to filter the contacts list by group ready!

We have to create the bean that manages the groups list, the group adding, and deletion—let's create a new class called `GroupsListHelper` inside the new package `book.richfaces.advcm.modules.main.groups` as follows:

```
@Name("groupsListHelper")
@Scope(ScopeType.CONVERSATION)
public class GroupsListHelper {
    @In(create = true)
    EntityManager entityManager;

    @In(required = true)
    Contact loggedUser;

    @In
    FacesMessages facesMessages;

}
```

Let's fill the empty Seam component with the logic to list the groups:

```
private List<ContactGroup> groups;

public List<ContactGroup> getGroups() {
    if (groups == null) {
        // Creating the query
        String query = "from ContactGroup cg where cg.contact.id=:
fatherId order by cg.name";

        // Getting the contacts list
        groups = (List<ContactGroup>) entityManager.createQuery(query)
                .setParameter("fatherId", loggedUser.getId())
                .getResultList();
    }
    return groups;
}

public void setGroups(List<ContactGroup> groups) {
    this.groups = groups;
}
```

We have seen this kind of code for the other features we developed — there is just one property with a getter and a setter; inside the getter, there is the code to lazy-load the list using standard JPA code.

Let's come back to the XHTML code — open the `contactsGroups.xhtml` file and add the logic to list the group inside the table.

Insert the following code just before the `</table>` closing tag of the file:

```
<a:repeat value="#{groupsListHelper.groups}" var="group">
  <tr>
    <td width="14" align="center" valign="top">
      <h:graphicImage value="/img/right_arrow_small.png"
        rendered="#{homeContactsListHelper.groupFilter.id==group.id}"/>
    </td>
    <td>
      <rich:spacer width="10" height="10"
                   style="background-color: #{group.color}"/>
      <a:commandLink value="#{group.name}"
                   reRender="contactsList, contactsGroups">
        <f:setPropertyActionListener value="#{group}"
                   target="#{homeContactsListHelper.groupFilter}"/>
        <f:setPropertyActionListener value="#{null}"
                   target="#{homeContactsListHelper.contactsList}"/>
```

```
        </a:commandLink>
        <rich:toolTip value="#{group.description}"/>
      </td>
    </tr>
  </a:repeat>
```

Using the `a:repeat` tag (that, as we have seen in the other chapters, works like the other data iteration components), we are able to insert a new table row for every group.

This time the first column arrow will be shown only if the group in that row is the one being shown at that moment.

We are also using `rich:spacer` with a background CSS property set to the group color, in order to show a small colored square for every group; we'll see how to set the color later in this chapter.

After the command link that activates the group filtering and re-renders the contacts list to show the new filtered contacts table, we can see a new tag called `rich:toolTip`—this tag is very useful for showing a tool tip with the group description when you go over the cell of the table containing the group name.

Here is a screenshot of what we have until now:

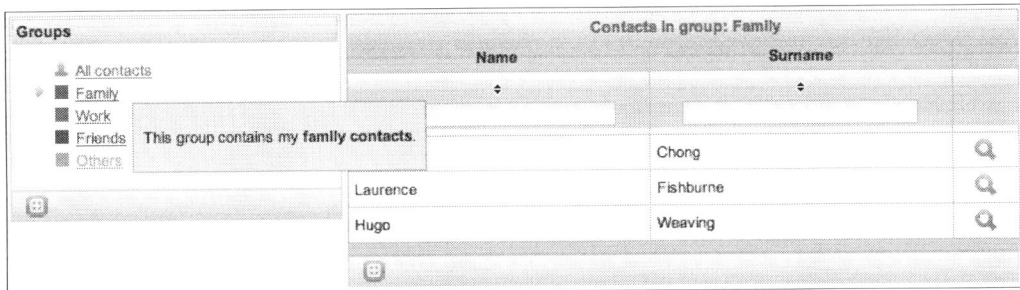

Other features of the rich:toolTip component

As we've seen, the simplest way to use the `rich:toolTip` component is to put it inside a container with the `value` attribute set, like the following code:

```
<a:outputPanel>
  <rich:toolTip value="This is the text of my tooltip!" />
</a:outputPanel>
```

Another way to attach a tool tip to a component is by using the `for` attribute as follows:

```
<a:outputPanel id="myPanel">
  <rich:toolTip value="This is the text of my tooltip!"
                for="myPanel"/>
</a:outputPanel>
```

Very simple!

Please notice that when using the `for` attribute, the `rich:toolTip` tag does not have to be nested inside the component (an `a:outputPanel` in our case).

Another important feature is the Ajax loading of the content:

```
<a:outputPanel>
  <rich:toolTip mode="ajax" value="#{myBean.myProperty}">
    <f:facet name="defaultContent">
      <h:outputText value="Loading... " />
    </f:facet>
  </rich:tooltip>
</a:outputPanel>
```

This code will show a tool tip with the `Loading...` text inside, until the content of the bound property (`myProperty`) is loaded using Ajax, and ready to be displayed.

There are other useful attributes (such as `showEvent`, `showDelay`, `hideDelay`, `followMouse`, and `direction`) that you can use to customize the tool tip behavior. You can also use the JavaScript API to call it from inside a JavaScript method!

Adding and editing groups

Let's go back to our application—what we need now is the ability to add and edit a group.

We are going to do this inside the group table, so that the group that is editing (or adding) is displayed as a form with inputs for adding or editing and not as a link.

To let you understand the meaning better, this is a screenshot of the completed feature:

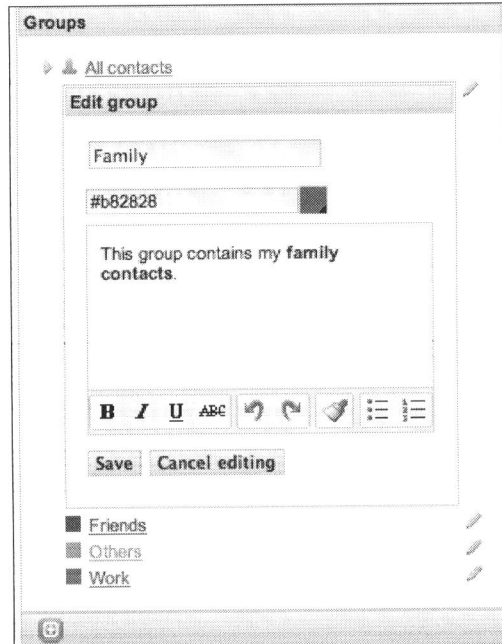

As you can see, the edit form is inside the table, at the place of the editing group (for adding the form will be at the last table row).

Let's start editing the GroupsListHelper Seam component, adding the new features we need.

First, let's add a groupEditing property that contains the group being edited:

```
private ContactGroup groupEditing;

public ContactGroup getGroupEditing() {
    return groupEditing;
}
public void setGroupEditing(ContactGroup groupEditing) {
    this.groupEditing = groupEditing;
}
```

Nothing new here—it's just a property with getter and setter.

Now, I have to make sure that the add and edit buttons would fill this property when I click on it.

For the editing feature, I can just add the following column to the group table inside the `contactsGroups.xhtml` file:

```
<td align="center" valign="top">
  <a:commandLink
     reRender="contactsGroups">
       <h:graphicImage value="/img/edit_small.png"/>
       <f:setPropertyActionListener value="#{group}"
          target="#{groupsListHelper.groupEditing}"/>
  </a:commandLink>
</td>
```

As you can see, `a:commandLink` just sets the `groupEditing` property and re-renders the contacts group table.

For the add button, we have to use a method that creates a new `ContactGroup` instance and inserts it into the list.

Let's open the `GroupsListHelper` class again, and add the following method:

```
public void addGroup() {
    ContactGroup newGroup = new ContactGroup();

    getGroups().add(newGroup);
    setGroupEditing(newGroup);
}
```

Now, we can add a toolbar with the add group button just below the groups table; let's switch to the `contactsGroups.xhtml` file and add this code after the `</rich:panel>` closing tag:

```
<rich:toolBar>
  <rich:toolBarGroup>
    <a:commandButton
        image="/img/addgroup.png"
        ajaxSingle="true"
        reRender="contactsGroups"
        action="#{groupsListHelper.addGroup}"/>
  </rich:toolBarGroup>
</rich:toolBar>
```

This button we've added just calls the `addGroup()` method and then re-renders the contact groups table.

The adding/editing form

We have the add/edit triggers ready, now we have to display the form (instead of a simple command link) when we encounter a group that is in editing mode.

In order to do that, let's edit the `contactsGroups.xhtml` file, enclosing the code inside the second table column (the one that shows the square and the group link) inside the `a:outputPanel` tag with the `rendered` attribute set:

```
<td>
  <a:outputPanel
    rendered="#{groupsListHelper.groupEditing.id!=group.id}">
    <rich:spacer width="10" height="10"
                 style="background-color: #{group.color}"/>
    <a:commandLink value="#{group.name}"
                   reRender="contactsList, contactsGroups">
      <f:setPropertyActionListener value="#{group}"
                   target="#{homeContactsListHelper.groupFilter}"/>
      <f:setPropertyActionListener value="#{null}"
                   target="#{homeContactsListHelper.contactsList}"/>
    </a:commandLink>
    <rich:toolTip value="#{group.description}"/>
  </a:outputPanel>
</td>
```

On doing that, the enclosed code will be shown only if the group being rendered is not in the edit mode.

After that panel, we have to insert the panel that contains the code for groups in the edit mode, so that the user will be able to edit the properties of a group that is in the edit mode.

In order to do so, let's add the following code after the `<a/outputPanel>` closing tag:

```
<rich:panel rendered="#{groupsListHelper.groupEditing.id==group.id}">
  <f:facet name="header">
    <h:panelGroup>
      <h:outputText value="#{messages['editGroup']}"
        rendered="#{groupsListHelper.groupEditing.id!=null}"/>
      <h:outputText value="#{messages['addGroup']}"
        rendered="#{groupsListHelper.groupEditing.id==null}"/>
    </h:panelGroup>
  </f:facet>
  <a:region>
    <h:panelGrid columns="1">
      <h:inputText id="newGroupName"
                   value="#{groupsListHelper.groupEditing.name}"
                   required="true">
        <rich:beanValidator/>
```

```
    </h:inputText >
    <rich:message for="newGroupName"
                  styleClass="messagesingle"
                  errorClass="errormsg"
                  infoClass="infomsg"
                  warnClass="warnmsg"/>
    <rich:colorPicker
                  value="#{groupsListHelper.groupEditing.color}"/>
    <rich:editor
      value="#{groupsListHelper.groupEditing.description}"/>
    <a:outputPanel>
      <a:commandButton value="#{messages['save']}"
        action="#{groupsListHelper.saveGroupEditing}"
        reRender="contactsGroups"/>
      <a:commandButton
        value="#{messages['cancelEditing']}"
        ajaxSingle="true"
        reRender="contactsGroups">
      <f:setPropertyActionListener
        value="#{null}"
        target="#{groupsListHelper.groupEditing}"/>
      </a:commandButton>
    </a:outputPanel>
  </h:panelGrid>
 </a:region>
</rich:panel>
```

We've highlighted one new component— rich:colorPicker.

This component permits the user to select a color in a visual way and is very useful and simple to use.

The next screenshot shows the component when opened:

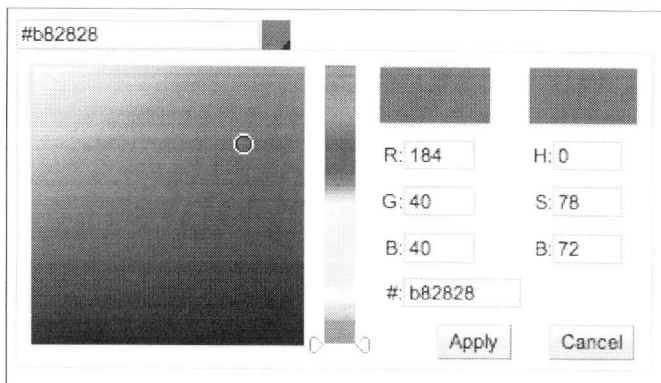

You can use the CSS to customize it (as with every RichFaces component), and use two facets to override the standard ones — by setting the `icon` facet, you can customize the icon that opens the panel, whereas, with the `arrows` facet, you can change the color selection arrows.

If you look at the other component, the working logic of this form is clean — when the group is in the editing mode, we show this form with the `ContactGroup` property bound to the input component; at the end of the form, we have two buttons — one to confirm and save the edited group into the database and the other to cancel the editing (that just sets `groupEditing` property to null and `reRender` the groups list).

To save the group into the database we have to add another method to the `GroupsListHelper` class:

```
public void saveGroupEditing() {
  if (entityManager.contains(getGroupEditing())) {
    // Save the object changes
    entityManager.merge(getGroupEditing());
  } else {
      // Associate the new group to the current logged user
      getGroupEditing().setContact(loggedUser);

      // Persist the object into the database
      entityManager.persist(getGroupEditing());
  }

  // Empty the instance (exits from edit mode)
  setGroupEditing(null);
}
```

The last feature for group management is the delete button; first let's add the method into the `GroupsListHelper` class as follows:

```
@In (create = true)
HomeContactsListHelper homeContactsListHelper;

public void deleteGroup(ContactGroup group) {
    // If the group to be deleted is selected
    if (homeContactsListHelper.getGroupFilter().getId()==

                group.getId()) {
        // Deselect it
        homeContactsListHelper.setGroupFilter(null);
        homeContactsListHelper.setContactsList(null);
    }
```

```
    // Remove the group from the database
    entityManager.remove(group);
}
```

In the first part of the method, we check if the group to delete is the selected one: if so, we deselect it and then remove it from the database. We have to get and set the `groupFilter` property that is inside the `homeContactsListHelper` component, that is why we injected it in a local property using the code outside the method.

Now we have to create the button in XHTML and link it with this method. Let's open the `contactsGroups.xhtml` file and add another column after the one for the edit:

```
<td align="center" valign="top">
  <a:commandLink
               action="#{groupsListHelper.deleteGroup(group)}"
               reRender="contactsGroups,contactsList">
    <h:graphicImage value="/img/delete_small.png"/>
    <f:setPropertyActionListener value="#{null}"
            target="#{groupsListHelper.groups}"/>
  </a:commandLink>
</td>
```

We have finished our group management features; now we have to make it possible for the user to insert contacts into the groups.

Adding contacts to a group using the drag 'n' drop

We are going to use the RichFaces drag-and-drop support to implement this feature, so we can show you how easy it is to do that.

When a user drags a contact over a group name, the contact will be inserted into that group, so let's start defining the contact table's columns, which contain the contact name and surname as a *draggable* area.

Let's open the `contactsList.xhtml` file and change the two columns containing the name and the surname in this way:

```
<rich:column width="45%"
             sortBy="#{contact.name}"
             filterBy="#{contact.name}">
  <h:outputText value="#{contact.name}"/>
  <rich:dragSupport dragType="contact"
              dragIndicator="contactDragIndicator"
              dragValue="#{contact}">
```

```
    <rich:dndParam type="drag" name="label"
                   value="#{contact.name} #{contact.surname}"/>
  </rich:dragSupport>
</rich:column>
<rich:column width="45%"
             sortBy="#{contact.surname}"
             filterBy="#{contact.surname}">
  <h:outputText value="#{contact.surname}"/>
  <rich:dragSupport dragType="contact"
                    dragIndicator="contactDragIndicator"
                    dragValue="#{contact}">
    <rich:dndParam type="drag" name="label"
                   value="#{contact.name} #{contact.surname}"/>
  </rich:dragSupport>
</rich:column>
```

We highlighted the important code (the one for the second column is
the same)—we are defining a draggable area of the contact type that uses
a personalized drag indicator (we'll see it very soon) and carries the dragged
contact instance as dragValue.

We also defined a drag parameter named label containing the name and surname
of the contact. We are going to use it in the drag indicator.

A drag indicator is an html panel following the mouse while dragging; we don't
have to define our personal ones. However, in this case, we want to show some
information about the dragged item (the name and surname) inside the panel.

This is the standard drag panel without dragIndicator:

	Chong
	Fishburne
	Moss
	Weaving

It's just a dotted rectangle that becomes green when the dragged item is over a
drop panel, which accepts it.

The basic usage of the dragIndicator is really simple—just put the following
code at the end of the page, before the closing </ui:composition> tag:

```
<rich:dragIndicator id="contactDragIndicator" />
```

In our application, we are just passing the label value using the dndParam parameter you have seen, so the result of having a drag indicator is:

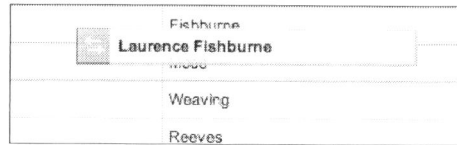

When the dragged object is over a drop panel that accepts it, the icon of the drag indicator changes, as shown in the following screenshot:

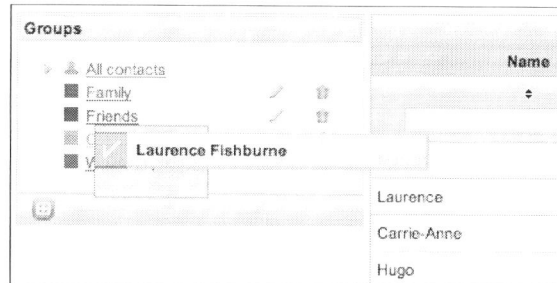

We can customize every part of the drag indicator using CSS and facets.

Now we have to create a drop area from every group that accepts the dragged items of the contact type.

Let's open the contactsGroups.xhtml file and add this code inside the commandLink group:

```
<a:commandLink value="#{group.name}"
               style="color: #{group.color};margin-left: 5px;"
               reRender="contactsList, contactsGroups">
  <f:setPropertyActionListener value="#{group}"
           target="#{homeContactsListHelper.groupFilter}"/>
  <f:setPropertyActionListener value="#{null}"
           target="#{homeContactsListHelper.contactsList}"/>
  <rich:dropSupport acceptedTypes="contact"
               dropListener="#{groupsListHelper.
                     processDropAddContactToGroup}"
               dropValue="#{group}"/>
</a:commandLink>
```

The highlighted code adds the drop support to every group link. It accepts only contact type dragged elements and carries a drop value containing the current group instance.

The drop listener defined will be called every time an element is dropped; let's define it inside the `GroupsListHelper` class:

```
public void processDropAddContactToGroup(DropEvent dropEvent) {
    // Get the Contact instance
    Contact droppedContact = (Contact) dropEvent.getDragValue();

    // Get the ContactGroup instance
    ContactGroup droppedGroup = (ContactGroup) dropEvent.
                                            getDropValue();

    // Check if the contact exists
    ContactInGroupId cingid = new ContactInGroupId
                (droppedGroup.getId(), droppedContact.getId());

    // If it doesn't exist
    if (entityManager.find(ContactInGroup.class, cingid) == null) {
    // Create the association
    ContactInGroup cing = new ContactInGroup(cingid,
                                droppedGroup,droppedContact);

    // Save into the database
    entityManager.persist(cing);facesMessages.
    addFromResourceBundle(StatusMessage.Severity.INFO,
    "contactAddedToTheGroup");
    } else {   // If it exists
                facesMessages.addFromResourceBundle
                            (StatusMessage.Severity.INFO,
                                "contactAlreadyInTheGroup");

    }
}
```

In this method, we get the `dragValue` and `dropValue` values, and use them to check if the contact is inside the group and whether or not to insert it.

This is a very simple and effective way to add drag-and-drop support to your application!

> The drag/drop type is very useful to define different drag-and-drop logic depending on the type of dragged item.

Removing contacts from a group using drag'n'drop

We also want to define an area below the group's `toolBar` where you can drop contacts that are to be deleted, inside a group.

This area must be shown only when the contact list is showing the content of a group therefore, it is shown when the `homeContactsListHelper.groupFilter` property is not null.

This might look like this:

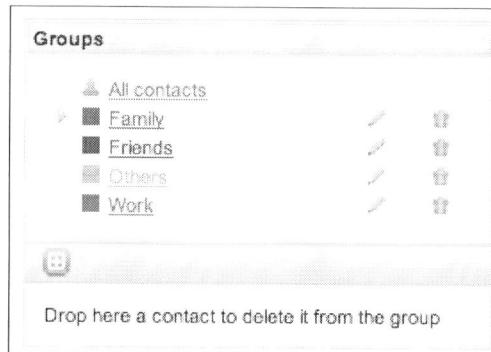

We leave it as an exercise for the reader. You can find the complete source code on downloading the application code.

Attaching files

We would like to attach one or more files to each contact. For example, we can attach some image, or the CV, or other useful information about the contact.

By implementing this feature, we are going to introduce three new components and explain how to use them in a productive way.

Creating the wizard

Let's start creating the upload file wizard—this is a simple two-page wizard that enables the user to upload and then review files, eventually adding a note to each one.

Let's create the `/view/main/uploadFiles/` directory and, inside it, an empty file called `wizardFirstStepUploadFiles.xhtml` (that will be the first step page of our wizard) with the following content:

```
<!DOCTYPE composition PUBLIC "-//W3C//DTD XHTML 1.0 Transitional//EN"
        "http://www.w3.org/TR/xhtml1/DTD/xhtml1-transitional.dtd">
<ui:composition xmlns="http://www.w3.org/1999/xhtml"
                xmlns:s="http://jboss.com/products/seam/taglib"
                xmlns:ui="http://java.sun.com/jsf/facelets"
                xmlns:f="http://java.sun.com/jsf/core"
                xmlns:h="http://java.sun.com/jsf/html"
                xmlns:rich="http://richfaces.org/rich"
                xmlns:a="http://richfaces.org/a4j">

  <!-- my code -->

</ui:composition>
```

Now we have to insert (replacing the `<!-- my code -->` comment) the form with the RichFaces file upload:

```
<h:form>
  <h:outputText value="#{messages['selectFilesToUpload']}" />
  <rich:fileUpload acceptedTypes="gif,jpg,png,pdf,doc,xls"
                   allowFlash="auto" autoclear="false"
                   maxFilesQuantity="10" immediateUpload="true"
                   fileUploadListener="#{filesUploadHelper.listener}">
  <a:support event="onuploadcomplete" reRender="nextBtn" />
  </rich:fileUpload>
</h:form>
```

The working way is very intuitive—for every file we upload, a listener method is called, so the application can manage the uploaded file.

The other attributes we have set are easy to understand, but a special mention goes to the `allowFlash` attribute, which permits the enabling of a Flash uploading panel component. If the Flash plugin is enabled, it allows the user to select more than one file to upload at a time.

Where the uploaded files are stored depends on `createTempFile`, an `init-param` set in `web.xml` file. By default, its value is `true`, and the files are stored in a temporary folder. If the parameter is set to `false`, then the uploaded files will be kept in the RAM (it is a better mode if you have uploaded small files).

In order to change the parameter value, you have to open the `web.xml` file and add this code:

```
<init-param>
  <param-name>createTempFiles</param-name>
  <param-value>false</param-value>
</init-param>
```

Before creating the bean, we have to define the path where the uploaded files will be saved, and we can use the `uiOptions` component for that. Just open the `UIOption` class and add the following property:

```
private String fileSavePath;
public String getFileSavePath() {
  return fileSavePath;
}
public void setFileSavePath(String fileSavePath) {
  this.fileSavePath = fileSavePath;
}
```

Now we have to configure it in the `components.xml` file. Let's open it and add a property to the `uiOption` component initialization:

```
<property name="fileSavePath">/my/file/path/</property>
```

For security reasons, it's highly recommended to put the file path outside the application—we will see how to enable the access through the application later on.

Now, we need the Seam component that manages the file upload process (`filesUploadHelper`). Let's create a new class called `FilesUploadHelper` inside the `book.richfaces.advcm.modules.main.files` package:

```
@Name("filesUploadHelper")
@Scope(ScopeType.CONVERSATION)
public class FilesUploadHelper {      @In(create = true)
    EntityManager entityManager;

    @In(required = true)
    HomeSelectedContactHelper homeSelectedContactHelper;

    @In
    UIOptions uiOptions;

}
```

Besides the `entityManager`, we need the `uiOptions` component because of the `fileSavePath` property. We also need `homeSelectedContactHelper` to get the selected contact to associate files with.

Now let's insert the `listener()` method:

```
public void listener(UploadEvent event) throws Exception {
    UploadItem item = event.getUploadItem();

    // Creating the instance
    ContactFile newFile = new ContactFile(homeSelectedContactHelper.
                        getSelectedContact(), item.getFileName(),
                        item.getContentType());

    // Persisting it into the database
    entityManager.persist(newFile);

    // Copying the files into the disk using the new id
    copyFile(new FileInputStream(item.getFile()),
                    new FileOutputStream(uiOptions.
getFileSavePath()
                                    + newFile.getId())));
}
```

As you can see, this method gets the `UploadItem` instance of the uploaded file, creates the association with the selected contact, and persists it into the database. After that it copies the temporary file to our preferred position, the following `copyFile` method is used to this:

```
private void copyFile(FileInputStream sourceStream,
                    FileOutputStream destinationStream)
        throws IOException {
    FileChannel inChannel = sourceStream.getChannel();
    FileChannel outChannel = destinationStream.getChannel();
    try {
        inChannel.transferTo(0, inChannel.size(),
                outChannel);
    }
    catch (IOException e) {
        throw e;
    }
    finally {
        if (inChannel != null) {
                try {
                        inChannel.close();
```

```
                    } catch (IOException ioe) { }
        }
      if (outChannel != null) outChannel.close();
    }
  }
```

This is an almost general bean that you can use in your application by just changing the database code.

The file review step

The wizard has two steps—we've seen the first one that permits the user to select and upload files. The second one is used to review the files and to eventually add a note to each one.

Before creating the second page, let's add the navigation code to the first one, after the `</rich:fileUpload>` closing tag:

```
<a:commandLink id="nextBtn" action="next"
              style="float:left;" styleClass="image-command-link">
  <h:graphicImage value="/img/next.png" />
  <h:outputText value="#{messages['next']}" />
</a:commandLink>
```

This button permits the user to navigate to the next page using the JSF navigation rules from the `next` outcome. Let's open the `faces-config.xml` file and add the following code after the `</application>` closing tag:

```
<navigation-rule>
  <from-view-id>/main/uploadFiles/wizardFirstStepUploadFiles.xhtml
  </from-view-id>
  <navigation-case>
    <from-outcome>next</from-outcome>
    <to-view-id>/main/uploadFiles/wizardSecondStepUploadFiles.xhtml
    </to-view-id>
  </navigation-case>
</navigation-rule>
<navigation-rule>
  <from-view-id>
    /main/uploadFiles/wizardSecondStepUploadFiles.xhtml
  </from-view-id>
<navigation-case>
  <from-outcome>previous</from-outcome>
```

```
        <to-view-id>
          /main/uploadFiles/wizardFirstStepUploadFiles.xhtml
        </to-view-id>
    </navigation-case>
    </navigation-rule>
```

This is standard JSF that permits navigation to the second step page in case of the next outcome, and going back to the first one in case of the previous outcome.

The screenshot of the first step of the wizard is as follows:

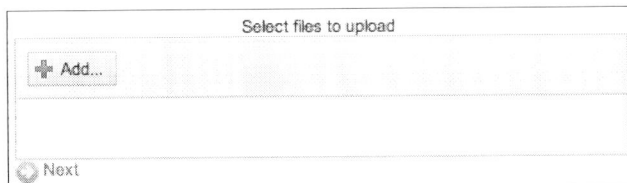

Now let's create an empty file (using the previously shown template) again called wizardSecondStepUploadFiles.xhtml and add the following code:

```
<h:form>
    <ui:include src="showCurrentContactFiles.xhtml">
        <ui:param name="edit" value="true"/>
        <ui:param name="columns" value="2"/>
    </ui:include>
    <a:commandLink ajaxSingle="true" action="previous"
                   reRender="uploadImagesWizard" style="float:left;"
                   styleClass="image-command-link">
        <h:graphicImage value="/img/previous.png"/>
        <h:outputText value="#{messages['previous']}"/>
    </a:commandLink>
</h:form>
```

You can notice that there is an included file (using the ui:include Facelets tag) with two passed parameters—that's because we will reuse the code to show the files' list for another feature (you will see it later).

The other component to go back to the first step is commandLink.

Now, let's create the showCurrentContactFiles.xhtml file using the empty template and add the following code:

```
<a:outputPanel style="width: 500px; height: 400px;
                overflow: auto;" layout="block">
    <rich:dataGrid value="#{filesListHelper.files}"
                   var="file" columns="#{columns}">
```

```
    <a:outputPanel layout="block" rendered="#{edit==true}"
            style="text-align: center;">
      <h:outputText value="#{file.fileName}"/>
            <br/><br/>
      <h:inputTextarea value="#{file.description}"
                style="width: 150px; height: 50px;"/>
    </a:outputPanel>
  </rich:dataGrid>
  <h:outputText value="#{messages['noFilesFound']}"
            rendered="#{empty filesListHelper.files}"/>
</a:outputPanel>
```

Here, we have `rich:dataGrid` with the number of columns passed as
a Facelets parameter (`columns`) that renders an edit box for every uploaded file
with `h:inputTextarea` to let the user add the file description.

As you can see (the highlighted code), this panel is shown only when the Facelets
parameter `edit` is set to `true`. We will later add another panel to manage the case
when `edit` is set to `false`.

This is the result with some associated files:

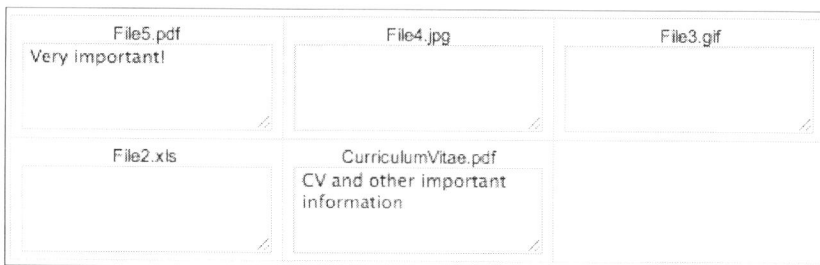

Creating the modal panel

We want to show the upload wizard inside a modal panel. Therefore, let's start
creating the code to show it.

Let's create a new file (with the empty template we've seen) inside the `/view/main/`
`uploadFiles/` folder, called `uploadFilesModalPanel.xhtml`, and put the following
code inside the `ui:component` tag:

```
<rich:modalPanel id="uploadFilesMP"
                minHeight="300"
                minWidth="350"
                autosized="true"
                moveable="true"
```

```
                         resizeable="false">
    <f:facet name="header">
      <h:outputText value="#{messages['uploadNewFiles']}"/>
    </f:facet>
  <!-- my code -->
  </rich:modalPanel>
```

Here, I defined the `rich:modalPanel` component setting the `id` and some attributes like `minWidth`, `minHeight`, `autosized`, `movable`, and `resizable`. Also, I have added the `f:facet` tag to customize the panel header.

This is a sample of what we have done:

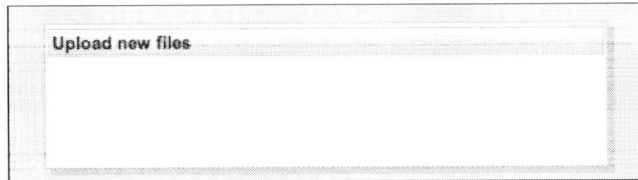

The code to open the modal panel is very simple.

Let's open the `contactEdit.xhtml` file and add the new `rich:toolBar` group to the latest `rich:toolBar` component:

```
<rich:toolBarGroup location="right">
  <a:commandLink
                  onclick="#{rich:component('uploadFilesMP')}.show();"
                  styleClass="image-command-link">
    <h:graphicImage value="/img/upload.png"/>
    <h:outputText value="#{messages['uploadFiles']}"/>
  </a:commandLink>
</rich:toolBarGroup>
```

The highlighted line is the one that does the trick to close the panel (for example, by using a button inside it). We can use the same code, but call the JavaScript `hide()` method instead of `show()`, very simple!

Remember that to make it work, we have to include the file into our page, so let's open the `home.xhtml` file and add the following code at the end, after the `</h:panelGrid>` closing tag:

```
<ui:include src="main/uploadFiles/uploadFilesModalPanel.xhtml" />
```

Control components without JavaScript

Another way of controlling the `rich:modalPanel` component (and the other components that have JavaScript API, which permits controlling them) is to use the `rich:componentControl` component. It allows, in fact, to call JavaScript functions of a component after a specific event.

Let's make an example of use by calling the `show()` function of our modal panel using `rich:componentControl`:

```
<a:commandLink styleClass="image-command-link">
  <h:graphicImage value="/img/upload.png"/>
  <h:outputText value="#{messages['uploadFiles']}"/>
  <rich:componentControl for="uploadFilesMP"
                         event="onclick" operation="show"/>
</a:commandLink>
```

By inserting the component inside the `a:commandLink`, we automatically attached to it—however, it is also possible to specify the component to attach to using the `attachTo` attribute:

```
<a:commandLink id="showPanelBtn" styleClass="image-command-link">
  <h:graphicImage value="/img/upload.png"/>
  <h:outputText value="#{messages['uploadFiles']}"/>
</a:commandLink>


<rich:componentControl for="uploadFilesMP" attachTo="showPanelBtn"
                       event="onclick" operation="show"/>
```

Inserting the wizard inside the modal panel

We are now ready to insert the wizard inside the modal panel and enable Ajax navigation using standard navigation rules. We are going to use the `a:include` component to make this possible!

Let's open the `/view/main/uploadFiles/uploadFilesModalPanel.xhtml` again and replace the `<!-- my code -->` comment with the code to include (the Ajax way!) the first step of the wizard:

```
<a:outputPanel id="uploadFilesWizard">
  <a:include ajaxRendered="true"
    viewId="/main/uploadFiles/wizardFirstStepUploadFiles.xhtml"/>
</a:outputPanel>
```

Now, let's add the close button into the first wizard step (to the `/view/main/uploadFiles/wizardFirstStepUploadFiles.xhtml` file):

```
<a:commandLink onclick="#{rich:component('uploadFilesMP')}.hide();"
            style="float:right;" styleClass="image-command-link">
  <h:graphicImage value="/img/close.png" />
  <h:outputText value="#{messages['close']}" />
</a:commandLink>
```

This is just the standard code we've seen for closing a modal panel (notice the call to the `hide()` method).

In the second step, we also want to save the modification before closing the panel, so the code to add (to the `/view/main/uploadFiles/wizardSecondStepUploadFiles.xhtml` file) is slightly different:

```
<a:commandLink
            action="#{filesListHelper.updateList}"
            oncomplete="#{rich:component('uploadFilesMP')}.hide();"
            style="float:right;" styleClass="image-command-link">
    <h:graphicImage value="/img/close.png"/>
    <h:outputText value="#{messages['finish']}"/>
</a:commandLink>
```

Here, the framework first calls the `filesListHelper.updateList` action method and then (`oncomplete`) closes the panel.

Here are the two screenshots of the steps inside the modal panel:

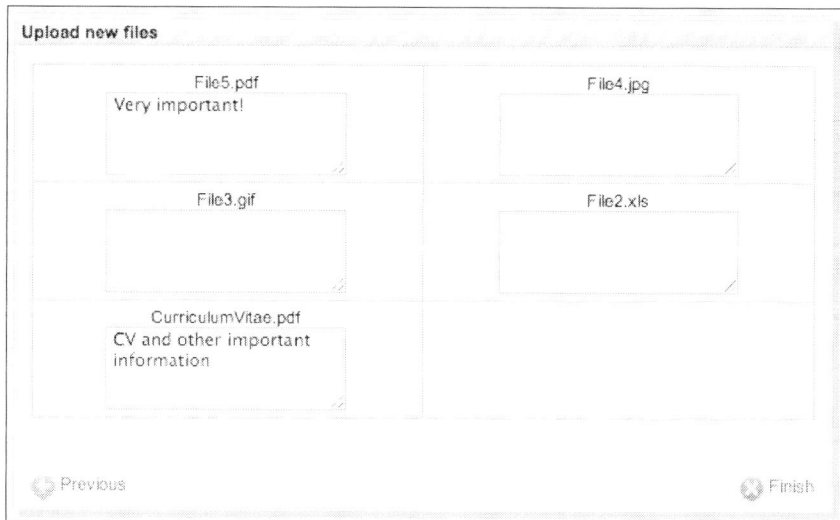

Finishing the file upload feature

The last feature we are going to add is the Files panel to show (or edit if in `edit` mode) the files associated to a contact.

In order to do that, we are going to use what we've seen uptil now, so let's start creating a new XHTML file with a modal panel called `showFilesModalPanel.xhtml` containing the following code:

```
<ui:component
        xmlns="http://www.w3.org/1999/xhtml"
        xmlns:ui="http://java.sun.com/jsf/facelets"
        xmlns:h="http://java.sun.com/jsf/html"
        xmlns:f="http://java.sun.com/jsf/core"
        xmlns:s="http://jboss.com/products/seam/taglib"
        xmlns:a="http://richfaces.org/a4j"
        xmlns:rich="http://richfaces.org/rich">

   <rich:modalPanel id="showFilesMP" minHeight="400"
                 minWidth="500" autosized="true"
                 moveable="true" resizeable="false">
      <f:facet name="header">
         <h:outputText value="#{messages['showFiles']}"/>
      </f:facet>

      <h:form>
         <a:outputPanel id="showFilesWizard">
```

```
        <ui:include src="showCurrentContactFiles.xhtml">
          <ui:param name="edit"
                    value="#{homeSelectedContactHelper.
                             selectedContactEditing}"/>
          <ui:param name="columns" value="3"/>
        </ui:include>
        <br/>
        <h:panelGroup style="float:right;">
          <a:commandLink action="#{filesListHelper.updateList}"
            oncomplete="#{rich:component('showFilesMP')}.hide();"
            rendered="#{homeSelectedContactHelper.
                         selectedContactEditing}"
            styleClass="image-command-link">
           <h:graphicImage value="/img/files.png"/>
           <h:outputText value="#{messages['save']}"/>
          </a:commandLink>
          <rich:spacer width="5"/>
          <a:commandLink action="previous"
            onclick="#{rich:component('showFilesMP')}.hide();"
            styleClass="image-command-link">
            <h:graphicImage value="/img/close.png"/>
            <h:outputText value="#{messages['close']}"/>
          </a:commandLink>
        </h:panelGroup>
      </a:outputPanel>
    </h:form>
  </rich:modalPanel>
</ui:component>
```

Here, we've created a modal panel that includes the showCurrentContactFiles.
xhtml (the one we created) file to show the files data grid. This time the edit Facelets
parameter depends on homeSelectedContactHelper.selectedContactEditing
property (you can see it highlighted in the code)—so, it will be set to true in edit
mode, but false otherwise.

After the ui:include, we have two buttons—one is the *Save* button (shown only
in edit mode) and the other is the *Close* button.

It's time to implement the panel rendered when not in the edit mode inside the
showCurrentContactFiles.xhtml file—let's open it again and add the following
code right after the <rich:dataGrid ..> tag:

```
<a:outputPanel layout="block"
               rendered="#{edit==false}"
               style="text-align: center;">
  <h:outputText value="#{file.fileName}"
```

```
                    style="font-weight: bold;"/>
    <br/><br/>
    <h:outputText value="#{file.description}" escape="false"/>
    <br/><br/>
    <s:link action="#{fileDownloadHelper.download}"
            styleClass="image-command-link">
      <f:param name="cid" value="#{file.id}"/>
      <h:graphicImage value="/img/download.png"/>
      <h:outputText value="#{messages['download']}"/>
    </s:link>
  </a:outputPanel>
```

This panel is rendered when the `edit` Facelets parameter is set to `false`.

The `download` method of the `FileDownloadHelper` bean we implemented is the following:

```java
public void download() {
    ContactFile contactFile = entityManager.find(ContactFile.class,
                                                  contactFileId);

    try {
        // Get the file
        File file = new File(appOptions.getFileSavePath() +
contactFile.getId());
        long fileLength = file.length();

        // Create the stream
        FileInputStream fileIS = new FileInputStream(file);

        // Get the data
        byte fileContent[] = new byte[(int) fileLength];
        fileIS.read(fileContent);

        // Stream the content
        FacesContext facesContext = FacesContext.getCurrentInstance();
        if (!facesContext.getResponseComplete()) {
            HttpServletResponse response = (HttpServletResponse)
            facesContext.getExternalContext().getResponse();
            response.setContentType(contactFile.getFileType());
            response.setContentLength((int) fileLength);
            response.setHeader("Content-disposition",
          "attachment; filename=" + contactFile.getFileName());

            ServletOutputStream out;

            out = response.getOutputStream();
```

```
        out.write(fileContent);
        out.flush();

        facesContext.responseComplete();
    }
  } catch (IOException e) {
     e.printStackTrace();
  }
}
```

It is useful for the download of small files (less than `Integer.MAX_VALUE`); for big ones it's better you use a servlet or a custom Seam resource.

The last step is adding the code to open the modal panel, both in view and in edit mode.

Let's open the `contactView.xhtml` file and add another `rich:toolBarGroup` tag inside `rich:toolBar`:

```
<rich:toolBarGroup location="right">
  <a:commandLink oncomplete="#{rich:component('showFilesMP')}.show();"
               ajaxSingle="true" reRender="showFilesPanel"
               styleClass="image-command-link">

    <f:setPropertyActionListener value="#{null}"
                                 target="#{filesListHelper.files}"/>
    <h:graphicImage value="/img/files.png"/>
    <h:outputText value="#{messages['files']}"/>
  </a:commandLink>
</rich:toolBarGroup>
```

The `commandLink` will force the re-read of the files list (by setting it to `null`) and will re-render `showFilesPanel` to synchronize the changes—after that the modal panel will be opened by the `oncomplete` JavaScript code.

Here is a screenshot of the final `rich:toolBar` in view mode:

The same `commandLink` must be added inside the `contactEdit.xhtml` file, near the *Upload* button, as it appears in the next screenshot:

Our new panel is ready; let's see how it looks in view mode:

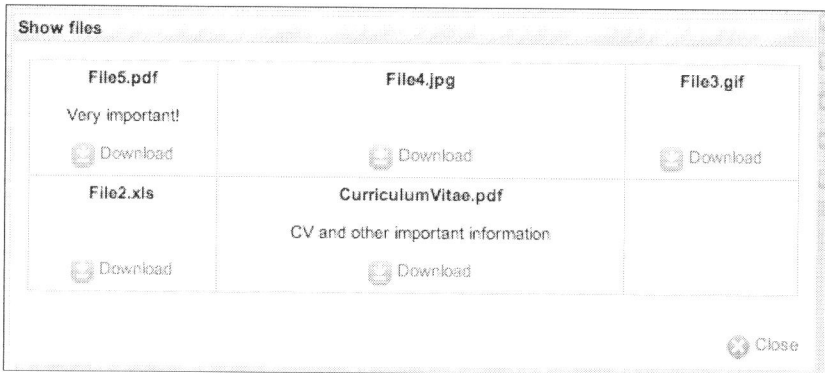

And in edit mode it appears as follows:

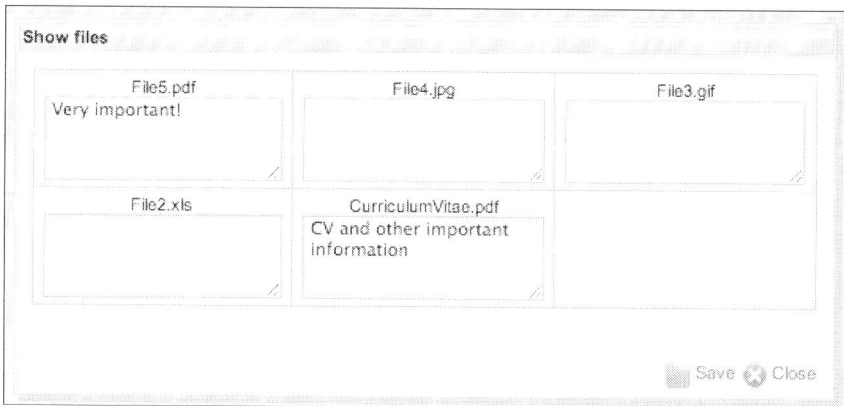

Summary

In this chapter, we've finished our application!

Until now, we've learned how to use the RichFaces components and how to customize them.

In the coming chapters, we will touch on topics such as skin customizing and creation, advanced techniques, and an introduction to the Component Development Kit, in order to develop our JSF Ajax components using the RichFaces framework.

8
Skin Customization

We have finished our application and now we would like to customize its look to follow the style we like. In this chapter, we will see how to change the style of existing skins (using CSS and XCSS) and how to create a new personalized skin starting from the built-in skins that the RichFaces framework offers.

Skinnability

In the Chapter 1, *First Steps*, we read an introduction of what RichFaces skinnability is about, and during the development of our application, we've learned how to set the default skin for a project and even how to change it dynamically.

Summarizing, every RichFaces component gives the support for skinnability and it means that just by changing the skin, we change the look for all of the components. That's very good for giving our application a consistent look and not repeating the same CSS values for each component every time.

RichFaces still uses CSS, but it also enhances it in order to make it simpler to manage and maintain.

Customize skin parameters

A skin file contains the basic settings (such as font, colors, and so on) that we'll use for all the components—just by changing those settings, we can customize the basic look and feel for the RichFaces framework.

As you might know, RichFaces comes with some built-in skins (and other external plug 'n' skin ones)—you can start with those skins in order to create your own custom skin.

The built-in skins are:

- Plain
- emeraldTown
- blueSky
- wine
- japanCherry
- ruby
- classic
- deepMarine

The plug 'n' skin ones are:

- laguna
- darkX
- glassX

The plug 'n' skin skins are packaged in external jar files (that you can download from the same location as that of the RichFaces framework) that must be added into the project in order to be able to use them. We will see how to create our custom plug 'n' skin in the next chapter.

Remember that the skin used by the application can be set as `context-param` in the `web.xml` file:

```
<context-param>
  <param-name>org.richfaces.SKIN</param-name>
  <param-value>emeraldTown</param-value>
</context-param>
```

This is an example with the `emeralTown` skin set:

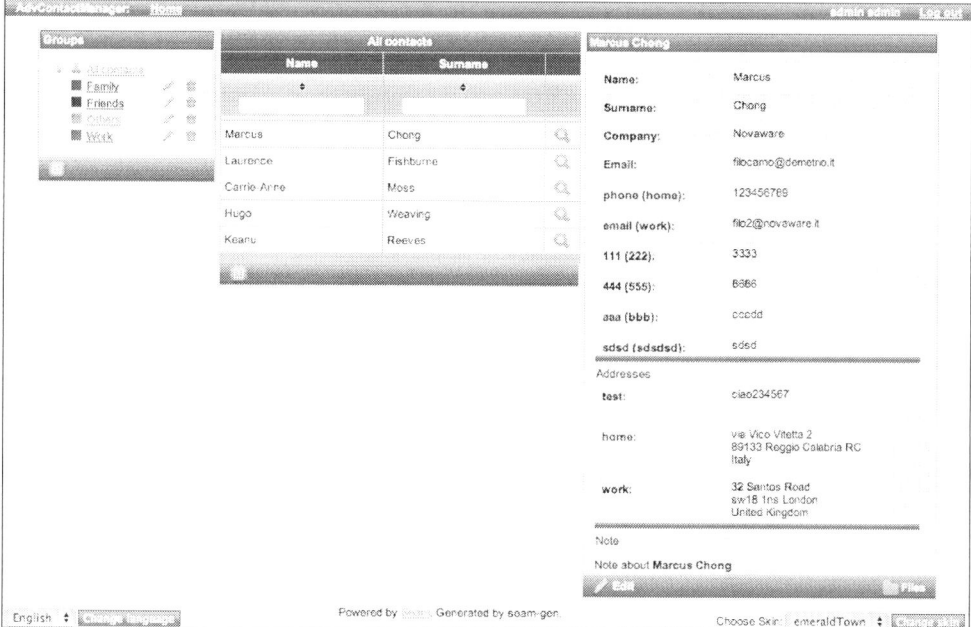

If we change the skin to `japanCherry`, we have the following screenshot:

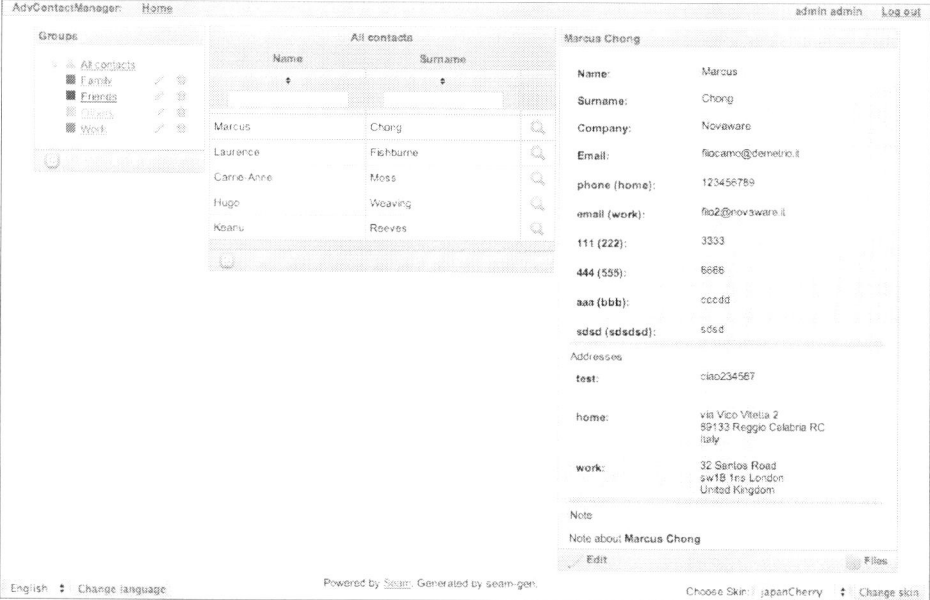

That's without changing a single line of CSS or XHTML!

Edit a basic skin

Now let's start creating our own basic skin. In order to do that, we are going to reuse one of the built-in skin files and change it. You can find the skin files in the `richfaces-impl-3.x.x.jar` file inside the `META-INF/skins` directory.

Let's open the file and then open, for example, the `emeraldTown.skin.properties` file that looks like this (yes, the skin file is a `.properties` file!):

```
#Colors
headerBackgroundColor=#005000
headerGradientColor=#70BA70
headerTextColor=#FFFFFF
headerWeightFont=bold

generalBackgroundColor=#f1f1f1
generalTextColor=#000000
generalSizeFont=18px
generalFamilyFont=Arial, Verdana, sans-serif

controlTextColor=#000000
controlBackgroundColor=#ffffff
additionalBackgroundColor=#E2F6E2

shadowBackgroundColor=#000000
shadowOpacity=1

panelBorderColor=#C0C0C0
subBorderColor=#ffffff

tabBackgroundColor=#ADCDAD
tabDisabledTextColor=#67AA67

trimColor=#BBECBB

tipBackgroundColor=#FAE6B0
tipBorderColor=#E5973E

selectControlColor=#FF9409


generalLinkColor=#43BD43
hoverLinkColor=#FF9409
visitedLinkColor=#43BD43
```

```
# Fonts
headerSizeFont=18px
headerFamilyFont=Arial, Verdana, sans-serif

tabSizeFont=11
tabFamilyFont=Arial, Verdana, sans-serif

buttonSizeFont=18
buttonFamilyFont=Arial, Verdana, sans-serif

tableBackgroundColor=#FFFFFF
tableFooterBackgroundColor=#cccccc
tableSubfooterBackgroundColor=#f1f1f1
tableBorderColor=#C0C0C0
tableBorderWidth=2px

#Calendar colors
calendarWeekBackgroundColor=#f5f5f5

calendarHolidaysBackgroundColor=#FFEBDA
calendarHolidaysTextColor=#FF7800

calendarCurrentBackgroundColor=#FF7800
calendarCurrentTextColor=#FFEBDA

calendarSpecBackgroundColor=#E2F6E2
calendarSpecTextColor=#000000


warningColor=#FFE6E6
warningBackgroundColor=#FF0000

editorBackgroundColor=#F1F1F1
editBackgroundColor=#FEFFDA

#Gradients
gradientType=plain
```

In order to test it, let's open our application project, create a file called `mySkin.skin.properties` inside the directory `/resources/WEB-INF/`, and add the above text.

Then, let's open the `build.xml` file and edit it, and add the following code into the `war` target:

```
<copy
  tofile="${war.dir}/WEB-INF/classes/mySkin.skin.properties"
file="${basedir}/resources/WEB-INF/mySkin.skin.properties"
overwrite="true"/>
```

Also, as our application supports multiple skins, let's open the `components.xml` file and add support to it:

```
<property name="defaultSkin">mySkin</property>
<property name="availableSkins">
    <value>mySkin</value>
    <value>laguna</value>
    <value>darkX</value>
    <value>glassX</value>
    <value>blueSky</value>
    <value>classic</value>
    <value>ruby</value>
    <value>wine</value>
    <value>deepMarine</value>
    <value>emeraldTown</value>
    <value>japanCherry</value>
</property>
```

> If you just want to select the new skin as the fixed skin, you would just edit the `web.xml` file and select the new skin by inserting the name into the context parameter (as explained before).

Just to make an (bad looking, but understandable) example, let's change some parameters in the skin file:

```
#Colors
headerBackgroundColor=#005000
headerGradientColor=#70BA70
headerTextColor=#FFFFFF
headerWeightFont=bold

generalBackgroundColor=#f1f1f1
generalTextColor=#000000
generalSizeFont=18px
generalFamilyFont=Arial, Verdana, sans-serif

controlTextColor=#000000
controlBackgroundColor=#ffffff
additionalBackgroundColor=#E2F6E2

shadowBackgroundColor=#000000
```

```
shadowOpacity=1

panelBorderColor=#C0C0C0
subBorderColor=#ffffff

tabBackgroundColor=#ADCDAD
tabDisabledTextColor=#67AA67

trimColor=#BBECBB

tipBackgroundColor=#FAE6B0
tipBorderColor=#E5973E

selectControlColor=#FF9409
generalLinkColor=#43BD43
hoverLinkColor=#FF9409
visitedLinkColor=#43BD43

# Fonts
headerSizeFont=18px
headerFamilyFont=Arial, Verdana, sans-serif

tabSizeFont=11
tabFamilyFont=Arial, Verdana, sans-serif

buttonSizeFont=18
buttonFamilyFont=Arial, Verdana, sans-serif

tableBackgroundColor=#FFFFFF
tableFooterBackgroundColor=#cccccc
tableSubfooterBackgroundColor=#f1f1f1
tableBorderColor=#C0C0C0
tableBorderWidth=2px

#Calendar colors
calendarWeekBackgroundColor=#f5f5f5

calendarHolidaysBackgroundColor=#FFEBDA
calendarHolidaysTextColor=#FF7800

calendarCurrentBackgroundColor=#FF7800
calendarCurrentTextColor=#FFEBDA

calendarSpecBackgroundColor=#E2F6E2
calendarSpecTextColor=#000000


warningColor=#FFE6E6
warningBackgroundColor=#FF0000
```

```
editorBackgroundColor=#F1F1F1
editBackgroundColor=#FEFFDA

#Gradients
gradientType=plain
```

Here is the screenshot of what happened with the new skin:

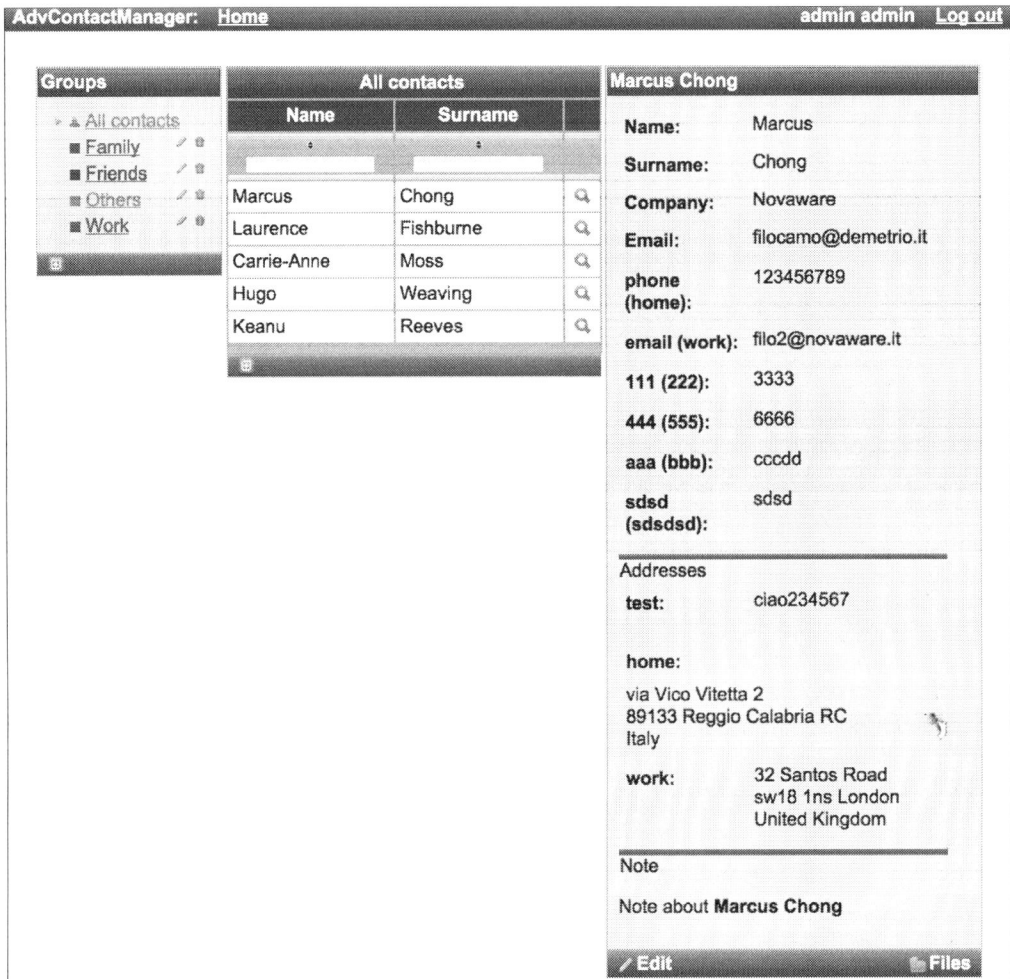

How do I know which parameters to change? The official RichFaces Developer Guide contains, for every component, a table with the correspondences between the skin parameters and the CSS properties they are connected to.

Using CSS

What about when we need to change just a specific component's look? And what if we need to change it just for a specific page?

In these cases, we can use the CSS framework to accomplish the tasks.

For the first case, we can redefine the skin-inserted CSS classes, and for the second, we can specify our specific CSS classes for every component.

Redefine the skin-inserted CSS classes

Let's come back to our example, we want to change the background for all of the panel headers.

In the official RichFaces Developer Guide, we can see that we have to redefine the CSS class `rich-panel-header`. Let's open the `/view/stylesheet/theme.css` and add the following code:

```
.rich-panel-header {
    color: #FF0000;
    background: #9999ff repeat scroll 0 0;
}
```

The result is as follows:

By now, all of the `rich:panel` components have a new header redefined by the CSS class.

Specify our specific CSS classes

If we want to change the style for a specific component, we can just pass our custom CSS classes using the `*Class` attributes.

In order to give an example, we are going to customize just the `rich:toolBar` component of the **All contacts** table—let's open the `/view/stylesheet/theme.css` file and add our custom CSS class as follows:

```
.my-custom-toolbar {
    background: #cccc00 repeat scroll 0 0;
}
```

Now, let's open the `/view/main/contactsList.xhtml` file and set the `styleClass` attribute with our newly created CSS class:

```
...
<rich:toolBar styleClass="my-custom-toolbar">
...
```

The result of this customization is as shown in the following screenshot:

You can see that only the **All contacts** table toolbar is customized.

You can also insert inline CSS code using the `style` attribute of the component:

```
...
<rich:toolBar styleClass="my-custom-toolbar"
              style="border: 2px solid #FF0000;">
...
```

You can see the following result:

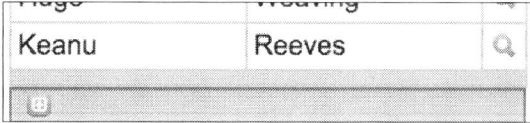

Even if we change the skin, our custom CSS settings will still be valid:

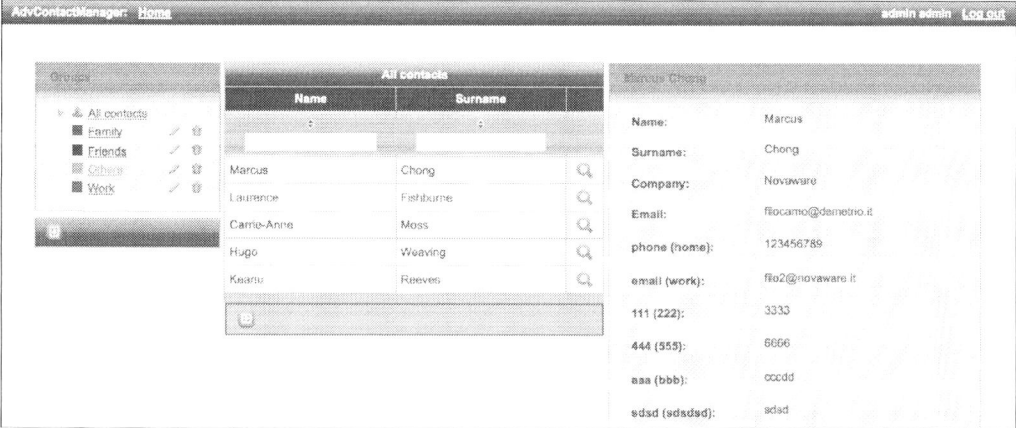

Using skins with non-skinnable components

The skinnability feature works only for RichFaces components, so, the same problems for which this feature was created would be found using other framework components (also using the standard JSF ones!).

In order to be able to use the skin parameters also for non-RichFaces components, the framework declares an object called `richSkin` that permits access to the skin values.

Let's see this code as an example:

```
#{richSkin.tabBackgroundColor}
```

Therefore, if we have a seam `div` component (`s:div`) and we still want to use the border color defined by the skin, we can use this code:

```
<s:div
    style="border: 10px solid #{richSkin.panelBorderColor}">
    <h:outputText value="Example text" />
</s:div>
```

And the color will be the one selected by our skin, so, for our new custom skin it will be as follows:

Example text

Instead, for the `japanCherry` skin, it will be:

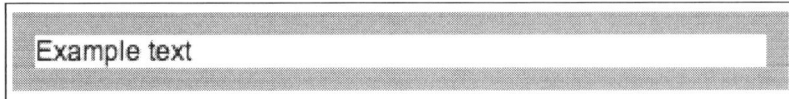

Example text

Standard controls skinning

For the standard XHTML controls, we have the options of customizing the style the RichFaces way.

RichFaces, in fact, unifies the application's appearance by skinning the standard HTML elements the same way it does with the other components of the library.

There are two levels of skinning:

- Standard: For customizing only the basic properties (applies to IE 6, IE 7 in BackCompat mode and Safari)
- Extended: For customizing more properties with more styles (it applies to Mozilla Firefox and IE 7 in standards-compliant mode)

In order to activate the Standard controls skinning, it is sufficient to add a new `context-param` inside the `web.xml` file, like this:

```
<context-param>
  <param-name>org.richfaces.CONTROL_SKINNING</param-name>
  <param-value>enable</param-value>
</context-param>
```

This will enable the feature for our application.

Enabling the parameter in our application will skin the standard controls from this:

So it appears like this:

If you want to customize the standard controls using the CSS framework, you can also enable the org.richfaces.CONTROL_SKINNING_CLASSES context parameter (inside the web.xml file)—by doing so, you will be able to edit a set of CSS classes for skinning the XHTML components (some examples of CSS classes you can redefine are rich-select, rich-input-text, and so on that follow the rich-<elementName>[-<elementType>] pattern).

> **Extended skinning in Opera and Safari**
>
> In order to resolve some problem with extended skinning in Opera and Safari, you can activate a JavaScript script that detects the browser and enables extended skinning only where supported.
>
> For doing that, just add the following code to the XHTML page (in our case, we would add it to the `/view/layout/template.xhtml` file):
>
> ```
> <script type="text/javascript">
>   window.RICH_FACES_EXTENDED_SKINNING_ON = true;
> </script>
> ```

XCSS

Another way to use skin properties values for CSS classes is the XCSS. It is an XML version of the CSS used to extend the CSS feature and add extra functionalities. It is widely used inside the RichFaces framework, because of its flexibility. In short, it is an XML version of the CSS file that contains skin parameters and dynamic resource generator classes. It is automatically converted in a standard CSS file suitable for all browsers.

In our application, you can open the `/view/stylesheet/theme.xcss` file and look at the definition created by Seam-gen for the project.

As you can see, you have to use the `<u:selector>` and `<u:style>` XML tags to create a CSS selector.

Let's see the following code for example:

```
<u:selector name=".rich-panel-header">
  <u:style  name="background-color"
            skin="headerBackgroundColor" />
  <u:style name="color"
            skin="headerTextColor" />
</u:selector>
```

This will read the values from the current skin and produce the following CSS code (if `mySkin` is selected):

```
.rich-panel-header {
    background-color: #005000;
    color: #FFFFFF;
}
```

As you can see, the `name` attribute of the `u:selector` tag defines the CSS selector name, and the `name` attribute of the `u:style` tag defines the name of the CSS property.

You can also use comma-separated CSS selector names into the `u:selector` name attribute to specify more selector at a time:

```
<u:selector name=".rich-panel-header, .rich-panel-body">
...
```

Another feature is the possibility to use Java resources inside the CSS to dynamically generate images; in `theme.xcss`, you can find some examples to generate gradients:

```
<u:selector name=".rich-table-subheadercell">
  <u:style name="background-image">
    <f:resource f:key="org.richfaces.renderkit.images.TabGradientB"/>
  </u:style>
</u:selector>
```

XCSS is very powerful and extends the CSS framework for skinning every component we need to skin!

Summary

In this chapter, we've seen all the powerful customization capabilities that the RichFaces framework offers.

In the next chapter, we will create a new skin using the plug 'n' skin technology.

9
Creating a New plug 'n' skin

The plug 'n' skin feature is a powerful way to create, customize, and deploy new skins for the RichFaces framework.

In this chapter, we'll learn how to create a new skin, edit it, and build it in order to have it ready to be deployed in our project.

In order to use the plug 'n' skin feature, we are going to use Apache Maven for the template creation and compiling. This is very useful, as we don't have to worry about dependencies and versioning that are completely managed by the Apache technology.

Installing Maven

If you haven't installed it yet, you'll need to download and install Maven before starting. In order to do that, visit the Maven website (`http://maven.apache.org`), download the latest version, and follow the instructions to complete the installation.

After that, we have to add the RichFaces profile to that of Maven. Let's open the `<maven_root_directory>/conf/settings.xml` file and add the following code into the `<profiles>` section:

```
<profile>
<id>RichFaces</id>
<repositories>
  <repository>
    <releases>
      <enabled>true</enabled>
    </releases>
    <snapshots>
      <enabled>false</enabled>
      <updatePolicy>never</updatePolicy>
```

```
      </snapshots>
      <id>repository.jboss.com</id>
      <name>Jboss Repository for Maven</name>
      <url>
        http://repository.jboss.com/maven2/
      </url>
      <layout>default</layout>
    </repository>
    <repository>
      <releases>
      <enabled>false</enabled>
      </releases>
      <snapshots>
        <enabled>true</enabled>
        <updatePolicy>always</updatePolicy>
      </snapshots>
      <id>maven2-snapshots.jboss.com</id>
      <name>Jboss Repository for Maven Snapshots</name>
      <url>http://snapshots.jboss.org/maven2</url>
      <layout>default</layout>
    </repository>
  </repositories>

  <pluginRepositories>
    <pluginRepository>
      <id>maven2-snapshots.jboss.com</id>
      <name>Jboss Repository for Maven Snapshots</name>
      <url>http://snapshots.jboss.org/maven2</url>
      <releases>
        <enabled>false</enabled>
      </releases>
      <snapshots>
        <enabled>true</enabled>
        <updatePolicy>always</updatePolicy>
      </snapshots>
    </pluginRepository>
    <pluginRepository>
      <releases>
        <enabled>true</enabled>
      </releases>
      <snapshots>
        <enabled>false</enabled>
        <updatePolicy>never</updatePolicy>
      </snapshots>
```

```
    <id>repository.jboss.com</id>
    <name>Jboss Repository for Maven</name>
    <url>
     http://repository.jboss.com/maven2/
    </url>
    <layout>default</layout>
   </pluginRepository>
  </pluginRepositories>
 </profile>
```

Now we have to activate the new profile. In order to do so, let's move to the bottom of the file, uncomment the `<activeProfiles>` section, and add the new profile. The section must appear as follows:

```
<!-- activeProfiles
 | List of profiles that are active for all builds.
 | -->
<activeProfiles>
  <activeProfile>RichFaces</activeProfile>
</activeProfiles>
```

Let's save the file and we're done with the Maven configuration!

Creating the new skin

Now it's time to start creating the new skin!

Create a folder called `PlugNSkin` wherever you like, open the terminal inside this directory, and type (all in one line) the following:

```
mvn archetype:create
    -DarchetypeGroupId=org.richfaces.cdk
    -DarchetypeArtifactId=maven-archetype-plug-n-skin
    -DarchetypeVersion=3.3.1.GA
    -DartifactId=newSkin
    -DgroupId=newSkin
    -Dversion=1.0
```

This command creates a generic template of a Maven project for creating the new skin. After the execution, we will have, a new folder called `newSkin` (the name we specified as `artifactId`) that contains all the Maven configuration files we need to start our new skin project.

Having the template ready, we have to create the custom skin. Optionally, we can use an existing one as the base skin (and we are going to do so—therefore, it will be simpler to start).

Let's go back to our terminal window and enter the following commands:

```
cd newSkin
```

```
mvn cdk:add-skin -Dname=myNewSkin -Dpackage=book.newSkin -
DbaseSkin=blueSky -DcreateExt=true
```

The last two parameters are optional and can be used to select a base skin for the new one and to add the Standard Controls Skinning CSS classes to the new project respectively.

The next screenshot shows the structure of the just generated skin:

- ▼ 📁 newSkin
  - 📄 pom.xml
  - ▼ 📁 src
    - ▼ 📁 main
      - ▼ 📁 config
        - ▼ 📁 resources
          - 📄 myNewSkin-resources.xml
          - 📄 resource-config.xml
      - ▼ 📁 java
        - ▼ 📁 book
          - ▼ 📁 newskin
            - ▼ 📁 mynewskin
              - ▼ 📁 images
                - 📄 BaseImage.java
      - ▼ 📁 resources
        - ▼ 📁 book
          - ▼ 📁 newskin
            - ▼ 📁 mynewskin
              - ▼ 📁 css
                - 📄 calendar.xcss
                - 📄 color-picker.xcss
                - 📄 combobox.xcss
                - 📄 context-menu.xcss
                - 📄 core.xcss
                - 📄 data-filter-slider.xcss
                - 📄 data-table.xcss
                - 📄 datascroller.xcss
                - 📄 drag-drop.xcss
                - 📄 dropdown-menu.xcss
                - 📄 editor.xcss
                - 📄 extended_classes.xcss
                - 📄 extended-data-table.xcss
                - 📄 extended.xcss
                - 📄 file-upload.xcss
                - 📄 gmap.xcss
                - 📄 inplace-input.xcss
                - 📄 inplace-select.xcss
                - 📄 inputnumber-slider.xcss
                - 📄 inputnumber-spinner.xcss
                - 📄 layout.xcss
                - 📄 list-shuttle.xcss
                - 📄 menu-components.xcss
                - 📄 message.xcss
                - 📄 modal-panel.xcss
                - 📄 ordering-list.xcss
                - 📄 paint2d.xcss
                - 📄 panel.xcss
                - 📄 panelbar.xcss
                - 📄 panelmenu.xcss
                - 📄 pick-list.xcss
                - 📄 progress-bar.xcss
                - 📄 scrollable-data-table.xcss
                - 📄 separator.xcss
                - 📄 simple-toggle-panel.xcss
                - 📄 spacer.xcss
                - 📄 suggestionbox.xcss
                - 📄 tab-panel.xcss
                - 📄 toggle-panel.xcss
                - 📄 tool-bar.xcss
                - 📄 tooltip.xcss
                - 📄 tree.xcss
                - 📄 virtual-earth.xcss
              - ▼ 📁 images
                - 📄 README.txt
        - ▼ 📁 META-INF
          - ▼ 📁 skins
            - 📄 myNewSkin-ext.xcss
            - 📄 myNewSkin.skin.properties
            - 📄 myNewSkin.xcss
          - 📄 README.txt
    - ▼ 📁 test
      - ▼ 📁 java
        - ▼ 📁 book
          - ▼ 📁 newskin
            - ▼ 📁 mynewskin
              - ▼ 📁 images
                - 📄 BaseImageTest.java

As you can see from the preceding screenshot, the folder contains the following files:

- Configuration files: Both Maven and skin configuration files in order to define the skin properties. Notice that the `myNewSkin.skin.properties` file contains the properties of the skin.

- XCSS files: Define the CSS classes of the new skin; they are based on the ones coming from the `blueSky` skin, as we added the `baseSkin` option.

- A class to store images called `BaseImage.java` and its test class (called `BaseImageTest.java`).

Customizing the new skin

Everything is set in order to start editing and customizing the new skin—we'll change some parameters to make the editing of the new skin evident to you. For this reason, the produced skin will be not good looking at all!

We need to change the standard colors and we can do that by redefining the skin parameters.

If we look at the `myNewSkin.skin.properties` file, we'll find some interesting options:

```
gradientType=glass
generalStyleSheet=resource:///META-INF/skins/myNewSkin.xcss
baseSkin=blueSky
extendedStyleSheet=resource:///META-INF/skins/myNewSkin-ext.xcss
```

The `generalStyleSheet` and the `extendedStyleSheet` options contain the path to include all of the needed stylesheets, the `baseSkin` (as we've seen) contains the name of the skin we used to generate the new one, the `gradientType` contains the type of gradient used by the new skin (other options are `plastic` and `plain`, and it is possible to generate new ones).

Inside this file, we can put the skin parameters we would like to redefine, for example:

```
headerBackgroundColor=#d5a32b
headerTextColor=#FF0000
myNewProperty=#d5a32b
```

We changed some parameters to show you how you can control the skin base options. As you can see, you can also define new properties to use inside the XCSS code (we'll use the `myNewProperty` value later).

The second thing we have to do is edit the `.xcss` files. As you can see on opening one of them, there are two different ways to edit CSS information—by using plain CSS or XCSS language.

In the first case, we can insert our CSS inside the `f:verbatim` tag in this way:

```
<f:verbatim>
  <![CDATA[
    // my css code
  ]]>
</f:verbatim>
```

In the second case, we can use XCSS tags outside the `f:verbatim` section.

For example, let's open the `tool-bar.xcss` file and define a border for the `rich:toolBar` component in plain CSS, by just adding the following definition inside the `.rich-toolbar` selector:

```
border: 1px solid red;
```

Now we will use XCSS to redefine the background gradient. Add the following code after the `f:verbatim` block:

```
<u:selector name=".rich-toolbar">
  <u:style name="padding" value="0px 5px 0px 5px" />
  <u:style name="background-position" value="0% 50%" />

  <u:style name="background-image">
    <f:resource
      f:key="org.richfaces.renderkit.html.CustomizeableGradient">
    <f:attribute name="valign" value="middle" />
    <f:attribute name="gradientHeight"
                 value="22px" />
    <f:attribute name="baseColor"
                 skin="myNewProperty" />
    <f:attribute name="gradientColor"
                 skin="headerGradientColor" />
    </f:resource>
  </u:style>
</u:selector>
```

As you can see, we have used the `CustomizedGradient` class to generate our gradient with the color set by the `myNewProperty` value.

The final version of the content of the `tool-bar.xcss` file is:

```xml
<?xml version="1.0" encoding="UTF-8"?>
<f:template xmlns:f="http://jsf.exadel.com/template"
  xmlns:u="http://jsf.exadel.com/template/util"
  xmlns="http://www.w3.org/1999/xhtml">
  <f:verbatim>
    <![CDATA[
      .rich-toolbar {
      border: 1px solid red;
      }
      .rich-toolbar-item {
      }
      .rich-toolbar-separator {
      }
    ]]>
  </f:verbatim>
  <u:selector name=".rich-toolbar">
    <u:style name="padding" value="0px 5px 0px 5px" />
      <u:style name="background-position" value="0% 50%" />

      <u:style name="background-image">
        <f:resource
          f:key="org.richfaces.renderkit.html.CustomizeableGradient">
        <f:attribute name="valign"
                     value="middle" />
        <f:attribute name="gradientHeight"
                     value="22px" />
        <f:attribute name="baseColor"
                     skin="myNewProperty" />
        <f:attribute name="gradientColor"
                     skin="headerGradientColor" />
        </f:resource>
      </u:style>
  </u:selector>
</f:template>
```

Packaging and deploying the new skin

Having edited our skin, we can go on to deploy it in our project. Let's come back to the terminal and from the skin root directory, let's digit:

```
mvn clean install
```

After the command completes its work, we'll have a new `target` directory containing all of the compiled files and the `jar` package named `newSkin-1.0.jar`, which we can use for deploying the new skin in our project.

We have explained how to deploy a new skin to our project, so we leave this as an exercise for the reader.

This is how our application looks, using the `blueSky` skin:

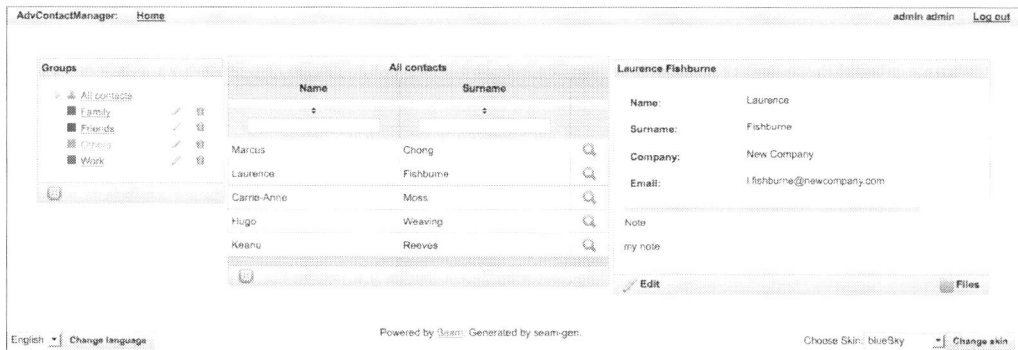

The result of our new deployed skin is as shown in the following screenshot:

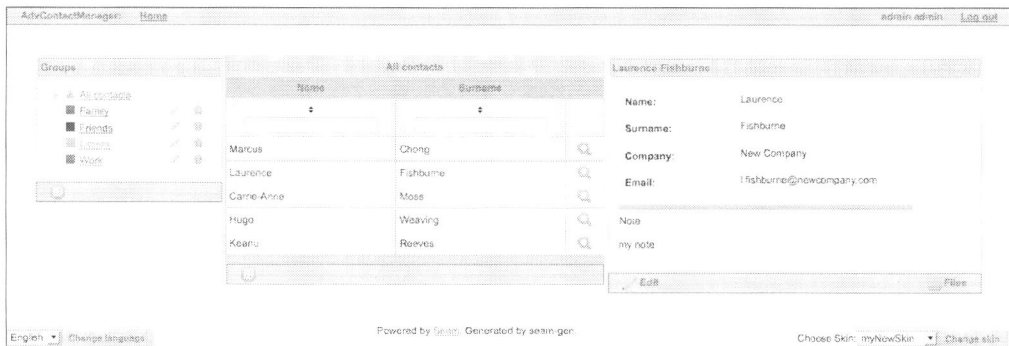

That's all! You can make and plug as many skins as you like in a very simple way!

Summary

In this chapter, we learned how simple it is to make a new pluggable skin!

In the next chapter, we'll see some advanced topics for optimizing your applications using the RichFaces framework.

10
Advanced Techniques

This chapter is going to talk about some "advanced" RichFaces topics. You will discover with single examples how to use and implement pushing, partial updates, session expiration handling, and so on.

Poll

By using the `a:poll` component, you can periodically poll the server for data and updates using an Ajax request. The use is the same as for `a:commandButton` and `a:commandLink`, so you can invoke an action and re-render one or more page areas.

This component uses a form-based request, so, it is required to put the `a:poll` component inside `h:form`.

Here there is a little example that shows how to use it:

```
<h:form>
  <a:poll
    id="poll"
    action="#{aBean.pollAction}"
    interval="500"
    reRender="result" />
</h:form>
<h:outputText
  id="result"
  value="Polling result: #{aBean.pollResult}" />
```

In this piece of code, we used the `a:poll` component to execute an action (the method `pollAction()` of the `aBean` bean) every 500 milliseconds (using the `interval` attribute) and, after the execution finished, to update the component with `id = "result"` (that writes the value the `pollAction()` method set in the `pollResult` property of the web page).

As we've said, we need h:form surrounding the a:poll component in order to make it work.

Let's do another simple example—we want to show a seconds counter updated every second with a checkbox that enables or disables it.

First, let's do our backing bean: in our project, by creating the book.richfaces. advcm.modules.main.examples.poll package and, inside that, a new class called PollExample. This class would look like this:

```
package book.richfaces.advcm.modules.main.examples.poll;

@Name("pollExample")
public class PollExample {

    private boolean pollingEnabled = true;

    public boolean getPollingEnabled() {
        return pollingEnabled;
    }

    public void setPollingEnabled(boolean pollingEnabled) {
        this.pollingEnabled = pollingEnabled;
    }

    public int getSeconds() {
        Calendar cal = Calendar.getInstance();
        return cal.get(Calendar.SECOND);
    }
}
```

As you can see, it is a simple Seam component with the boolean property (pollingEnabled) having the getter and setter, and a method that returns the current time in seconds (getSeconds()).

Now, let's create the pollExample.xhtml page inside the /view/examples/poll/ directory. It might look like:

```
<!DOCTYPE composition PUBLIC "-//W3C//DTD XHTML 1.0 Transitional//EN"
"http://www.w3.org/TR/xhtml1/DTD/xhtml1-transitional.dtd">
<ui:composition xmlns="http://www.w3.org/1999/xhtml"
                xmlns:ui="http://java.sun.com/jsf/facelets"
                xmlns:h="http://java.sun.com/jsf/html"
                xmlns:a="http://richfaces.org/a4j"
                template="/layout/template.xhtml">
```

```
<ui:define name="body">
  <h:form>
    <a:poll id="myPoll" interval="1000"
            enabled="#{pollExample.pollingEnabled}"
            reRender="pollUpdate"
            ajaxSingle="true"/>

      <h:selectBooleanCheckbox
                  value="#{pollExample.pollingEnabled}">
        <a:support event="onchange"
                    reRender="myPoll,pollUpdate"
                    ajaxSingle="true"/>
      </h:selectBooleanCheckbox>

      <h:panelGroup id="pollUpdate">
        <h:outputText value="Polling active: "
                      rendered="#{pollExample.pollingEnabled}"/>
        <h:outputText value="Polling NOT active: "
                      rendered="#{!pollExample.pollingEnabled}"/>
        <h:outputText value="#{pollExample.seconds}"/>
      </h:panelGroup>

  </h:form>
</ui:define>
</ui:composition>
```

Here, we have defined the `a:poll` component inside `h:form`, setting the polling interval to 1000 ms (that is, one second) and re-rendering the text section at every update. Also, we have set the `ajaxSingle` attribute to `true`, because we don't want to process the checkbox value every time the poll is fired (we should also use two different forms for that).

Inside the `h:selectBooleanCheckbox`, we inserted the `a:support` component to fire an Ajax action when the user clicks on the checkbox, submitting the form, updating the model with the new checkbox value, and re-rendering the `a:poll` component that is enabled or disabled, depending on the `boolean` value controlled by the checkbox (`pollingEnabled`).

Finally, the `outputText` component renders the information back to the user; those are updated every second by the `a:poll` component.

The result of the enabled polling is:

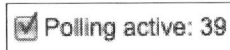

☑ Polling active: 39

As we have said, the text is updated every second with the current time in seconds from the server clock.

When the poll component is disabled, nothing is updated and the text stays with the value of the latest update:

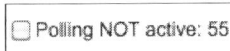

☐ Polling NOT active: 55

Creating images dynamically

In order to add something interesting to this example and also to explain another useful component, we are going to edit it by adding a dynamic graphical counter. We will use the a4j:mediaOutput RichFaces component to render an image (each second) with the current value of seconds from the server.

First of all, let's open PollExample.java and add the paint method to create the image:

```
public void paint(OutputStream out, Object data)
                          throws IOException {
  // Creating an image
    BufferedImage img = new BufferedImage(40, 40, BufferedImage.TYPE_
                                          INT_RGB);
  // Getting the Graphics2D object
    Graphics2D graphics2D = img.createGraphics();

  // Setting background color, foreground color and font size
    graphics2D.setBackground(Color.WHITE);
    graphics2D.setColor(Color.RED);
    graphics2D.setFont(graphics2D.getFont().deriveFont(25f));

  // Clearing the background with the color set
    graphics2D.clearRect(0, 0, 40, 40);

  // Drawing the number value
    graphics2D.drawString(String.valueOf(getSeconds()),4,36);

  // Writing the image into the output stream as PNG
    ImageIO.write(img,"png",out);
}
```

As you can notice, the paint method has two parameters—the first one is `OutputStream` used to write the output image to and the second one contains the `Serializable` object, passed by the `value` attribute of the component (in our case, we are not using it).

This method creates `BufferedImage`, fills it with the current seconds value, and writes it as a `PNG` image to the output stream.

Now, let's open `pollExample.xhtml` and insert the `mediaOutput` component:

Replace the following component:

```
<h:outputText value="#{pollExample.seconds}"/>
```

With this code:

```
<a:mediaOutput element="img" cacheable="false"
               value="#{pollExample.seconds}"
               createContent="#{pollExample.paint}"
               mimeType="image/png"/>
```

As we can see, we have set the `element` attribute as `img`, which is why the component supports the dynamical generation of other kinds of objects such as Flash movies, applets, or scripts.

The `cacheable` attribute defines the caching strategy both for the client and the server. Anyway, for our frequent requests, it is possible that the client caches the image in any case. Therefore, it will not be refreshed each second.

In order to avoid this problem, it is sufficient to set the `value` attribute with a different value for every update (in our case, the current value of the seconds from the server). As the serialized object passed becomes part of the image name, the name will change for every new generated image, which will therefore not be cached by the browser.

The object passed using the `value` attribute is passed to the paint method, using the `data` parameter.

For specifying which method to call in order to generate the object, we use the `createContent` attribute and we've set the MIME type of the returned image (`image/png`) using `mimeType`.

The result, when polling is active, is as follows:

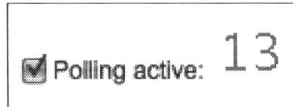

When it is not active, we will see the last image sent:

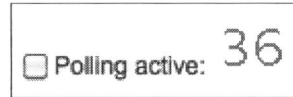

Push

The `a:push` component simulates push data from the server. It sends (according to the `interval` attribute) a very small, (and fast) non-JSF request to the server, in order to check if there are new messages in the queue and if this is true, it performs a standard JSF request.

Example code:

```
<a4j:push
  reRender="myComponent"
  interval="3000"
  eventProducer="#{messageBean.addListener}" />
```

In this example, it will check in every 3 seconds (3000 milliseconds) whether there is a message in the queue. If so, the component with `id = "myComponent"` will be re-rendered.

The `eventProducer` attribute is needed to point at a method that accepts the `PushEventListener` instance and registers it, in order to use it inside the bean.

It can be very useful, for example, for asynchronous actions that need periodic page updates.

Let's see a practical use—we want to do a complex (and long) job in the background, updating the user about the job status percentage; the *Start job* button must be disabled after the job calculation starts, and enabled again at the end.

Let's create our backing bean called `PushExample` inside the `book.richfaces.advcm.modules.main.examples.push` package and insert this code:

```
package book.richfaces.advcm.modules.main.examples.push;

@Name("pushExample")
@Scope(ScopeType.CONVERSATION)
public class PushExample implements Runnable {

    private Integer completedPercentage = 0;

    public Integer getCompletedPercentage() {
        return completedPercentage;
    }

    public void sand setCompletedPercentage(Integer completedPercentage)
{
        this.completedPercentage = completedPercentage;
    }

    public void startJob() {
        new Thread(this).start();
    }

    public void run() {
        // This is a heavy job
        for (int c = 0; c < 10; c++) {
            try {
                Thread.sleep(1000);  // Wait for 1 second

                completedPercentage += 10;

                // If I finished
                if (completedPercentage == 100) {
                    // Reset
                    completedPercentage = 0;
                }
            } catch (InterruptedException e) {
                completedPercentage = 0; // Reset on error
            }
        }
    }
}
```

The component we have created has an `Integer` property that contains the job status percentage value (from 0 to 100). Also, the component implements the `Runnable` interface so we can run the job in background (inside a Thread instance) without blocking the frontend during the calculation.

The `startJob()` method is called by a button (we'll see it soon) and returned immediately after creating a new thread that does the job in the background. As we have made our class `Runnable`, we need to implement the `run()` method, that is the one called after the thread creation, for doing the job. The code inside the `run()` method simulates a job that updates the `completedPercentage` value every second and resets it when the job is completed.

Now, we have to connect the push component to the backend, in order to be able to communicate with it when new data is ready to be pushed into the frontend.

Let's add the `PushEventListener` property and a method that will be called by the push component in order to register the listener:

```
@Name ("pushExample")
@Scope (ScopeType.CONVERSATION)
public class PushExample implements Runnable {

    private PushEventListener listener;

    public void addListener(EventListener listener) {
        synchronized (listener) {
            if (this.listener != listener) {
                this.listener = (PushEventListener) listener;
            }
        }
    }

    // Other code
}
```

The `addListener` method just saves the listener object that can be used to fire a push update, by calling the `onEvent` method of the listener this way:

```
listener.onEvent(new EventObject(this));
```

We can also pass a customized `EventObject` if we need that.

Coming back to our example, we need to modify the `run()` method to make it notify the push component at every step (so, every second in our case):

```
public void run() {
    // This is a heavy job
    for (int c = 0; c < 10; c++) {
        try {
            Thread.sleep(1000);  // Wait for 1 second

            completedPercentage += 10;

            // If I finished
            if (completedPercentage == 100) {
                // Reset
                completedPercentage = 0;
            }

            listener.onEvent(new EventObject(this));
        } catch (InterruptedException e) {
            completedPercentage = 0; // Reset on error
        }
    }
}
```

After every completed part (or in general, when we think there is important data to push), we have just to call the onEvent method, in order to notify the push component that there is new data ready to be pushed.

The /view/examples/push/pushExample.xhtml file is quite simple to understand:

```
<!DOCTYPE composition PUBLIC "-//W3C//DTD XHTML 1.0 Transitional//EN"
"http://www.w3.org/TR/xhtml1/DTD/xhtml1-transitional.dtd">
<ui:composition xmlns="http://www.w3.org/1999/xhtml"
                xmlns:ui="http://java.sun.com/jsf/facelets"
                xmlns:h="http://java.sun.com/jsf/html"
                xmlns:a="http://richfaces.org/a4j"
                template="/layout/template.xhtml">

    <ui:define name="body">
      <h:form>
        <a:push interval="1000"
        eventProducer="#{pushExample.addListener}"
        reRender="pushUpdate"/>
      </h:form>

      <h:form id="pushUpdate">
        <h:outputText
              value="Job status: #{pushExample.completedPercentage}%"/>
```

```
                        <a:commandButton value="Start job"
                          action="#{pushExample.startJob}"
                          disabled="#{pushExample.completedPercentage>0}"
                          reRender="pushUpdate"/>
            </h:form>

        </ui:define>
    </ui:composition>
```

You can notice we have connected the push component to the backend using the eventProducer attribute—every time there is new data, the push component will re-render the pushUpdate form that shows the completed job percentage and the *Start job* button. This will be disabled when the first data is pushed and enabled again at the end of the job (when the completedPercentage property is set again to 0).

In order to start the conversation and make the example URL simpler, we are going to add another page (in the same directory of the example) called pushExample.page.xml that contains the configuration we need:

```
<?xml version="1.0" encoding="UTF-8"?>
<page xmlns="http://jboss.com/products/seam/pages"
      xmlns:xsi="http://www.w3.org/2001/XMLSchema-instance"
      xsi:schemaLocation="http://jboss.com/products/seam/pages http://
jboss.com/products/seam/pages-2.1.xsd">

    <begin-conversation join="true" />

  <rewrite pattern="/pushExample" />
</page>
```

This is what we see when the job has not been started:

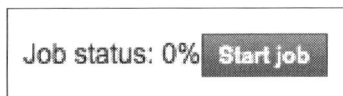

Job status: 0% Start job

And this is what we see when our job is running:

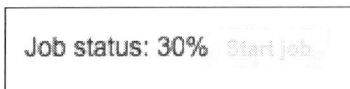

Job status: 30% Start job

Creating a RichFaces JavaScript function

This component is very useful when you need to perform an Ajax request using JavaScript code and to pass server-side data (serialized in JSON format) to a JavaScript function.

The following is an example:

```
<a:jsFunction
            data="#{myBean.myData}"
            name="myJSMethod"
            action="#{myBean.myAction}"
            oncomplete="externalScript(data.subProperty1,
                                        data.subProperty2)"
            reRender="myObj" />
```

In this example, we defined a JavaScript function called myJSMethod that will first get the data from the myBean bean and call the myAction method of myBean. When the action is completed, it will pass the data to another JavaScript function (that was already defined somewhere). After that, the framework will reRender the myObj component.

The component uses a standard JSF call to send the request, for it must stay inside a form component.

Let's see a simple use of a:jsFunction.

The bean we are going to use is very simple— it just has the currentDate property (with a getter and setter) and a method (updateCurrentDate()) that updates the property with the current date and time.

Our class will be in the book.richfaces.advcm.modules.main.examples. jsFunction package and will be called JsFunctionExample:

```
package book.richfaces.advcm.modules.main.examples.jsFunction;

import java.util.Date;

@Name("jsFunctionExample")
public class JsFunctionExample {

    private Date currentDate=new Date();

    public Date getCurrentDate() {
```

```
        return currentDate;
    }

    public void setCurrentDate(Date currentDate) {
        this.currentDate = currentDate;
    }

    public void updateCurrentDate() {
        setCurrentDate(new Date());
    }
}
```

We want to use a JavaScript function (defined by the jsFunction component) to call a backend method and fire an Ajax update. In order to achieve that, we can use this code inside the /view/examples/jsFunction/jsFunctionExample.xhtml page:

```
<!DOCTYPE composition PUBLIC "-//W3C//DTD XHTML 1.0 Transitional//EN"
"http://www.w3.org/TR/xhtml1/DTD/xhtml1-transitional.dtd">
<ui:composition xmlns="http://www.w3.org/1999/xhtml"
                xmlns:ui="http://java.sun.com/jsf/facelets"
                xmlns:h="http://java.sun.com/jsf/html"
                xmlns:a="http://richfaces.org/a4j"
                template="/layout/template.xhtml">
  <ui:define name="body">
    <h:form>
      <a:jsFunction
                name="updateDate"
                action="#{jsFunctionExample.updateCurrentDate}"
                reRender="dateSection"/>
    </h:form>
    <h:panelGroup id="dateSection">
      <h:outputText value="Last update: "/>
      <h:outputText
                value="#{jsFunctionExample.currentDate}"/>
    </h:panelGroup>
    <br/>
    <h:outputLink value="#" onclick="updateDate()">
      <h:outputText value="Update now!"/>
    </h:outputLink>
  </ui:define>
</ui:composition>
```

First, we defined the JavaScript function using the `a:jsFunction` component, then we've created a simple HTML link (using the `h:outputLink` component) that calls the generated JavaScript function when clicked (`onClick` event).

The JavaScript function will call the `updateCurrentDate()` method of our bean and then `reRender dateSection` to show the new updated date.

If you need to integrate a lot of JavaScript code, this is a very powerful component!

Here you can see a screenshot of the example in action:

Last update: Tue Jul 14 19:18:18 BST 2009
Update now!

Partial update of data iteration components

The simplest way to update a data iteration component (for example, a `rich:dataTable`) is to re-render the entire table even if just one row was changed.

There is a more powerful way to optimize this process and it is the capability to choose which rows have to be updated during the re-rendering of the list. The good news is that this is a quite simple task and we are going to see it now.

First of all, let's create a `rich:dataTable` table. We are going to re-use the `GroupsListHelper` Seam component to get the list of the groups to fill in the table.

Let's create the `/view/examples/partialUpdate/partialUpdateExample.xhtml` file:

```
<!DOCTYPE composition PUBLIC "-//W3C//DTD XHTML 1.0 Transitional//EN"
        "http://www.w3.org/TR/xhtml1/DTD/xhtml1-transitional.dtd">
<ui:composition xmlns="http://www.w3.org/1999/xhtml"
            xmlns:ui="http://java.sun.com/jsf/facelets"
            xmlns:f="http://java.sun.com/jsf/core"
            xmlns:h="http://java.sun.com/jsf/html"
            xmlns:rich="http://richfaces.org/rich"
            xmlns:a="http://richfaces.org/a4j"
            template="/layout/template.xhtml">
```

```
<ui:define name="body">
  <h:panelGrid columns="2">
    <h:form>
      <rich:dataTable
                  value="#{groupsListHelper.groups}"
                  var="group">
                  <f:facet name="header">Groups renamer</f:facet>
        <rich:column>
          <f:facet name="header">Name</f:facet>
          <h:outputText value="#{group.name}"/>
        </rich:column>
      </rich:dataTable>
    </h:form>
  </h:panelGrid>
</ui:define>
</ui:composition>
```

That's very simple to understand—it's just a `rich:dataList` showing the names of the groups that we have in the database.

Now we want to put an *Edit* link button for every group to make it appear as a panel on the right side of the page, which is used to edit the selected group. After clicking on the *Save* button, the panel disappears and only the edited table row is updated.

Let's edit the `rich:column` inside the `rich:dataTable`; it might look like this:

```
<rich:column>
  <f:facet name="header">Name</f:facet>
  <h:panelGroup id="groupRow">
    <h:outputText value="#{group.name}"/>
    <h:panelGroup
                rendered="#{group.id!=partialUpdateExampleHelper.
                                              selectedGroup.id}">
        (<a:commandLink value="Edit" reRender="groupRow"
                    action="#{partialUpdateExampleHelper.
                                          editGroup(group)}"/>)
    </h:panelGroup>
  </h:panelGroup>
</rich:column>
```

We have just added and enclosed `h:panelGroup` with the id set as `groupRow` (we'll see later where we are going to use it) and the `a:commandLink` component that initiates the editing of the group at that row.

Now, let's add another attribute to the `rich:dataTable` component called `ajaxKeys`:

```
ajaxKeys="#{partialUpdateExampleHelper.ajaxUpdateRows}"
```

You can use this attribute to every data iteration component and it points to an array containing a list of row numbers of the rows that have to be updated.

Also, let's add the edit panel after the closing `</h:form>` tag:

```
<a:outputPanel ajaxRendered="true">
  <h:form
    rendered="#{partialUpdateExampleHelper.selectedGroup.id!=null}">
    <rich:panel>
      <f:facet name="header">
        Edit #{partialUpdateExampleHelper.selectedGroup.name} group
      </f:facet>

      <h:inputText id="groupName"
        value="#{partialUpdateExampleHelper.selectedGroup.name}"/>
      <a:commandButton value="Save" reRender="groupRow"
          process="groupName"
          action="#{partialUpdateExampleHelper.saveSelectedGroup}"/>
      <a:commandButton value="Cancel"
        reRender="groupRow"
        ajaxSingle="true"
        action="#{partialUpdateExampleHelper.cancelGroupEditing}"/>
    </rich:panel>
  </h:form>
</a:outputPanel>
```

We have enclosed everything inside `a:outputPanel` with the `ajaxRendered` attribute set to `true`, so that we don't have to explicitly re-ender it at every request (it is done automatically at every Ajax request). We can notice that the edit form is rendered only if there is a group selected.

You can also see that when the form is submitted (by clicking on **Save** button), we are re-rendering `h:panelGroup` inside the column and not the whole table.

Let's use the backing bean to manage the partial update. Let's create the Java class `book.richfaces.advcm.modules.main.examples.partialUpdate.PartialUpdateExampleHelper`; it might look like this:

```
package book.richfaces.advcm.modules.main.examples.partialUpdate;

@Name("partialUpdateExampleHelper")
```

```
@Scope(ScopeType.CONVERSATION)
public class PartialUpdateExampleHelper {
    @In(create = true)
    EntityManager entityManager;

    @In(create = true)
    GroupsListHelper groupsListHelper;

    private Set<Integer> ajaxUpdateRows;

    private ContactGroup selectedGroup;

    public void editGroup(ContactGroup group) {
        setSelectedGroup(group);

        // Tell RichFaces to reRender just the selected row
        reRenderRow();
    }

    public void cancelGroupEditing() {
        // Tell RichFaces to reRender just the selected row
        reRenderRow();

        // Empty the selected group
        setSelectedGroup(null);
    }

    public void saveSelectedGroup() {
        // Save the group data to database
        entityManager.merge(getSelectedGroup());

        // Tell RichFaces to reRender just the selected row
        reRenderRow();

        // This group is no more selected
        setSelectedGroup(null);
    }

    private void reRenderRow() {
        // We have to clear the list of elements to reRender
            // because this component scope is conversation
        getAjaxUpdateRows().clear();
```

```
        // Find the index of the selected group inside the
            // groups list
        int groupIndex = groupsListHelper.getGroups().
                            indexOf(getSelectedGroup());

        // Tell to RichFaces to reRender just this row
        getAjaxUpdateRows().add(groupIndex);      }

    public Set<Integer> getAjaxUpdateRows() {
        if (ajaxUpdateRows == null) {
            ajaxUpdateRows = new HashSet<Integer>();
        }
        return ajaxUpdateRows;
    }

    public void setAjaxUpdateRows(Set<Integer> ajaxUpdateRows)
    {
        this.ajaxUpdateRows = ajaxUpdateRows;
    }

    public ContactGroup getSelectedGroup() {
        return selectedGroup;
    }

    public void setSelectedGroup(ContactGroup selectedGroup) {
        this.selectedGroup = selectedGroup;
    }
}
```

After the injection of the `entityManager` component (used to merge the modified data submitted by the edit form) and the `groupListHelper` component (used to get the groups list shown into the `dataTable`), we can find two properties. The first one (`ajaxUpdateRows`) contains, as we've said, the list of the indexes of the groups list that has to be re-rendered (in our case only one row) and, the second one contains the pointer to the group that is being edited (if null, no groups are being edited). We can find the getter and setter for every property at the end of the class. In the middle, we see three methods called by the XHTML code that are used to start group editing (`editGroup`), cancel the editing of the selected group (`cancelEditingGroup`), and save the newly edited group data (`saveSelectedGroup`).

We can notice that every method clears and then adds the selected group row index in the `ajaxUpdateRows` list, to tell the `rich:dataTable` component to only re-render that row.

In order to do that, they call the `reRenderRow` method that clears the list of elements to re-render (we have to do that because the component has CONVERSATION scope and the list is kept for every request), and then, find the index of the selected group from the list of groups (inside the `groupsListHelper` bean).

The last task to do is to add a `partialUpdateExample.page.xml` file to begin the conversation when the page is accessed.

Here is the screenshot of the preceding example in **Edit** mode:

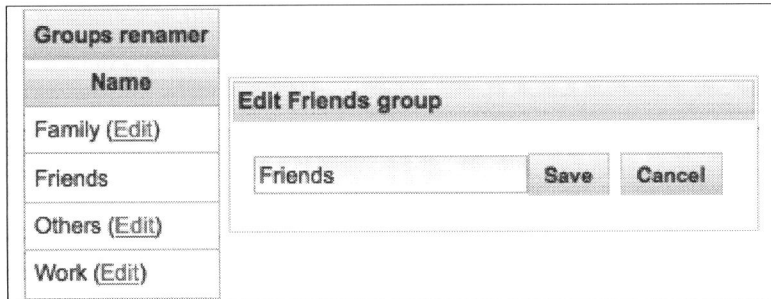

RichFaces component binding in JBoss Seam / JBoss Application Server environment

Sometimes we need to dynamically generate some part of the UI in a way that is difficult or impossible to achieve using the XHTML. In those cases, we can use the JSF binding feature to generate the JSF component on-the-fly using the Java code.

Also, RichFaces, being a standard JSF framework, gives the support for component binding.

Component binding, sometimes, is very useful to use complex logic to dynamically generate UI components in order to achieve some specific task. You can see it as the Swing GUI programming (as you know, JSF is also a component-based framework), but into the web context.

It's very important that you use the binding feature only if strictly necessary, as it makes the view depending on the application logic.

Moving all the libraries to the EAR

If you are packaging your project into an EAR structure, you might have some problem with the class loader.

In those cases (and if you have generated your project using seam-gen), just follow these simple steps:

- Open the /deployed-jars-war.list file and copy all the content
- Open the /deployed-jars-ear.list file and paste all the copied content
- Delete the /deployed-jars-war.list file
- Open the /build.xml file and delete the following code from the war file:

```
<copy todir="${war.dir}/WEB-INF/lib">
  <fileset dir="${lib.dir}">
    <includesfile name="deployed-jars-war.list"/>
    <exclude name="jboss-seam-gen.jar"/>
  </fileset>
</copy>
```

- Create the /view/META-INF/ directory
- Inside the directory just created, create a file called MANIFEST.MF and insert the code:

```
Class-Path: lib/
```

- Using ANT, call the following targets in order: unexploded, clean, explode

Now, all of your library files are in the lib directory of the EAR, and there will be no problem with the class loader while using the binding feature with RichFaces and Seam.

> We decided to move all of the files to the EAR lib directory for simplicity, because it is difficult to manage the right dependences for every library.

A simple binding example

Now that our environment is ready, we can create a simple example.

A very important thing to keep in mind is that you cannot use Seam conversational components to contain binding properties, because they are updated during the Restore View phase that occurs before the restoring of the Seam conversation context. You can see it in the Seam life cycle diagram shown in the next figure:

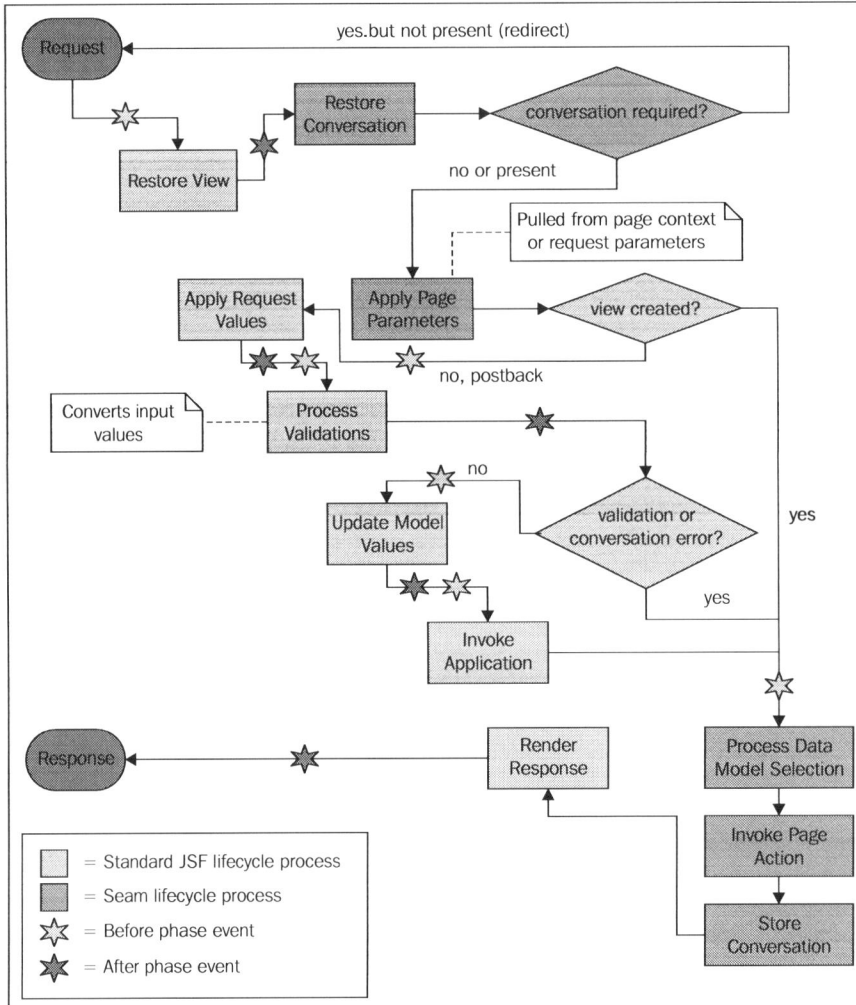

Another limitation of JSF component binding using the Seam framework is that you also can't inject conversational components inside EVENT scoped ones.

One solution you can adopt is to use the @Factory annotation (or, the @Out or @Unwrap annotations) to create a non-conversational component, which acts as a binding for the JSF object we need to customize.

The XHTML code for our example is very simple; let's add it to a file called /view/examples/binding/bindingExample.xhtml:

```
<!DOCTYPE composition PUBLIC "-//W3C//DTD XHTML 1.0 Transitional//EN"
"http://www.w3.org/TR/xhtml1/DTD/xhtml1-transitional.dtd">
<ui:composition xmlns="http://www.w3.org/1999/xhtml"
                xmlns:ui="http://java.sun.com/jsf/facelets"
                xmlns:rich="http://richfaces.org/rich"
                template="/layout/template.xhtml">

   <ui:define name="body">
      <rich:panel binding="#{myPanel}" />
   </ui:define>
</ui:composition>
```

Also, let's create a bindingExample.page.xml file in the same directory to initiate the conversation:

```
<?xml version="1.0" encoding="UTF-8"?>
<page xmlns="http://jboss.com/products/seam/pages"
      xmlns:xsi="http://www.w3.org/2001/XMLSchema-instance"
      xsi:schemaLocation="http://jboss.com/products/seam/pages http://
jboss.com/products/seam/pages-2.1.xsd"
      login-required="true">
   <begin-conversation join="true"/>
   <rewrite pattern="/bindingExample"/>
</page>
```

The login is required as we are going to use GroupsListeHelper that needs a logged user.

The bean (book.richfaces.advcm.modules.main.examples.binding.BindingExampleHelper) contains just a method that creates the object we need in the EVENT scope:

```
package book.richfaces.advcm.modules.main.examples.binding;

@Name("bindingExampleHelper")
@Scope(ScopeType.CONVERSATION)
```

```
public class BindingExampleHelper {
    @In(create = true)
    GroupsListHelper groupsListHelper;

    @Factory(value = "myPanel",
             scope = ScopeType.EVENT,
             autoCreate = true)
    public UIPanel createPanel() {
        FacesContext facesContext = FacesContext.getCurrentInstance();

        // Setting up the new panel
        UIPanel myPanel = new HtmlPanel();
        myPanel.setId("myPanel");
        myPanel.setHeader("Panel title");

        // A simple text
        HtmlOutputText txt = new HtmlOutputText();
        txt.setValue("My panel text.<br/>");
        txt.setEscape(false);
        myPanel.getChildren().add(txt);

        // Adding the groups names
        for (ContactGroup group : groupsListHelper.getGroups()) {
            // Ading the group name to the panel
            txt = new HtmlOutputText();
            txt.setValue(group.getName()+"<br/>");
            txt.setEscape(false);
            myPanel.getChildren().add(txt);
        }

        HtmlOutputText latestTxt = new HtmlOutputText();
        latestTxt.setValue("Latest panel text.<br/>");
        latestTxt.setEscape(false);
        myPanel.getChildren().add(latestTxt);

        // An Ajax link
        UIAjaxCommandLink link = new HtmlAjaxCommandLink();
        link.setValue("do something");
```

```
link.setAjaxSingle(true);
link.setReRender("myPanel");
link.setActionExpression(facesContext.getApplication().
getExpressionFactory().createMethodExpression(facesContext.
getELContext(), "#{someBean.someAction}",
Void.TYPE, new Class[0]));

// Adding the children (1 string and 1 link)
myPanel.getChildren().add(link);

return myPanel;
    }
}
```

The `myPanel` object (its type is `UIPanel`) is created and put in EVENT scope by the factory method `createPanel()` — it sets up the panel header and then creates some components (reading the groups list from the database) and adds them as children.

As you can notice, the "manager" Seam component (`BindingExampleHelper`) is conversational, but produces an EVENT scoped object.

The result of the code we have seen is as follows:

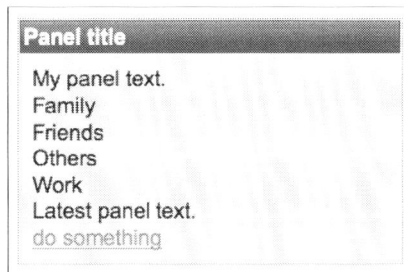

The tree component

The next example will show how to make and use a `rich:tree` component in an effective way.

First let's create the `/view/examples/tree/treeExample.xhtml` page, it might look like this:

```
<!DOCTYPE composition PUBLIC "-//W3C//DTD XHTML 1.0 Transitional//EN"
"http://www.w3.org/TR/xhtml1/DTD/xhtml1-transitional.dtd">
<ui:composition xmlns="http://www.w3.org/1999/xhtml"
                xmlns:ui="http://java.sun.com/jsf/facelets"
                xmlns:h="http://java.sun.com/jsf/html"
```

```
                    xmlns:rich="http://richfaces.org/rich"
                    template="/layout/template.xhtml">

   <ui:define name="body">
     <h:form>
       <rich:tree switchType="ajax" value="#{contactsTree}"
                 var="item">
         <rich:treeNode iconLeaf="/img/contact.png"
               icon="/img/files.png">
           <h:outputText value="#{item.name}"/>
         </rich:treeNode>
       </rich:tree>
     </h:form>
   </ui:define>
</ui:composition>
```

Here, we've defined a tree that gets the data model from the `contactsTree` variable and uses Ajax to render the changes (`switchType="ajax"`) during the user interaction.

Inside the tree, we've also defined what the standard tree node will look like.

Let's use the backing bean now—create a `book.richfaces.advcm.modules.main.examples.tree` package, and inside it, a Java class called `TreeExampleHelper`.

This class might look like the following code:

```
package book.richfaces.advcm.modules.main.examples.tree;

@Name("treeExampleHelper")
@Scope(ScopeType.CONVERSATION)
public class TreeExampleHelper {
    @In(create = true)
    EntityManager entityManager;

    @In
    FacesMessages facesMessages;

    @In(create = true)
    GroupsListHelper groupsListHelper;

    @In(create = true)
    HomeContactsListHelper homeContactsListHelper;

    @Factory(value = "contactsTree", autoCreate = true,
```

```
        scope = ScopeType.CONVERSATION)
public TreeNode fillInContactsTree() {
    TreeNode tree = new TreeNodeImpl();

    for (ContactGroup group : groupsListHelper.getGroups()) {

        TreeNode groupNode = new TreeNodeImpl();

        // Add the sub level

        // I want only the contacts inside the current
        // group
        homeContactsListHelper.setGroupFilter(group);
        // Force the reloading of the list with the new
        // filter
        homeContactsListHelper.sand so onontactsList(null);

        for (Contact contact : homeContactsListHelper.gand
                                    so onontactsList()) {

            TreeNode contactNode = new TreeNodeImpl();

            // Add the contact inside the group
            contactNode.setData(contact);
            groupNode.addChild(group.getId() + "_" +
contact.getId(), contactNode);
        }

        // Add the group with contacts inside
        groupNode.setData(group);
        tree.addChild(group.getId(), groupNode);
    }

    // Reset the filter
    homeContactsListHelper.setGroupFilter(null);
    homeContactsListHelper.sand so onontactsList(null);

    return tree;
}
}
```

The `fillInContactsTree()` method is the factory of `contactsTree` variable that contains the tree data model (an implementation of the `TreeNode` interface). Our tree will contain the Groups/Contacts structure read from the database, and would look like the next screenshot:

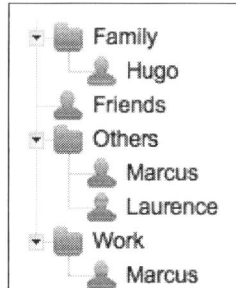

State saving

A feature we would like to add is **state saving** — this way, we can put the current tree state into a property and keep it between the requests, or store and then reset in another moment (for example, when the user comes back).

In order to achieve that, we have just to add the `DataComponentState` property (with getter and setter) inside our bean:

```
private DataComponentState dataState;

public DataComponentState getDataState() {
    return dataState;
}

public void setDataState(DataComponentState dataState) {
    this.dataState = dataState;
}
```

Then we set the `componentState` attribute of the `rich:tree` component in the XHTML file:

```
<rich:tree ... componentState="#{treeExampleHelper.dataState}"
```

Action listeners

We can define some listener to control user interaction with the tree.

The first one we are going to define is the `changeExpandListener`, let's add the following method into our bean:

```
public void changeExpandListener(NodeExpandedEvent event) {
  UITree tree = (UITree) event.gand so onomponent();

  facesMessages.add(StatusMessage.Severity.INFO,
  "Node changed/expanded: "+trefor exampleetRowData());
}
```

Notice how we get the `UITree` instance from the event passed to the method.

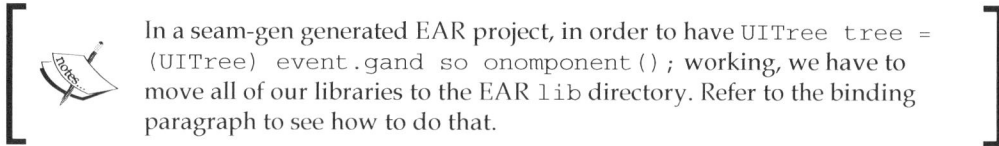

> In a seam-gen generated EAR project, in order to have `UITree tree = (UITree) event.gand so onomponent();` working, we have to move all of our libraries to the EAR `lib` directory. Refer to the binding paragraph to see how to do that.

Now let's set the `rich:tree changeExpandListener` attribute:

```
<rich:tree ... changeExpandListener="#{treeExampleHelper.
changeExpandListener}" ... >
```

Done! Now we can act when a user expands or closes a part of the tree.

Another useful listener we can set is the `nodeSelectListened`. It can be added the same way as the other listener. Let's add the following method into the bean:

```
public void selectionListener(NodeSelectedEvent event) {
    UITree tree = (UITree) event.getComponent();

    Object selectedObject = tree.getRowData();
    if (selectedObject instanceof ContactGroup) {
        facesMessages.add(StatusMessage.Severity.INFO,
     "Group selected: "+ ((ContactGroup)selectedObject).getName());
    } else {
        facesMessages.add(StatusMessage.Severity.INFO,
        "Contact selected: "+ ((Contact)selectedObject).getName()+"
                        "+((Contact)selectedObject).getSurname());
    }
}
```

And also add it to the XHTML file:

```
<rich:tree ...
          nodeSelectListener="#{treeExampleHelper.selectionListener}"
          ajaxSubmitSelection="true" ... >
```

We have also set the `ajaxSubmitSelection` attribute to `true` in order to "Ajaxize" every listener submission.

You can see the result of selecting a group in the following screenshot:

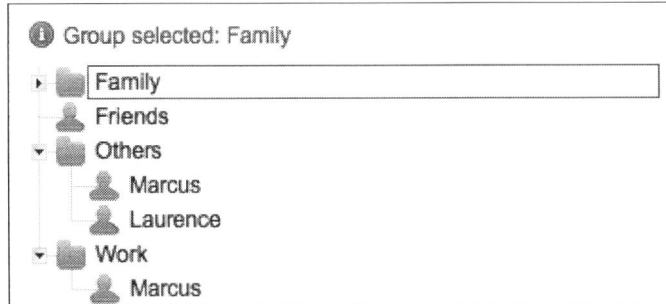

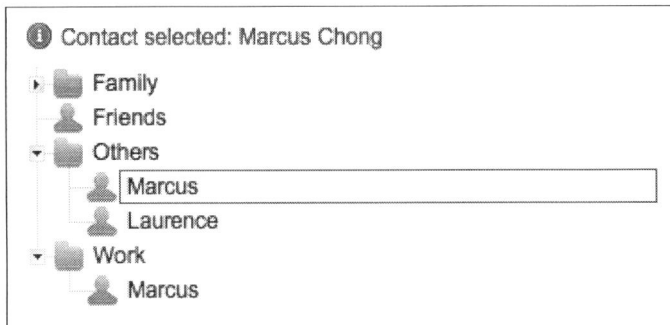

Controlling the session expiration

Using the RichFaces framework, it is possible to control the session expiration during an Ajax request in a better way—just redefine the `A4J.AJAX.onExpired` JavaScript method!

> You can keep the session alive by polling the server at a regular interval of time, by using the `a4j:poll` component (we have seen how to use it in this chapter).

Let's do an example using a modal panel to notify that the session expired—open the `/view/layout/template.xhtml` file and move at the end of it, just before the `</body>` tag.

Let's add the modal panel code first:

```
<rich:modalPanel id="sessionExpiredMP" resizeable="false"
                 width="300" height="200">
  <h:outputText value="The session has expired" />
  <br/>
  <s:button value="Click here to close it"
    onclick="#{rich:component('sessionExpiredMP')}.hide();" />
</rich:modalPanel>
```

This modal panel will be opened when the session will expire.

For doing that, let's redefine the JavaScript function `A4J.AJAX.onExpired`—after the modal panel code, let's add the following:

```
<script type="text/javascript">
  A4J.AJAX.onExpired = function(loc, expiredMsg) {
        $('sessionExpiredMP').show();
  };
</script>
```

Now every time the session will expire, the modal panel will be opened.

It is possible to redefine also the `onError` JavaScript error handler.

Session expiration time

In order to control the session expiration time, it is possible to set the `session-timeout` option into the `web.xml` file. If you don't find it, just put the following code:

```
<session-config>
    <session-timeout>10</session-timeout>
</session-config>
```

Where `10` means that the session will expire after 10 minutes of inactivity.

This feature doesn't work if you are using MyFaces, unless you disable its error handling, in this way:

```
<context-param>
  <param-name>org.apache.myfaces.ERROR_HANDLING</param-name>
  <param-value>false</param-value>
</context-param>
```

Summary

Advanced RichFaces topics are not as complex as you may think. Once you understand the basics about the framework, it's not difficult to *switch* to a more advanced level. The power of RichFaces can be seen also in this— you can start using it in a simple way, but you can still rely on it to do more complex tasks that, as you've seen, are simple to achieve with a bit of experience.

11
Component Development Kit

In this chapter, we are going to create a simple JSF component using the **Component Development Kit** (**CDK**). Developing a JSF component is not a simple task, and if you do it without the help of the CDK, you will have to write a lot of standard (and not component-specific) code that includes UIComponent class, Renderer class, Tag class, configuration files, and so on. The CDK offers a lot of advantages such as a pre-generated project skeleton to start quickly, a generator that does the task of repetitive task generation using simple configuration files, built-in Ajax functionalities, testing, optimization for specific JSF version, creation of the component renderer using a JSP-like markup code, support for JSF skinning, and more.

In order to show how to start and its basic features, we are going to develop a star rating component that accepts a float value and renders it as stars.

Let's start!

Configuring the environment

All the CDK is based on Apache Maven (`http://maven.apache.org/`) that is widely used to generate the skeleton code that we can use as a base to work on.

Maven is a tool used by a lot of Java projects in order to manage the project management and building phases. It is close (as a concept) to Apache Ant and very useful to build automation.

Maven can dynamically download dependencies needed to create a project and is very useful to create from scratch and maintain project templates.

Installing Maven

If you haven't installed Maven before starting we need to install it. In order to do so, visit the Maven website (`http://maven.apache.org`), download it, and follow the instructions to complete the installation.

Configuring

After we have correctly installed Maven, we have to configure it to use it with the CDK.

The `setting.xml` file contains all the general Maven settings we can use in our Maven projects.

In our case, we are going to add the `cdk` profile to the settings element; this profile enables general resources such as `cdk`-specific repositories and plugins, that will be shared among the `pom.xml` files used for our CDK components.

Go to the maven directory and open the `conf/settings.xml` file inside an editor, adding a new profile (inside the `profiles` section) for CDK:

```
<profile>
    <id>cdk</id>
    <repositories>
        <repository>
            <id>maven2-repository.dev.java.net</id>
            <name>Java.net Repository for Maven</name>
            <url>http://download.java.net/maven/1</url>
            <layout>legacy</layout>
        </repository>
        <repository>
            <releases>
                <enabled>true</enabled>
            </releases>
            <snapshots>
                <enabled>false</enabled>
                <updatePolicy>never</updatePolicy>
            </snapshots>
            <id>repository.jboss.com</id>
            <name>Jboss Repository for Maven</name>
            <url>http://repository.jboss.com/maven2/</url>
            <layout>default</layout>
        </repository>
    </repositories>
    <pluginRepositories>
```

```
        <pluginRepository>
            <id>maven.jboss.org</id>
            <name>JBoss Repository for Maven Snapshots</name>
            <url>http://snapshots.jboss.org/maven2/</url>
            <releases>
                <enabled>false</enabled>
            </releases>
            <snapshots>
                <enabled>true</enabled>
                <updatePolicy>always</updatePolicy>
            </snapshots>
        </pluginRepository>
        <pluginRepository>
            <releases>
                <enabled>true</enabled>
            </releases>
            <snapshots>
                <enabled>false</enabled>
                <updatePolicy>never</updatePolicy>
            </snapshots>
            <id>repository.jboss.com</id>
            <name>Jboss Repository for Maven</name>
            <url>http://repository.jboss.com/maven2/ </url>
            <layout>default</layout>
        </pluginRepository>
    </pluginRepositories>
</profile>
```

As you can see, we have added `repository` and `pluginRepository` resources that will be used by our `pom.xml` file.

After that, we have to activate the profile. In order to do that, just uncomment the `activeProfiles` section, as in the following code:

```
<activeProfiles>
   activeProfile>cdk</activeProfile>
</activeProfiles>
```

Now the environment is ready and we can start creating our new component project!

Creating the project

In order to generate our project, first let's create a directory to contain our component (it can contain more than one) and let's call it, for example, `sandbox`.

Inside the new directory, let's create a file called `pom.xml` and insert this code:

```xml
<?xml version="1.0" encoding="UTF-8"?>
<project xmlns="http://maven.apache.org/POM/4.0.0" xmlns:xsi="http://
www.w3.org/2001/XMLSchema-instance" xsi:schemaLocation="http://maven.
apache.org/POM/4.0.0 http://maven.apache.org/  xsd/maven-4.0.0.xsd">

    <modelVersion>4.0.0</modelVersion>
    <groupId>org.mycompany</groupId>
    <artifactId>sandbox</artifactId>
    <url>http://mycompany.org</url>
    <version>1.0-SNAPSHOT</version>
    <packaging>pom</packaging>
    <dependencies>
        <dependency>
            <groupId>javax.servlet</groupId>
            <artifactId>servlet-api</artifactId>
            <version>2.4</version>
            <scope>provided</scope>
        </dependency>
        <dependency>
            <groupId>javax.servlet</groupId>
            <artifactId>jsp-api</artifactId>
            <version>2.0</version>
            <scope>provided</scope>
        </dependency>
        <dependency>
            <groupId>javax.servlet.jsp</groupId>
            <artifactId>jsp-api</artifactId>
            <version>2.1</version>
            <scope>provided</scope>
        </dependency>
        <dependency>
            <groupId>javax.faces</groupId>
            <artifactId>jsf-api</artifactId>
            <version>1.2_12</version>
        </dependency>
        <dependency>
            <groupId>javax.faces</groupId>
             <artifactId>jsf-impl</artifactId>
```

```
            <version>1.2_12</version>
        </dependency>
    <dependency>
        <groupId>javax.el</groupId>
        <artifactId>el-api</artifactId>
        <version>1.0</version>
    <scope>provided</scope>
    </dependency>
    <dependency>
        <groupId>el-impl</groupId>
        <artifactId>el-impl</artifactId>
        <version>1.0</version>
    <scope>provided</scope>
    </dependency>
    <dependency>
        <groupId>javax.annotation</groupId>
        <artifactId>jsr250-api</artifactId>
        <version>1.0</version>
    </dependency>
        <dependency>
        <groupId>org.richfaces.ui</groupId>
        <artifactId>richfaces-ui</artifactId>
        <version>3.3.1.GA</version>
    </dependency>
    </dependencies>
</project>
```

With the exception of the `modelVersion`, `packaging`, and `dependencies` sections, you can change the other parameters (such as `groupId`, `artifactId`, and so on) with your custom values.

> What is a POM?
>
> If you don't know Maven, maybe you are wondering about what POM means. **POM** stands for **Project Object Model** and it is used as a description of the project to be built—inside it, you can specify not only dependencies but also the tasks to do during the process and a lot of advanced features. It can be customized with three-part plugins for specific tasks.

Having created the POM, we can move (in our terminal) inside the sandbox directory that we have just created (containing the pom.xml file) and launch the following command (it is all in one whole line):

```
mvn archetype:generate -DarchetypeGroupId=org.richfaces.cdk
-DarchetypeArtifactId=maven-archetype-jsf-component
-DarchetypeVersion=3.3.1.GA -DartifactId=starRating
```

By using this command, we are asking Maven to generate a project template for a component called starRating.

It will start the project generation phase stopping at a certain point to ask you some information:

```
Define value for groupId: : book.richfaces.cdk.example
```

Here, we've defined the prefix for the package structure of our library to be book.richfaces.cdk.example.

Pressing the *Enter* key, we can go over the next question:

```
Define value for version:  1.0-SNAPSHOT: :
```

Here, we can decide the component version. The system suggests the 1.0-SNAPSHOT value and we just confirm it by pressing *Enter*.

Also for the next question, we choose the predefined values by just pressing the *Enter* key:

```
Define value for package:  book.richfaces.cdk.example: :
```

After that, the script asks us to confirm the values, so we just press *Y* and go on by pressing the *Enter* key:

```
Confirm properties configuration:
groupId: book.richfaces.cdk.example
artifactId: starRating
version: 1.0-SNAPSHOT
package: book.richfaces.cdk.example
 Y: : Y
```

It generates the new component project structure that should appear as shown in the following screenshot:

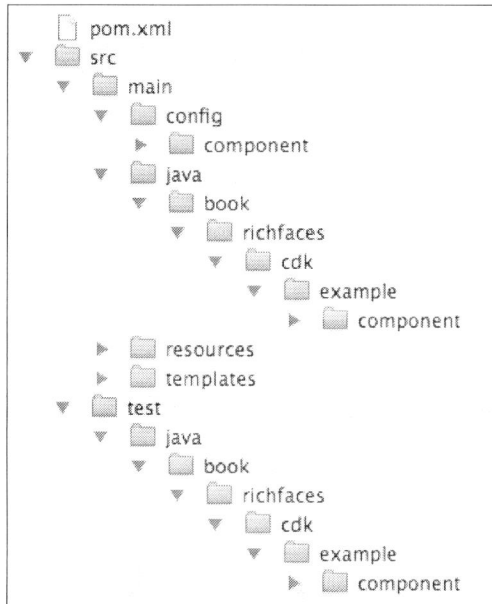

```
    pom.xml
▼   src
  ▼   main
    ▼   config
      ►   component
    ▼   java
      ▼   book
        ▼   richfaces
          ▼   cdk
            ▼   example
              ►   component
    ►   resources
    ►   templates
  ▼   test
    ▼   java
      ▼   book
        ▼   richfaces
          ▼   cdk
            ▼   example
              ►   component
```

A short explanation for the generated directory structure is as follows:

Directory	Description
src/main/config	Contains the metadata files related to the component configuration.
src/main/java	Contains the Java code.
src/main/resources	Contains every resource we are going to use in our component (images, JavaScript files, CSS files, and so on.).
src/main/templates	Contains the JSP-like template that describes the layout of the component.

Generating the template

As you can see, inside the new generated component directory (called `starRating`), you can find another `pom.xml` file. The next step is to edit this file by adding a new plugin inside the `plugins` section:

```
<plugin>
  <artifactId>maven-compiler-plugin</artifactId>
  <inherited>true</inherited>
  <configuration>
    <source>1.5</source>
    <target>1.5</target>
  </configuration>
</plugin>
```

Setting the `source` and `target` versions inside the `configuration` element of the plugin tells the Maven compiler plugin to pass those parameters to the `javac` compiler. Therefore, we obtain classes compatible with the version of Java we specified in the target element (1.5) for compiling 1.5-compatible source code.

We need to set those parameters, as the default source setting is 1.3, and the default target setting is 1.1—this is independent of the JDK you run Maven with.

We are now ready to create the skeleton for our new component: let's go inside the `starRating` directory and launch the following command:

mvn cdk:create -Dname=starRating

We have just executed the Maven goal called `cdk:create` passing the `name` as parameter (using the `-D` option to define a system property).

Testing the template

After the creation of the template skeleton, we can test it by just launching the following code:

mvn install

If, at the end of the process, it says BUILD SUCCESSFUL, then everything worked and you have generated a new (empty) component `jar` package. You can find the package inside the `target` directory that the process created.

> The next time you want to again rebuild the project, you should first clean everything and then regenerate it by using the following command:
>
> ```
> mvn clean install
> ```

Creating the component

As we've said, we have just generated an empty component—the next step is to edit the generated files (and add new ones) in order to create our custom files.

We've decided to develop a simple component in order to show you how to start in a simple way. Therefore, we are not going to use JavaScript or complex features—our component will just show the star rating we pass to it.

In order to make it more interesting we are also going to manage decimal values (showing a half star).

Component configuration

First of all, we need to configure our new component—let's open the `src/main/config/component/starRating.xml` file for editing and add the `value` property inside the `<component>` element, using the following code:

```xml
<property>
  <name>value</name>
    <classname>java.lang.Float</classname>
    <description>
      The value of the component.
    </description>
</property>
```

Also, we want to support the standard properties for style customizing (`style` and `styleClass`); instead of adding them by hand, we can use the predefined entities by adding this code:

```
&html_style_attributes;
```

There are other predefined entities for the common attributes you can use (refer to the CDK documentation for this purpose at `http://docs.jboss.org/richfaces/latest_3_3_X/en/cdkguide/html/`).

Component resources

The second thing we need are the images of two kinds of stars—full and half.

They are shown in the next image:

Let's create the `starRating/src/main/resources/book/richfaces/cdk/example/renderkit/html/images` directory and copy the two images (named `full.png` and `half.png`) inside it.

We will see how to use them in the next section.

Component renderer

The Renderer class of a component is responsible to make the representation of the component generating the chosen markup (such as HTML, WML, and so on.). It is also responsible for converting the client values to the right type that the component will use.

In order to go into the depth of the JSF components' structure and life-cycles, refer to the official JSF documentation.

Using the CDK framework, we can create our Renderer class using a JSP-like markup page that will be automatically converted into Java code during the package generation. Very convenient!

Let's open the generated template file `starRating/src/main/templates/book/richfaces/cdk/example/htmlStarRating.jspx` and start importing the resources we are going to use, by adding the highlighted code between the `f:clientId` and the `div` tags:

```
...
<f:clientid var="clientId"/>

<f:resource var="fullStar" name="images/full.png" />
<f:resource var="halfStar" name="images/half.png" />

<div ...
```

Now we can refer to them using the name set in the var attribute (fullStar and halfStar). For example, if we want to insert the full star image, we can use the following code:

```
<img src="#{fullStar}" />
```

In our application, we accept Float values in the value attribute (that we specified as a Float into the configuration file), so the first thing to do is to get a Float from the passed value.

In order to do so, we use a special tag called jsp:scriptlet that is very useful to insert Java logic inside the JSP-like code—it will be copied "as is" into the generated Renderer class.

Let's add the following Java logic code inside the div tag:

```
<jsp:scriptlet>
  <![CDATA[
  Float ratingValue =(Float) component.getAttributes().get("value");
              variables.setVariable("ratingValue", ratingValue);
  ]]>
</jsp:scriptlet>
```

In this code, we first get the passed Float value and then insert it into a variable named ratingValue (so, we can refer to it in the next code snippet we are going to insert).

After getting and setting the value, we have to get the integer part of the float value and write as many stars as the number we have found.

For that purpose, we use the following scriptlet (to be written after the first one):

```
<jsp:scriptlet>
<![CDATA[
    // Render the full stars
    int integerValue = (int)Math.floor(ratingValue);
    for (int b=0; b<integerValue; b++) {
]]>
</jsp:scriptlet>

<img src="#{fullStar}" alt="#{ratingValue}" />

<jsp:scriptlet>
<![CDATA[
    }
]]>
</jsp:scriptlet>
```

As you can see, we mixed the HTML code and Java code (properly closing and re-opening the `scriptlet` tags).

The code we've just inserted iterates over the integer part in order to write a list of full stars—for example, if we pass the number 3.4, it writes three full stars.

Now we have to consider the decimal part and decide what to do. We've made a simple logic:

- if the decimal part's value is more than 0.66, then we write another full star (rounding up)
- if it is between (included) 0.33 and 0.66, we write a half star
- if the value is less than 0.33, we don't write anything (rounding down)

We can implement this simple logic by appending the following code:

```
<jsp:scriptlet>
<![CDATA[
    // Decide if I have to render for the last star
    float decimalPart = (ratingValue-integerValue);
    if (decimalPart>0.66)  {
]]>
</jsp:scriptlet>


        <img src="#{fullStar}" alt="#{ratingValue}" />


<jsp:scriptlet>
<![CDATA[
    } else if (decimalPart>=0.33 && decimalPart<=0.66) {
]]>
</jsp:scriptlet>
        <img src="#{halfStar}" alt="#{ratingValue}" />
<jsp:scriptlet>
<![CDATA[
    }
]]>
</jsp:scriptlet>
```

We have finished (this is a very simple component), and we are ready to test it inside our application!

Testing the new component

First of all, we have to regenerate the component's JAR package using the following command from the `starRating` directory:

`mvn clean install`

After the process completes, we have to copy the JAR (named `starRating-1.0-SNAPSHOT.jar`) package inside the `lib` directory of our project (in our case, we are going to use the *AdvContactManager* project we've used for the examples in Chapter 10, *Advanced Techniques*).

After that, we have to add the new library into the produced package in a seam-generated project and edit the `deployed-jars-war.list` file by adding the following line:

```
starRating-1.0-SNAPSHOT.jar
```

In our case, we are adding it into the EAR list file (`deployed-jars-ear.list`), because we've moved all of the libraries there, while writing the examples for Chapter 10.

Now let's create the example bean class called `StarRatingTest` in the package `book.richfaces.advcm.modules.main.examples.component`:

```
package book.richfaces.advcm.modules.main.examples.component;

import org.jboss.seam.annotations.Name;

@Name("starRatingTest")
public class StarRatingTest {
    private Integer intTest;
    private Float floatTest;

    public Integer getIntTest() {
        return intTest;
    }

    public void setIntTest(Integer intTest) {
        this.intTest = intTest;
    }

    public Float getFloatTest() {
        return floatTest;
    }
}
```

```
    public void setFloatTest(Float floatTest) {
        this.floatTest = floatTest;
    }
}
```

It is just a "container" for an integer and a float variable.

Now let's use it inside the XHTML with our new component!

Let's create a file called componentExample.xhtml inside the /view/examples/ component/ directory and add the following code:

```
<!DOCTYPE composition PUBLIC "-//W3C//DTD XHTML 1.0 Transitional//EN"
"http://www.w3.org/TR/xhtml1/DTD/xhtml1-transitional.dtd">
<ui:composition xmlns="http://www.w3.org/1999/xhtml"
                xmlns:ui="http://java.sun.com/jsf/facelets"
                xmlns:h="http://java.sun.com/jsf/html"
                xmlns:a="http://richfaces.org/a4j"
                xmlns:test="http://mycompany.org/starRating"
                template="/layout/template.xhtml">

  <ui:define name="body">
    <h:form>
      <h:panelGrid columns="3">
        <h:outputText value="Integer test: "/>
        <h:inputText value="#{starRatingTest.intTest}">
          <a:support event="onchange"
                     reRender="sri" ajaxSingle="true"/>
        </h:inputText>

        <test:starRating id="sri" value="#{starRatingTest.intTest}"/>
        <h:outputText value="Float test: "/>
        <h:inputText value="#{starRatingTest.floatTest}">
          <a:support event="onchange"
                     reRender="srf" ajaxSingle="true"/>
        </h:inputText>
        <test:starRating id="srf"
                         value="#{starRatingTest.floatTest}"/>
      </h:panelGrid>
    </h:form>
  </ui:define>
</ui:composition>
```

As you can see, we've connected the bean values to an input text and two `starRating` components in order to show the value the user types into the input as stars.

For using the component, we've defined the namespace as you can notice by the highlighted line.

The last thing we can add (optionally, just to have a good looking URL for the page) is the Seam page descriptor in the same directory, with the name `componentExample.page.xml` and the following content:

```
<?xml version="1.0" encoding="UTF-8"?>
<page xmlns="http://jboss.com/products/seam/pages"
      xmlns:xsi="http://www.w3.org/2001/XMLSchema-instance"
      xsi:schemaLocation="http://jboss.com/products/seam/pages
      http://jboss.com/products/seam/pages-2.1.xsd">

   <rewrite pattern="/componentExample"/>
</page>
```

If we run the example, we can see the component updated by an Ajax request after the user's input focus leaves the `h:inputText` component.

The following screenshot shows the example in action:

Integer test:	4	
Float test:	3.35	

We can also try to set the `style` and `styleClass` elements to customize the component appearance, as shown in the following screenshot, for example:

Integer test:	3	
Float test:	8.5	

Here we added colored borders to our test components just to give you an example. You can also implement custom images for stars and so on: it's up to you!

Summary

CDK is a very useful "kit" to develop rich JSF components in a fast and solid way, without caring about all the standard (and repetitive) code that a normal JSF component creation requires.

In this chapter, we have seen how to start a project in order to develop a simple JSF Ajax component in a simple and effective way using the features the CDK offers.

Reading the documentation about CDK (`http://docs.jboss.org/richfaces/latest_3_3_X/en/cdkguide/html/`) and studying the source code of the RichFaces library (that can be downloaded from `http://www.jboss.org/richfaces/download/stable.html`) is a very useful way to go over and develop more complex components.

RichFaces Components Overview

The RichFaces framework has many JSF Ajax components for adding Ajax to your applications in very simple ways, without prior knowledge of JavaScript. However, if you know JavaScript, you have more framework features to use inside your own JavaScript code.

Here is a "fast" list of all of the components that the 3.2.2 version of RichFaces contains. In the following chapters, we are going to develop an application using RichFaces and while doing it, we'll see how those components work in practice using real examples that cover all their functionalities.

Ajax support

a4j:ajaxListener
The component has the same functionalities as that of `<f:actionListener>` or `<f:valueChangeListener>`, but it works in an Ajax container.

a4j:actionparam
It combines the functionality of `<f:param>` and `<f:actionListener>`.

a4j:commandButton
As we have seen in the previous paragraph, the component is very similar to the `<h:commandButton>` component, with built-in Ajax support.

a4j:commandLink

The `<a4j:commandLink>` component is very similar to the `<h:commandLink>` component, with built-in Ajax support.

a4j:form

It is very similar to `<h:form>`, with more Ajax capabilities (such as Ajax submission by default).

a4j:htmlCommandLink

It is same as the `<h:commandLink>`, but with correct link generation for RichFaces framework support.

a4j:jsFunction

This component allows the user to invoke the server-side data and return it in a JSON format to use in client JavaScript calls.

a4j:poll

As we have seen, the `<a4j:poll>` component allows periodical sending of Ajax requests to a server and is used for a page updating and/or action calling within a specified time interval.

a4j:push

The `<a4j:push>` simulates "push" data periodically, performing Ajax requests to the server.

a4j:region

This component defines an area that is decoded on the server and updated after Ajax submission.

a4j:status

This displays the current Ajax request's status when the Ajax request is in process or finished.

a4j:support

The `<a4j:support>` component adds Ajax support to an existing JSF component.

Resources/beans handling

a4j:keepAlive

This component allows keeping the state of a bean alive between requests.

a4j:loadBundle

The component loads a localized resource bundle and exposes it (as a map). It is similar to the component with the same name from the JSF Core library.

a4j:loadScript

This component inserts script links to the `head` element.

a4j:loadStyle

It inserts stylesheet links to the `head` element.

Ajax Validators

rich:ajaxValidator

Provides Ajax validation for JSF inputs.

rich:graphValidator

By using `<rich:graphValidator>`, you will be able to register Hibernate Validators for multiple input components.

rich:beanValidator

The component provides bean validation using Hibernate model-based constraints.

Ajax output

a4j:include

The component is used to implement an Ajax working wizard inside a JSF page.

a4j:mediaOutput

Using this component, you will be able to generate images, video, sounds, and other customized binary resources on-the-fly.

a4j:outputPanel

As we have seen, we can use this component as a placeholder for adding elements after an Ajax update.

Ajax miscellaneous

a4j:log

Using this component, you can get client-side debug information on an Ajax request.

a4j:page

The component encodes the full HTML page structure and is used to solve incompatibility problems in early Ajax4jsf versions.

a4j:portlet

This is a deprecated component—it defines the same functionality as `f:view`.

Data iteration

a4j:repeat

`<a4j:repeat>` is a basic iteration component allowing Ajax update capabilities to a set of its children.

rich:columns

This allows you to create a dynamic set of columns.

rich:columnGroup

This component groups columns together and is used in complex tables.

rich:column

This renders a row for a UIData component (such as `rich:dataTable` or `rich:dataGrid`).

rich:dataGrid

It renders data as a grid with built-in support for Ajax updates.

rich:dataList

The component renders an unordered list from a model.

rich:dataOrderedList

It renders an ordered list from a model.

rich:dataDefinitionList

It renders a definition list from a model.

rich:dataFilterSlider

It uses a slider to filter table data.

rich:datascroller

This provides the scrolling Ajax functionality for UIData components.

rich:dataTable

The component is similar to `h:dataTable` with more features and built-in support of Ajax updates. It also offers ordering and filtering support.

rich:subTable

It gives the possibility of inserting sub-tables into tables with built-in Ajax update support.

rich:extendedDataTable

It extends the standard `<rich:dataTable>` component, giving a lot of features such as integrated data-scrolling, built-in selection support, row grouping, ordering, filtering, and so on.

rich:scrollableDataTable

It adds additional features to standard table component such as integrated data scrolling, dynamical row fetch, ordering, filtering, drag-and-drop support, and so on.

Drag-and-drop support

rich:dndParam

This component is used for passing parameters during drag-and-drop operations.

rich:dragIndicator

It defines what appears under the mouse cursor during drag-and-drop operations. The displayed drag indicator can show information about the dragged elements.

rich:dragSupport

This component defines a "drag zone" that you can drag to any component that supports drop operations (that is a "drop zone").

rich:dropSupport

It defines a "drop zone" for drag-and-drop operations. When a draggable element is moved and dropped onto the drop area, an Ajax request for this event is started.

rich:dragListener

The component is used to execute an action listener method after a drag operation.

rich:dropListener

The component is used to execute an action listener method after a drop operation.

Rich Menu

rich:contextMenu

It is used to create a context menu, activated after a user-defined event on any element of the page.

rich:dropDownMenu

The component describes multilevel drop-down menus.

rich:menuGroup

It is used to define an expandable group of items.

rich:menuItem

It's the definition of a single menu item.

rich:menuSeparator

It is the definition of a horizontal separator that can be placed between menu groups or menu items.

Rich trees

rich:tree

This component renders a tree data structure with drag-and-drop capability.

rich:treeNode

This component describes a node in the `<rich:tree>` component.

rich:changeExpandListener

It is used to execute an action listener method on an expand/collapse event on a tree node.

rich:nodeSelectListener

It is used to execute an action listener method after the selection of a tree node.

rich:recursiveTreeNodesAdaptor

It defines data models and process nodes recursively. It is an extension of `<rich:treeNodesAdaptor>`.

rich:treeNodesAdaptor

It defines data models and creates representations for them.

Rich output

rich:modalPanel

The component implements a modal dialog window controlled by JavaScript code.

rich:paint2D

Same as "paint" (Graphics2D) in "SWING" components, it generates an image by using a managed bean method.

rich:panel

It is a panel (with or without header).

rich:panelBar

It renders a panel divided into sub-panels—the selected panel is shown, and users can display the other panels by clicking on their headers.

rich:panelBarItem

It implements a child panel inside `rich:panelBar`.

rich:panelMenu

The component renders an inline vertical menu on a page.

rich:panelMenuGroup

It implements an expandable group of items inside a panel menu or other groups.

rich:panelMenuItem

It is an item of `panelMenu`.

rich:progressBar

The `<rich:progressBar>` component displays a progress bar showing the current status of a process.

rich:separator

A customizable horizontal line to use as a separator in a layout.

rich:simpleTogglePanel

A collapsible panel that shows/hides content after activating a header control.

rich:spacer

It renders a transparent image to use as a spacer in a layout.

rich:tabPanel

A panel that contains other panels as tabs.

rich:tab

A tab child panel within a `rich:tabPanel` component.

rich:togglePanel

This component is a named facet container that can show a specific facet by invoking it using the `rich:toggleControl` component. Only one facet at a time is shown.

rich:toggleControl

Used to switch between `rich:togglePanel` facets.

rich:toolBar

A horizontal bar that accepts any of the JSF components as children.

rich:toolBarGroup

A group of tool bar items.

rich:toolTip

It renders a component that shows a non-modal pop up for a specified event.

Rich input

rich:calendar

The `<rich:calendar>` component renders a monthly calendar for date (and time) input.

rich:comboBox

This component renders an editable combobox.

rich:fileUpload

For file uploads with Ajax support.

rich:inplaceInput

This component is used for both displaying and editing data.

rich:inplaceSelect

This component is used for both displaying and editing (choosing from a list of options) data.

rich:inputNumberSlider

This component makes it possible to select a number from a defined range using an horizontal slider.

rich:inputNumberSpinner

This component makes it possible to select a number from a defined range using a spinner.

rich:suggestionbox

It adds an `inputText`-like component that shows a suggestion list based on the keys typed.

Rich Selects

rich:listShuttle

It is used for selecting items from a list; the selected items are shown in another list (there is also a reorder option for the selected items).

rich:orderingList

It is useful to order items in a list.

rich:pickList

It is used for selecting items from one list to another. The differences with `rich:listShuttle` are that it is simpler and doesn't use a custom model for items, only the `f:selectItem`(s) tag.

Rich miscellaneous

rich:componentControl

It allows calling JavaScript API functions on components after defined events.

rich:effect

It utilizes the *scriptaculous* JavaScript library to attach effects to other page elements.

rich:gmap

It renders the code necessary to show a Google map element.

rich:virtualEarth

It renders the code necessary to show a Virtual Earth map element.

rich:hotKey

This component allows the user to register hot keys for the page or particular elements and thus execute the client-side code.

rich:insert

It is used to insert source code and highlight it according to the type (for example Java, XHTML, C, Groovy, and so on).

rich:jQuery

It installs the jQuery JavaScript framework functionality and connects it to other DOM objects (or components).

rich:message

It renders a single message for a specific component (similar to `h:message`, but with Ajax support and other features).

rich:messages

The component renders all JSF messages for components (similar to `h:messages`, but with Ajax support and other features).

JSF 2 and RichFaces 4

The next version of RichFaces (still in Alpha status) will focus on JSF 2.0 support and integration. Except for some optimizations, both on the client and server code and a simplified CDK, it will be focused on extending the JSF 2 specification about Ajax support (JSF 2, in fact, now includes it too, thanks to the contribution of the RichFaces team).

The changes will not be that big, so if you learn RichFaces 3.3.X, you will be quickly able to switch to Version 4.0 when it's out.

We are going to see a simple example using the `a4j:support` tag, now included also in JSF 2.0 standard tags.

RichFaces 3.3.X

In RichFaces 3.3.X, you would write:

```
<h:inputText value="#{myBean.myProperty}" >
  <a4j:support
              event="onblur"
              action="#{myBean.doSomething}"
              reRender="myComponent"/>
</h:inputText>
```

We can understand this code—in this example, every time the text in `inputText` changes, RichFaces 3.3.X will fire the `#{myBean.doSomething}` method and re-render the component which has `id` equal to `myComponent`.

JSF 2.0

In order to do the same in JSF 2.0, you would use the following code:

```
<h:inputText value="#{myBean.myProperty}" >
  <f:ajax
        event="blur"
        execute="@form"
        listener="#{myBean.doSomethingListener}"
        render="myComponent"/>
</h:inputText>
```

As you can see, it is not very different—we can notice a name change (obviously), the listener instead of the action, `render` in place of `reRender`, and a new attribute called `execute`. It works a bit like the RichFaces `process` attribute, telling what to send with the request, but simplified (then not so powerful like the RichFaces one). In this case, the `@form` value tells that all the form should be sent (you can also use, for example, `@this` to just send the surrounding component).

RichFaces 4.X

You can see that the official JSF 2 specification has got a lot for the RichFaces framework experience. However, in RichFaces 4, the new `a4j:ajax` component (that replaces `a4j:support`) is going to support a complete set of RichFaces advanced features (that are not in JSF 2 specs) such as queues management, the `process` attribute to decide exactly which components to process, the regions, and more.

Here there is the same example using RichFaces 4:

```
<h:inputText value="#{myBean.myProperty}" >
  <a4j:ajax
            event="blur"
            listener="#{myBean.doSomethingListener}"
            render="myComponent"/>
</h:inputText>
```

The changes are minimal and you can easily understand this code without problems.

Finally, learning about RichFaces 3.3.X gets you ready to switch to RichFaces 4 and JSF 2 when they will be ready for production use!

Index

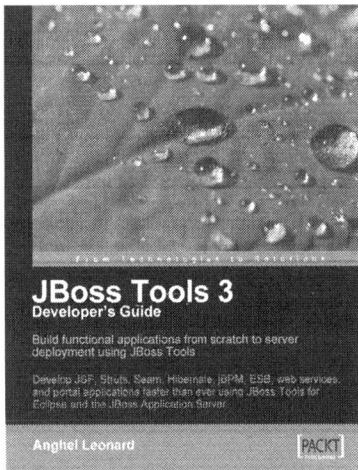

JBoss Tools 3 Developers Guide

ISBN: 978-1-847196-14-9   Paperback: 408 pages

Develop JSF, Struts, Seam, Hibernate, jBPM, ESB, web services, and portal applications faster than ever using JBoss Tools for Eclipse and the JBoss Application Server

1. Develop complete JSF, Struts, Seam, Hibernate, jBPM, ESB, web service, and portlet applications using JBoss Tools

2. Tools covered in separate chapters so you can dive into the one you want to learn

3. Manage JBoss Application Server through JBoss AS Tools

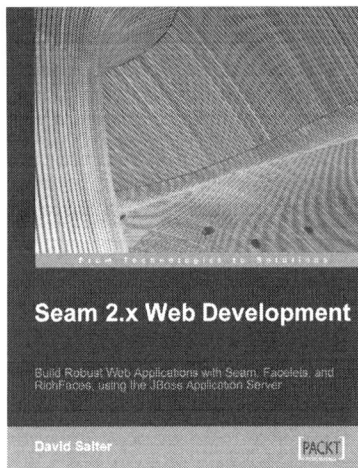

Seam 2.x Web Development

ISBN: 978-1-847195-92-0   Paperback: 300 pages

Build robust web applications with Seam, Facelets, and RichFaces using the JBoss application server

1. Develop rich web applications using Seam 2.x, Facelets, and RichFaces and deploy them on the JBoss Application Server

2. Integrate standard technologies like JSF, Facelets, EJB, and JPA with Seam and build on them using additional Seam components

3. Informative and practical approach to development with fully working examples and source code for each chapter of the book

Please check **www.PacktPub.com** for information on our titles

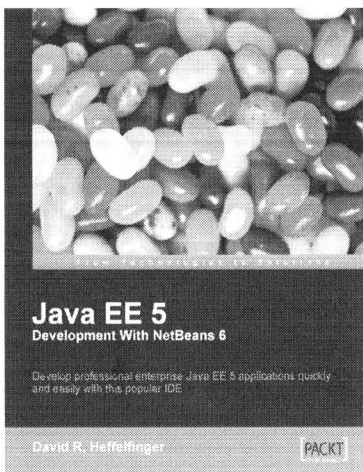

Java EE 5 Development with NetBeans 6

ISBN: 978-1-847195-46-3   Paperback: 400 pages

Develop professional enterprise Java EE applications quickly and easily with this popular IDE

1. Use features of the popular NetBeans IDE to improve Java EE development

2. Careful instructions and screenshots lead you through the options available

3. Covers the major Java EE APIs such as JSF, EJB 3 and JPA, and how to work with them in NetBeans

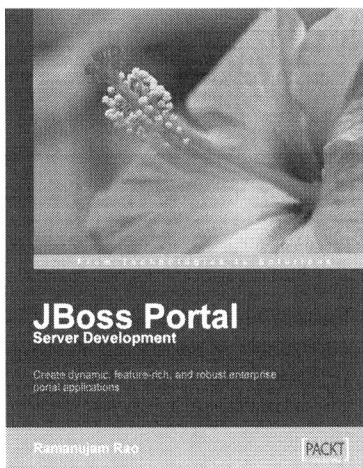

Java EE 5
Development With NetBeans 6

Develop professional enterprise Java EE 5 applications quickly and easily with this popular IDE

David R. Heffelfinger   PACKT

JBoss Portal Server Development

ISBN: 978-1-847194-10-7   Paperback: 276 pages

Create dynamic, feature-rich, and robust enterprise portal applications

1. Complete guide with examples for building enterprise portal applications using the free, open-source standards-based JBoss portal server

2. Quickly build portal applications such as B2B web sites or corporate intranets

3. Practical approach to understanding concepts such as personalization, single sign-on, integration with web technologies, and content management

JBoss Portal
Server Development

Create dynamic, feature-rich, and robust enterprise portal applications

Ramanujam Rao   PACKT